UNDERSTANDING
SOCIETIES

UNDERSTANDING
SOCIETIES

READINGS FOR
INTRODUCTORY SOCIOLOGY

Edited by
Gillian Balfour

Fernwood Publishing • Halifax & Winnipeg

Editing and text design: Brenda Conroy
Printed and bound in Canada by Hignell Book Printing

Published in Canada by Fernwood Publishing
32 Oceanvista Lane, Black Point, Nova Scotia, B0J 1B0
and 748 Broadway Avenue, Winnipeg, Manitoba, R3G 0X3
www.fernwoodpublishing.ca

Fernwood Publishing Company Limited gratefully acknowledges the financial support of the Government of Canada through the Canada Book Fund and the Canada Council for the Arts, the Nova Scotia Department of Communities, Culture and Heritage, the Manitoba Department of Culture, Heritage and Tourism under the Manitoba Publishers Marketing Assistance Program and the Province of Manitoba, through the Book Publishing Tax Credit, for our publishing program.

Library and Archives Canada Cataloguing in Publication

Understanding societies : readings for introductory sociology / edited by Gillian Balfour.

Includes bibliographical references.

ISBN 978-1-55266-536-7

1. Sociology. I. Balfour, Gillian, 1965-

HM586.U53 2012   301   C2012-903242-5

Contents

Introduction vii

1 Sociology and the Study of Society 1

Revitalizing the Classics
Tony Simmons (Fernwood, forthcoming)... 1

2 Is Human Behaviour the Result of Our Biology? 12

Racialized Policing: Aboriginal Peoples' Encounters with the Police
Elizabeth Comack (Fernwood, 2012).. 13

3 Culture, Society and History 22

"Resisting Conformity: Women Talk About Their Tattoos"
Jessica Antony, in Les Samuelson and Wayne Antony (eds.),
Power and Resistance, 5th ed. (Fernwood, 2012) 22

4 The Basis of Modern Societies 31

"Inequality, the Profit System and Global Crisis"
David McNally, in Julie Guard and Wayne Antony (eds.),
Bankruptcies and Bailouts (Fernwood, 2009)............................ 32

5 Analyzing Social Class 36

"The Economic Crisis: Class Warfare from Reagan to Obama"
Robert Chernomas, in Julie Guard and Wayne Antony (eds.),
Bankruptcies and Bailouts (Fernwood, 2009)............................ 36

6 Living in Capitalist Societies 43

"Alienation and Discipline in High-Performance Sport"
Gamal Abdel-Shehid and Nathan Kalman-Lamb,
in *Out of Left Field* (Fernwood, 2011)...................................... 43

7 The Social Construction of Ideas and Knowledge 48

Missing Women, Missing News
David Hugill (Fernwood, 2010) 48

8 The Role of the State... 59

"Crime as a Social Problem: From Definition to Reality"
Les Samuelson, in Les Samuelson and Wayne Antony (eds.),
Power and Resistance, 5th ed. (Fernwood, 2012) 60

9 Neoliberalism and Globalization 69

Cops, Crime and Capitalism: The Law-and-Order Agenda in Canada
Todd Gordon (Fernwood, 2006) 70
"Towards a Theory of Terrorism"
Gary Teeple, in Sandra Rollings-Manusson (ed.), *Anti-Terrorism:
Security and Insecurity after 9/11* (Fernwood, 2009) 73

10 Inequality of Wealth and Income 87

"On the Streets There's No Forgetting Your Body"
Jeff Shantz, in Diane Crocker and Val Marie Johnson (eds.),
Poverty, Regulation, and Social Justice (Fernwood, 2010) 87

11 Race and Ethnicity 90

"Race and Racism as Determinants of Health"
Josephine B. Etowa and Elizabeth A. McGibbon, in
Elizabeth McGibbon *Oppression: A Social Determinant
of Health* (Fernwood, 2012) 90

12 Gender Issues 102

"The Social Construction of 'Dangerous' Girls and Women"
Karlene Faith and Yasmin Jiwani, in Carolyn Brooks and
Bernard Schissel (eds.), *Marginality and Condemnation*,
2nd edition (Fernwood, 2008) 102

13 Looking Toward the Future 128

"Squat the City, Rock the Courts: Challenging the Criminal
Marginalization of Anti-Poverty Activism in Canada"
Lisa Freemen, in Diane Crocker and Val Marie Johnson (eds.),
Poverty, Regulation, and Social Justice (Fernwood, 2010) 129

Notes 141

References 145

Introduction

The kids aren't alright.... since the economic recession of 2008 youth unemploy-ment has continued to climb: today almost one million young Canadians are out of school and out of work (Statistics Canada 2012), including university graduates with staggering student loan debts. Unemployment is gendered and racialized: Aboriginal and Black young men are hardest hit by the collapsing job market as they are more likely to drop out of school, but all young men as a group have the highest rate of unemployment. So, are the "shock jocks" at Sun Media, CNN and the *Globe and Mail* right when they describe youth today as lazy, entitled and selfish? Probably not. But such stereotypes make it easier to police and criminalize young people, like we see in the media accounts of student protestors in Quebec in 2012 and the G20 protests in Ontario in June 2010. What do economics and politics have to do with sociology? Sociology is about you, but also how you are connected to and impacted by structures like the political and economic systems and how these systems shape your everyday world, like the coffee you drink in the morning on the way to class, the clothes you buy, the courses you take at university and the food you eat. Sociology tackles the big questions of police brutality, suicide and human trafficking in ways that might surprise you.

This collection of critical essays written by Canadian sociologists is intended to animate or illustrate some of the key conceptual arguments you will learn in *How Societies Work: Class, Power and Social Change* (Naiman 2012). Most introductory text books try to cover a lot concepts and theories of several different aspects of the discipline. These two books are different. Instead we hope that you become deeply engaged in a key sociological debate over the role of capitalism in human societies — and begin to explore capitalism as an inherently social practice of power that organizes all aspects of our daily lives. These books are not like those you will likely find in your economics, political studies or business courses: sociologists look at capitalism as the scaffolding of contemporary social life: what movies come to theatres, the music you can download, even if you get married and have children. To understand the place of capitalism's logic and demands in our personal lives, we need to think sociologically about our place in history, our own biographies as immigrants or Indigenous peoples, our sexualities and our spiritual beliefs. As much as the social world stems from the demands of capitalism, we are agents of change. The deepening of poverty and exclusivity of affluence is not inevitable; we can alter how capitalism shapes our lives — we just need to know how it works. That's what these books are about: understanding how societies work.

1 Sociology and the Study of Society

In this chapter, you will be introduced to a new way of thinking about yourself — using your "sociological imagination." C.Wright Mills (1959) coined the expression "sociological imagination" to encourage us to see the linkages between public issues and private troubles; rather than blame ourselves as individuals we need to see the connections between what we experience and how the world works, or does not work. A sociologist's imagination is animated by theory and research; it is not common sense. Sociological theories are sets of assumptions woven together to explain social problems and to create possible solutions. Sociological research is conducted in various ways (for example, interviews, case studies, surveys, participant observation, focus groups and content analysis of media or government documents). Research makes sociology a social science; our theories are grounded in the material world of peoples' lives. Some theories are orientated towards social change to improve the conditions of peoples' lives, and other theories seek to devise systems of social order and control. Sociology of "change" is grounded in the ideas of Karl Marx and later of Max Weber. Sociology of social order asks a different set of questions about how the world works and human nature and is informed by the ideas of Emile Durkheim.

Revitalizing the Classics

Tony Simmons (Fernwood, forthcoming).

"The Historical Materialism of Marx"

A spectre is haunting the office towers and boardrooms of the failed banks and mortgage companies. It is the spectre of Karl Marx. More than any other theorist covered in this book, the ghost of Karl Marx refuses to rest in peace; his critique of capitalism has never seemed as relevant as it does today.... The past few years have revealed a steadily deepening crisis in the global financial system — a crisis unprecedented in recent memory. The early symptoms of this downward spiral were first seen in 2007 with the start of what became known as the sub-prime mortgage crisis. After a decade or more of conspicuous consumption — often borrowing on the equity of their own homes — many American homeowners were suddenly faced with plummeting house values, soaring mortgage interest rates, an end to easy credit and crippling levels of personal debt. The results of this economic meltdown were catastrophic for many ordinary people: mortgage foreclosures, personal bankruptcy, dispossession and eviction from their homes. And much more was to come. Like a toxic virus, the financial crisis spread from the banks and mortgage companies to other institutions in the economy — insurance companies, credit rating agencies and bond markets. And having infected the financial centres of the United States, the contagion then migrated to Europe, Asia and the rest of the planet. In just a few years we have witnessed a complete cycle of boom-bubble-bust: a crisis that originated in the housing market but which has spread to every corner of the economy.

It was during the 1980s that the neoliberal agenda was first unleashed on an unsuspecting public: tax cuts for the rich and super rich and cutbacks in social spending for middle and low income families; as well as increased militarization and bloated defence budgets.... Unsecured mortgages were offered to unqualified applicants, and credit was extended to anyone who requested it. But this bubble of infinite consumption was doomed to burst, and when it did — several decades later — the results were disastrous for almost everyone. The crunch came in 2008. After the first wave of foreclosures and evictions in the housing market, the bank failures followed.

For many working people, the financial collapse that led to the loss of their homes was exacerbated by contractions in the energy, manufacturing and retail sectors of the economy. In order to cut their production and distribution costs, many corporations — and public sector employers — resorted to measures such as workforce cutbacks, wage rollbacks, layoffs, reduced benefits and outsourcing to shore up declining profit margins. The consequences of these measures have been depressingly similar for a growing percentage of the workforce — unemployment, underemployment and declining real incomes. But perhaps the most shocking picture to emerge from the carnage of the financial crisis is the ever widening gap in income and wealth between the super rich and the rest of society. While the top corporate elite has experienced an unprecedented gain in wealth and income over the past few decades, the disappearing middle class and lower income groups have seen their standards of living rapidly eroded — in many cases — into poverty.

None of this would have surprised Karl Marx. Over 150 years ago, he predicted that capitalist societies would remain vulnerable to recurrent boom-bubble-bust crises. His critical analysis of capitalism convinced him that boom periods of production and accumulation would inevitably slump into recessions or even depressions. During these economic meltdowns, it was only the capitalist elite that would profit from its financial speculation while the majority of the working-class population would slide downwards into greater poverty and insecurity. Indeed, he believed that capitalism was an inherently unjust system of social and economic relations in which those who produced the wealth in society — whether in fields, factories, mines, drilling sites or offices — were doomed to have this wealth extracted from them as profit for the capitalist class, which owned the means of production.

Whatever we may think about Karl Marx, his diagnosis and prognosis of capitalism as an unjust and unstable economic system remain as relevant today as on the day he completed the first volume of his famous three-volume work, *Das Kapital,* in 1867. Indeed, during 2011, we witnessed the rise of a grassroots movement, Occupy Wall Street, that is protesting against the excessive salaries, bonuses and profits pocketed by the financial elite, which has, through its ruinous policies of speculation and accumulation, put private greed far above any consideration of public need. Although the Occupy Movement has so far resisted demands to formulate a detailed political platform or program, there can be no doubt about its main concern: the growing gap between the super rich and the rest of the population — in the U.S. and beyond. Unsurprisingly, these concerns have been echoed in many other parts of the world. The movement identifies itself with what it calls the 99 percent of the population, in opposition to the 1 percent, who own and control an inordinate share of global wealth and income and who exercise disproportionate political influence. In other words, the Occupy Movement wants an end to the system in which a privileged elite is able to exploit and dominate the overwhelming majority of the population in contemporary capitalist society. The ghost of Karl Marx casts a long shadow.

So what is it like to live in these difficult times of economic uncertainty where wages are falling and the cost of living is rising? Using our sociological imagination means that we try to understand people's choices in context; how we behave or think is shaped endlessly by our social worlds.

"The Skeptical Modernism of Max Weber"

On October 21, 2009 ... Patrick Clayton walked into the Workers' Compensation Board (WCB) in Edmonton, Alberta, with a loaded shotgun and took nine people hostage. Clayton announced that he was trying to publicize his long-standing and unresolved grievance against the WCB. Apparently, after his benefits had been cut off, he was forced to turn to street drugs as an alternative source of pain medication — resulting in his subsequent addiction. Later that day, he released all the hostages unharmed before he was arrested, charged and taken into custody. In November 2011, he finally went to trial where he pleaded guilty to a number of criminal offences arising from this incident and was sentenced to eleven years' imprisonment. Besides the obvious drama of the hostage-taking, this event focused greater public scrutiny on the WCB in particular and, more generally, on how individuals are treated by large bureaucratic organizations in our society.

Plenty of opinions have been expressed about the hostage taking. Most editorials found it safest to simply condemn the incident as a serious criminal offence and to empathize with the hostages, who were traumatized — although physically unhurt — by their experience. At the same time, however,

Edmonton hostage-taker was "prisoner of corporate bullying"
CTVNews.ca Staff
Updated: Thu. Nov. 17, 2011 5:10 PM ET

Two years ago, Patrick Clayton walked into the downtown Edmonton offices of the Workers' Compensation Board and took nine people hostage at gunpoint. On Thursday, the 40-year-old Clayton apologized to his victims and attempted to explain his actions as a cry for help. Though some people supported Clayton after the incident, he was charged with hostage-taking, possession of a weapon for dangerous purposes and pointing a firearm. Ten days ago, he pleaded guilty to those charges. But on Thursday Clayton told an Edmonton courtroom that the hostage situation resulted from anger and frustration that left him feeling like a "political prisoner of corporate bullying." On the day of the incident, Clayton walked into the downtown building and pulled out a firearm, forcing nine people into a boardroom. Over the next hours, Clayton slowly let his captives go. Ten hours after the incident began, Clayton was arrested peacefully by police. While the standoff shocked Edmonton's downtown business community, it was the culmination of a long-standing ordeal for Clayton. Six years before the Oct. 21, 2009, standoff, Clayton was injured on the job and soon became embroiled in the bureaucratic process of getting compensation. Three years after the injury, Clayton had a standoff with police on a city bridge. And finally, on a Wednesday morning, Clayton stormed the WCB armed with a gun.

From the Canadian Press

while no one has condoned the kidnapping of hostages, there has also been an outpouring of sympathy for the hostage taker. Whatever the merits of Patrick Clayton's own case, it is clear from other testimonials that many individuals feel they have been poorly treated by the WCB.

[This story of Patrick Clayton] exemplifies some of the worst features of large bureaucracies. Many people perceive the treatment they've received at the hands of bureaucratic officials to have been unfair, unreasonable and unjust. Besides the WCB, complaints of callous, dismissive or indifferent officials have involved Immigration, Customs and Excise and Revenue Canada, to name a few government departments. Most of these stories share a similar profile: the impersonal application of rules and regulations without any concern for the individual case; a wooden obedience to a hierarchical chain of command; secrecy and unaccountability; ensuring that the operational requirements of the organization always trump the demonstrated needs of the individual; an overemphasis on "red tape" and documentation; and the triumph of authority over humanity.

In the public mind, bureaucracies are frequently been seen in negative terms — sometimes as shadowy and sinister unelected centres of power and secret information or, more commonly, as time-wasting and inefficient government agencies. Recent events have fuelled popular concerns over the growing power and global reach of large government bureaucracies. Since 9-11, for example, many individuals have been apprehended at airports or other public places and relocated — through the extra-judicial practice of "extraordinary rendition" — to secret sites for "enhanced interrogation." Individuals caught up in this shadowy web of the secret state — such as Canadian Maher Arar, for example — have found themselves transported into a Kafkaesque world without any due process, constitutional or legal protection and stripped of their human rights (see, for example, such movies as *Rendition* [2007], *Extraordinary Rendition* [2007] and *Taxi to the Dark Side* [2007]).

At the same time, the growing power and secrecy of public and private sector bureaucracies have generated countermovements of resistance and revelation. The age of the giant bureaucracy has also become the age of the whistleblower. Perhaps the most famous of all whistleblowers today is the web-based organization WikiLeaks, along with its celebrity founder, Julian Assange. But other whistleblowers — such as Daniel Ellsberg (in the U.S. during the Vietnam War) and Richard Colvin (in Canada during the Afghan detainee controversy) — have also tried to hold powerful government bureaucracies accountable for their concealment, or distortion, of the truth.

Today, in the post-9-11 world, most of us have become sensitive to the fact that large government and corporate bureaucracies collect and share information about us as never before. The "Beyond the Border" agreement between Canada and the U.S. (the Perimeter Security and Economic Competitiveness Action Plan 2011) gives the Canadian government unparalleled powers to share information on Canadian citizens, permanent residents and others with U.S. national security and law enforcement agencies. Within Canada, the Privacy Commissioner and a number of civil liberties organizations have expressed grave reservations concerning these greatly enhanced powers of surveillance and information sharing. And even while working on our laptops or desktops, in the privacy of our own homes, most of us realize that every keystroke is tracked by private marketing companies, which use this information to send us pop-up advertisements based on our recorded interests and purchases.

But, of course, this is not the whole story; bureaucracies also play a vital and indispensable role in our everyday lives. Without bureaucracies, even the most routine tasks — such as registering a motor vehicle, renewing a driver's licence, submitting a healthcare expense claim or paying taxes — would be infinitely more complicated and drawn out. Notwithstanding their popular reputation as inefficient and time-wasting organizations, bureaucracies actually save most of us a lot of time and effort. Whatever our own feelings about bureaucracies, they have become a quintessential part of modern life. Most of us work in bureaucracies, study in bureaucracies, consume in bureaucracies and are entertained and amused in bureaucracies. Bureaucracies have become an inescapable part of our urban landscape.

Max Weber was one of the earliest theorists to recognize the historical significance of the large, complex, formal organization — i.e., the modern bureaucracy. Weber saw beyond his own time into the future — which is our present — when bureaucracies, for better or worse, would become a definitive feature. Weber saw both the promise and the threat that bureaucracies offered to the modern world and to the life of the individual in modern society. Even now, Weber's name is often invoked whenever the negative effects of bureaucratic rules and regulations hit the headlines. It doesn't take much for any of us to feel like victims when confronted with an implacable bureaucracy.

While Weber foretold the rise of large state and corporate bureaucracies as part of the trend towards increasing rationalization, he remained highly ambivalent about its impact on society. Rationalization, according to Weber, was an irreversible historical trend towards ever greater efficiency, standardization and uniformity. At the same time, rationalization also led to increasing impersonality, regimentation and conformity. It was like a historical tidal wave that swept everything before it; out with the old beliefs and practices based on tradition, faith and religion, and in with the new forces of secularization, science and modernization. Weber famously described this process in the following quote: "The fate of our times is characterised by rationalisation and intellectualisation and above all by the 'disenchantment of the world'" (Weber 1946: 155; see also Ritzer 1999; Koshul 2005).

Weber distinguished between several different types of rationality. But it was formal rationality — the instrumental logic that emphasizes above all else the drive for greater efficiency — which has been responsible for the rationalization of our worldview and our institutions. It is formal rationality that has led to the disenchantment and modernization of our contemporary world. Although Weber anticipated many of the ways in which formal rationality has transformed our lives through scientific and technological innovation, he was also keenly aware that some of these rational innovations could result in negative or even irrational social consequences. Indeed, Weber sometimes darkly alluded to the potential "irrationality of rationality." Thus while a bureaucracy may provide officials with far more efficient means for mass processing a large number of cases — whether these are clients, patients, customers, citizens or inmates — the same bureaucracy may also lead to greater impersonality and insensitivity when dealing with individual cases. [For example] the rationality of nuclear physics has also produced the irrationality of the nuclear bomb. The bureaucratic rationality that founded McDonald's restaurants or Wal-Mart box stores was also responsible for the bureaucratic irrationality of Auschwitz and Treblinka (see Ritzer 2008a; and Bauman 1989). … For Weber, the world-historical process of rationalization conjured up the prospect of a new age in which the "iron cage" of bureaucracy would dominate and suppress the human spirit. Weber also described the rationalization of society (especially the process of bureaucratization) as "the polar night of icy darkness" (Weber 1994: xvi). Rationalization was a sword with a double edge: while it could enhance the struggle for liberty and eliminate scarcity and want; it could also — either through intended or unintended consequences — result in new forms of slavery and inhumanity. Once the genie had escaped from the bottle, there was no way to recapture it. Weber helped to transform the study of society from a traditional scholarly discipline into a modern social science.

Change theories such as those provided by Karl Marx and Max Weber provide us with an understanding of how conflict and resistance are seeds of social transformation that may not always be what we had intended. Order theories focus on how social stability can be reproduced to ensure individuals are socially integrated and morally regulated. Emile Durkheim is the classical sociologist who understood society to be an organism that responds to external pressures (such as an economic recession or outbreak of an infectious disease like HIV/AIDS) through adapting its social institutions to restore social order (such as immigration restrictions from countries with high rates of HIV/AIDS infection, public school sex education programs to include information on safer sex or mandatory HIV/AIDS testing of pregnant women). Ultimately, equilibrium and social stability (order) are natural states of human society; conflict is best contained and managed.

"Emile Durkheim: Summer of Discontent"

In Vancouver, London and many other cities in the United Kingdon, the summer of 2011 will be remembered as a summer of discontent. It was marked by some of the worst riots seen in Canada and Britain for many years. The riot in Vancouver on June 15, which began in the downtown core, was apparently started by disgruntled hockey fans angered over the defeat of their team, the Vancouver Canucks, by the Boston Bruins during the seventh game in the National Hockey League's series of Stanley Cup playoffs. Television viewers across Canada were astounded to see graphic images of young people smashing store windows, looting stores, burning buildings and setting fire to automobiles — including police cars — in a spectacular "bonfire of the vanities." It was, by any account, a night to remember. Perhaps the eeriest aspect of these disturbances was the fact that many rioters and vandals made no effort to conceal their identities. Indeed, they appeared to pose for the camera: assuming heroic and defiant postures on top of burning vehicles or in front of police lines. Many rioters recorded their exploits on smart phones and posted these video clips later — via Facebook — onto the internet. For the crowds of spectators, these events appeared to unfold like a wild and uninhibited reality show on the streets of Vancouver and — via TV — into the living rooms of the nation.

But although the destruction in downtown Vancouver horrified most Canadians, this vandalism was minor in comparison to the widespread urban violence that broke out in many English cities two months later — on August

7, 2011. These disturbances began in the London borough of Tottenham and were precipitated by the police shooting of an unarmed Black man — an Afro-Caribbean motorist named Mark Duggan. Within hours, the riot had spread to other London boroughs and to other cities — including Manchester, Salford, Liverpool, Nottingham and Birmingham. Some observers concluded that London had not seen devastation on this scale since the Blitz.

In the aftermath of these riots there was a predictable flurry of soul searching, hand wringing and recrimination — among media pundits, politicians, clergy and the general public. Everyone, it seemed wanted to offer an instant explanation for these disturbances, as well as an instant fix. In Vancouver, both Mayor Gregor Robertson and Police Chief Jim Chu initially blamed the violence on "anarchists," until it became clear that no real anarchists had taken part in these disturbances. In the U.K., Secretary for Justice Kenneth Clarke blamed the riots on "a feral underclass" — a description that demonized the rioters as wild animals, devoid of any humanity, though the acting commissioner of the Metropolitan Police, Tim Godwin, felt obliged to disassociate himself from these comments. Meanwhile, the mayor of London, Boris Johnson, impatiently dismissed what he labelled "economic and sociological justifications" for the riots. Even before the dust from the riots had settled and the fires had been extinguished, the war of words had already begun: in the newspapers, on TV and radio talk shows, and on Internet blog sites. The orgy of violence and destruction had left in its wake a host of competing explanations, as well as proposals designed to prevent a recurrence of these events. Predictably, attempts to make sense of the chaos ranged widely across the political spectrum — from the far right to the far left and everywhere in-between.

For conservative leading commentators, the riots were explained quite simply in terms of the "pure criminality" of the rioters. Images of looters hauling away stolen merchandise, often in labelled store bags, only served to reinforce the conviction of many observers that these were opportunistic crimes. The looters wanted the same things as the rest of us, except that they were unwilling, or unable, to pay for them. There were even some published reports of looters who tried on store clothes to check their fit, before stealing them. There appeared to be no political motive for these actions — only hyper-consumerism.

In addition to emphasizing the wanton criminality of the rioters, conservatives speculated on other factors that may have contributed to the disturbances. These included the alleged failure of the penal system to adequately punish or deter juvenile crime, the high incidence of family breakdown and single parent households — especially among low income groups — and a perceived decline in public morality and traditional values. Needless to say, these tough-minded explanations were often followed by equally tough-minded proposals for dealing with these and any future disturbances. Some British tabloids —the *Daily Mail* for example — advocated the use of plastic bullets and water canons, as well as the deployment of the Army, to contain the violence on the streets. Previously, these measures had only ever been used within the U.K. in Northern Ireland. Almost everyone insisted on tougher sentences for law breakers, with far less leniency for juvenile offenders. Many Facebook and Twitter feeds went even further, some calling for "shoot to kill" crowd control policies, others for the return of such Victorian remedies as compulsory sterilization of those convicted of civil disorders.

On the other hand, liberal and left-wing commentators were more willing to ascribe the causes of the riots to underlying social and economic conditions. Many blamed government cutbacks and other neoliberal policies that have led to increasing economic inequality and social polarization. Socially marginalized inner-city neighbourhoods and toxic housing estates are also seen as breeding grounds for crime, substance abuse and family breakdown. In some ethnic communities, racist police attitudes and practices are cited as reasons for a general distrust and disrespect of the law. Others believe that the sense of entitlement and impunity displayed by many rioters is a direct result of recently exposed corruption at the very top of society — at least in the U.K. The series of scandals that have plagued the financial, media and political elites has created a pervasive climate of cynicism and disrespect for law and order and a widespread contempt for the authority of the state. For some observers, the rot in British society began at the top and has simply worked its way down to the bottom. Whereas the conservatives argue for a stronger law-and-order agenda and a return to more traditional family and civic values, the liberal left is calling for greater income redistribution, youth employment programs, more educational and training opportunities and greater social inclusion. Each side of the political spectrum believes that while it has pin-pointed the underlying causes of the present social crisis, the opposition is only addressing the symptoms.

The question of what causes social unrest and political upheaval has preoccupied generations of social thinkers. It was certainly a question that the French social theorist Emile Durkheim took very seriously. Indeed, had Durkheim witnessed the riots in London and Vancouver, he undoubtedly would have seen these events as examples of a pathological social condition he called "anomie." "Anomie," for Durkheim, was a state in which individuals no longer felt any real connection to each other, nor any sense of responsibility to a collective social order. More than anything else, anomie is experienced as a state of social detachment in which the individual no longer feels any strong bonds of group membership — whether to the family, the local community, the church or the state. In the modern world, the demands of group membership have become increasing remote and abstract. We have fewer social ties than ever that last for a lifetime and fewer fixed loyalties or codes of conduct. Once we become adults, we are pretty much alone out there to blaze our own trail and determine our own destiny. This is the individualism that has come to define the modern world. But as

Durkheim suggested, if all social ties are eventually dissolved and traditional moral restraints are dismissed as irrelevant, we have reached a pathological state of hyper-individualism — or "anomie. And this is a state when bad things are more likely to happen — such as suicide, homicide, crime, deviance and civil disorder. Durkheim would have instantly recognized the riots as clear symptoms of anomie — of a deep underlying disconnect between the individual and society.

When Durkheim first announced that one of the most serious issues of modern society was the problem of "anomie," he really hit the jackpot. For while Marx may have foreseen the growth of monopoly and global capitalism and Weber may have anticipated the coming perils of totalitarianism, it was Durkheim who first diagnosed the social malaise that would eventually spread in so many different directions. As we shall see, there has always been some academic disagreement over the best way to translate the concept of "anomie." But, most social theorists recognize that the term signifies a fundamental problem in the way modern individuals fit into contemporary society. In a nutshell, Durkheim realized that during periods of rapid social change, many individuals find great difficulty in adjusting to the impersonal and anonymous conditions of modern life, especially when uprooted from more traditional communities. To Durkheim's trained eye, traditional communities provided most individuals with a well-defined social identity, as well as a strong sense of meaning and purpose. People who lived and worked in small communities — such as a Newfoundland outport, a First Nation's reserve, a rural Quebec village or a small town on the Prairies — normally knew who they were, accepted their place in society and understood their purpose in life. Small communities were tightly integrated through such local institutions as the family, the church, the school, the village council, the volunteer fire department and the baseball team. These institutions not only reinforced the identities of members of the community but also helped to socialize individuals into a common set of norms and values. Most people were well integrated into their local community and were guided and regulated by its customary rules and beliefs.

All this began to change with the growth of towns and cities and with the inevitable migration of people from rural areas to urban centres. In the big city, people truly became individuals for the first time in history — alone and often unattached to traditional networks of kinship, religion or community. Life in the big city or the boom town seemed to offer unlimited new experiences and opportunities, while many of the old community-based norms and values no longer served as a practical guide for living. But without their traditional standards of right and wrong, many individuals succumbed to a state of moral confusion and social isolation — Durkheim's "anomie."

The irony of today's information society is that the culture of hyper-individualism is accompanied by ever more frenetic efforts of individuals to stay "fully networked" and "connected" to each other, through a battery of mobile communication devices. Nowadays, many individuals try to stay connected wherever they happen to be — at home, at work, in their cars, in busses, airports, restaurants and — most visibly — on the street. It almost seems as though we are fearful of losing our connection to each other, however momentary and contrived these connections may be. Social networking sites such as Facebook and Twitter provide further evidence of this desperate search for friendship, companionship or simple social contact. Our contemporary culture remains afflicted by an endemic state of anomie, which helps to explain some of the remarkable displays of collective sentiment that followed public events such as the Stanley Cup riot in Vancouver and the riots in London and other U.K. cities . Each of these incidents, in its own way, provided an excuse for a collective sharing of emotion and an opportunity (albeit temporary) for group inclusion and heightened social solidarity.

According to Durkheim, the problem of anomie is especially acute during periods of rapid economic change — whether downward cycles of recession or depression or upward cycles of rapid growth and sudden prosperity. Both boom and bust cycles contribute to a weakening of collective norms and values (moral deregulation) and to a loosening of social ties (social disintegration). Besides the endemic symptoms of loneliness and estrangement, anomie can also contribute to other social problems. The age of hyper-individualism is an age of unregulated appetite and overblown ambition. It is an age in which anything seems possible and everything appears available. Today, the symptoms of public anomie are manifested in a number of different ways — some more pathological than others. At the lower end of the anomic scale is the desperate search for self-affirmation and recognition that preoccupies so many individuals in our society. The rise of the celebrity culture, [the popularity of reality TV shows like *The Biggest Loser* and *Say Yes to the Dress*] and the relentless tide of self-promotion through social media and networking sites all testify to a widespread need for self-celebration and self-celebritization. ...

The culture of anomie has produced some destructive social side effects. Although it is often associated with withdrawal, depression and even suicide, anomie can also contribute to more aggressive forms of behaviour. Some theorists (Reich 1933; Poulantzas 1970; Hoffer 1951) have suggested a link between the widespread public anomie that invariably follows the social fragmentation and demoralization of war and revolution — and the rise of demagogues and populist political leaders. An obvious example is the rise of Adolph Hitler in the aftermath of the defeat and post-war humiliation of Germany in 1914. ... Today, in the second decade of the new millennium, the Tea Party in the U.S. appears to be thriving on a state of anomie that has gripped some sections of the American public in the aftermath of the financial crisis and two costly overseas wars — in Afghanistan and Iraq. Perhaps the most extreme expression of this trend was seen in the horrific mass murder in Norway committed by Andreas Brevik in July 2011.

2 Is Human Behaviour the Result of Our Biology?

Oftentimes when left to make sense of horrific events such as mass murder our analytical toolbox is empty, except for labelling such actions as monsterous and those who commit them as monsters deserving of suffering themselves. But as we have started to explore, using a sociological approach we ask different questions and come to different conclusions. Order theories, such as those rooted in the classical works of Emile Durkheim, discussed in Chapter 1, view social order and social control as the essence of how human societies work because human nature is comprised of instinctual and innate drives such as aggression and lust. Therefore, when people do horrific things, we cast them as pathological or sick, or not having acquired appropriate morality or empathy because of how their brain is "wired' or how poorly controlled they are due to a lack of proper parenting in the home or lax criminal justice policies.

Classical biological determinism has been disproven through advancements in human genome studies; most social scientists agree that human behaviour is a result of a complex interplay between environment, experience and genetics. Social history however shows us how influential biological determinism has been in the protection of elite interests, for example, as that expressed in slavery and colonialism. In this chapter we look at racial profiling by police as a practice of social control that is informed by stereotypes about racialized young men. Naiman (2012)argues that race remains as salient today in how we construct categories of dangerousness and inferiority as it was in the early twentieth century, when governments authorized the forcible sterilization of "mental defectives" using rudimentary intelligence tests, and systems of land ownership by white Europeans were built upon the enslavement of "negroes," whose darker skin and facial features deemed them to be savages undeserving of the privileges of citizenship. Although race as a biological measure of the causes of criminality or conformity has been debunked, young Black and Aboriginal men are more likely to be arrested, charged, confined and, in some cities, shot by police than any other social group. In the readings that follow, Elizabeth Comack documents cases of racial profiling in Winnipeg and Toronto to reveal the social construction of the inner-city crime problem as a race problem.

Racialized Policing:
Aboriginal Peoples' Encounters with the Police
Elizabeth Comack (Fernwood, 2012)

"Race and Racism"

On the early afternoon of January 31, 2005, Winnipeg 911 operators received a call about a robbery that had just occurred at a residence in East Kildonan, an older suburb of the city. The perpetrators were reported to have left the scene in a taxicab. After the police determined that the cab was headed towards Winnipeg's North End, one of the city's inner-city communities, they quickly flooded the area with officers and began doing spot checks of likely suspects. An eighteen-year-old Aboriginal man named Matthew Dumas was walking down a North End street when a police cruiser with a lone officer in it pulled up. When the officer called to him, Matthew took off and ran down a back lane. The officer followed in pursuit. Less than fifteen minutes after this first encounter, Dumas lay dying on a sidewalk. A bullet from a police-issue revolver was lodged in his abdomen.

Following normal protocol for cases in which police officers take the life of a civilian, the Winnipeg Police Service (WPS) Homicide Unit conducted an investigation into the shooting death. The investigation found no basis for criminal negligence or liability on the part of the officers involved. Some three years later an inquest was held into the death. Held over a two-week period in June 2008, the inquest proceeded in typical fashion. Civilian and police witnesses were called to testify before a provincial court judge. Several lawyers were also present — an attorney appointed to represent the Crown, counsel for the Dumas family, and counsel representing the Winnipeg Police Service. The focus of the inquest rested squarely on individual actions and the application of standard police operating procedures. The net result was that members of the Winnipeg Police Service were exonerated. Instead, Matthew Dumas was the one held responsible for his own death. The presiding judge concluded, "Mr. Dumas' behavior and choices drove the events that led to his death on January 31, 2005." In her report the judge also wrote that she "found nothing in the evidence to support the claim that Mr. Dumas' death was a result of racism" (Curtis 2008: 67). ...

"Starlight Tours"

On the morning of November 29, 1990, two construction workers discovered the frozen body of a young Aboriginal man, partially clad and wearing only one shoe, in a field on the outskirts of Saskatoon. The young man was later identified as Neil Stonechild. He had been last seen on the night of November 24, when the temperature had dropped to minus 28 degrees Celsius. Cuts and marks on his body suggested that he had been assaulted, but an autopsy concluded that he had died of hypothermia. The Stonechild family suspected that Neil Stonechild had been driven to the area and abandoned. A police investigation concluded that no foul play was involved in his death.

Some ten years later the frozen bodies of two more Aboriginal men were found on the outskirts of Saskatoon. The shirtless body of Rodney Nastius was discovered on January 29, 2000. He was last seen alive in the early morning hours of that same day in downtown Saskatoon. The frozen body of Lawrence Wegner was found five days later, February 3, 2000. He was wearing a T-shirt, blue jeans, and no shoes. Wegner was last seen alive on January 30, 2000. The day after his body was discovered Darrel Night and his uncle were talking to a police officer they happened to meet and told him about a similar experience. Night said he had been taken out of town by two Saskatoon police officers on January 28, 2000, and dropped off not far from where the bodies of Nastius and Wegner were found. Despite being dressed in only a jean jacket and summer shoes, Night managed to survive by attracting the attention of a worker at the nearby Queen Elizabeth Power Plant. The worker let him into the building to warm up and phone for a taxi.

The freezing deaths of Stonechild, Nastius, and Wegner and Night's revelation that police officers had dropped him off on a bitterly cold Saskatchewan night on the outskirts of the city generated a tidal wave of controversy over what came to be referred to as "Starlight Tours" — a seemingly benign term that connotes the police practice of detaining people, driving them to another location, and leaving them there to find their own way home. That all of these men were Aboriginal also raised the spectre of racism.

As the news about the Saskatoon Starlight Tours spread, Aboriginal organizations reported receiving hundreds of phone calls about similar incidents across the province (Brass 2004; McNairn 2000). A reporter for the Saskatoon StarPhoenix was also receiving calls. He said that "everyone seemed to know someone who had been taken on a starlight tour, and now they were calling him" (Reber and Renaud 2005: 177). Demands for a public inquiry into the matter of Aboriginal-police relations in the province grew louder. Not confident in the criminal justice system's response, the Federation of Saskatchewan Indian Nations (which represents 74 First Nations in the province) hired its own investigator to look into allegations of police brutality against Aboriginal people.

Shortly after Night disclosed his experience to a Saskatoon police officer, Constables Dan Hatchen and Ken Munson were suspended from the Saskatoon Police Service (SPS) and an RCMP task force named Project Ferric was launched to investigate Night's allegations and the deaths of Nastius, Wegner, and Stonechild. In 2001 Hatchen and Munson were found guilty of unlawful confinement and sentenced to eight months' imprisonment. In February 2003 the Saskatchewan Justice Minister announced an inquiry into the death of Neil Stonechild and the investigations carried out by the SPS and the RCMP. Headed by the Honourable Mr. Justice David

Wright, the Commission of Inquiry into Matters Relating to the Death of Neil Stonechild began sitting in September 2003. When the report of the inquiry was submitted in October 2004, Justice Wright made it clear that he was highly critical of the police investigation into Stonechild's death. He characterized it as "insufficient and totally inadequate" (Wright 2004: 212). Following the release of the report, Constables Larry Hartwig and Bradley Senger, the officers involved in the Stonechild case, were dismissed from the Saskatoon Police Service. ...

The response to revelations of Starlight Tours was split into two opposing camps. Aboriginal activists and organizations declared the practice to be evidence of the racism rampant in the Saskatoon police force; police and their supporters said Starlight Tours were a myth perpetrated by special interest groups, and they denied the claims of racism and any wrongdoing on the part of the officers involved in the Night case and the deaths of the other Aboriginal men. But in the broader context of racialized policing these competing positions about Starlight Tours take on a different cast. William King and Thomas Dunn (2004: 341) suggest that the police practice of transporting troublesome persons to another location — otherwise known as "dumping" — is an informal policy that "is generally acknowledged by police practitioners." In Prairie cities such as Saskatoon, this racialized policing practice appears to have become one of the strategies that police utilize to reproduce order in their dealings with troubled and troublesome people.

Life and Death of Darrell Night

With only a Grade 11 education and no current job, thirty-four-year-old Darrel Night was typical of many Aboriginal people living in Saskatoon. Depending on various estimates, from one-third to almost one-half of Aboriginal adults in Saskatoon had less than a Grade 12 level of education. The unemployment rate for Aboriginal people in the city was about 22 percent, compared to 4.8 percent for the non-Aboriginal population (Anderson 2005: 36, 43). Also like many Aboriginal people, Night was in poor health. He regularly suffered from dizziness as a result of a bout with tuberculosis and meningitis. He coped with the imbalance it caused by keeping one eye closed. Also not uncommon, Night had a drinking problem and was no stranger to the police; he had received some twenty-two criminal convictions (Renaud and Reber 2005: 123). While the relationship between Darrel Night and the Saskatoon police was probably already strained, characterized by mistrust and suspicion on both sides, the events of January 28, 2000, brought the strain into bold relief.

On that night Night had been at a house party but left when a fight broke out in the early morning hours. He set off to walk the few blocks to his sister's home, where he was staying. After he left, the police were called to the house on a weapons disturbance because one of the men at the party had been threatening people with a knife. Constables Dan Hatchen and Ken Munson were two of the officers on patrol that night. Each of them had logged some sixteen years on the Saskatoon police force. They had been partners for six years. When they reached the house they were among the last of the police cars to arrive, and so they left the scene. It was then that they met up with Night, who was walking down the street.

As the patrol car slowed down alongside him, Night became belligerent, yelling at the officers: "About fucking time you guys showed up, get the fuck up and stop those fights. I have to tell you what to do?" He also gave them the finger (R. v. Munson and Hatchen 2003 at 6). As the vehicle went by, Night pounded on the side panel and the trunk. In return, the officers called Night a "drunken fucking Indian" (Zakreski 2000). Arresting Night for "causing a disturbance," they handcuffed him and put him in the back of their cruiser. Night assumed that he was being taken to the drunk tank. Instead, the officers drove him to the outskirts of the city, more than two kilometres from the Queen Elizabeth Power Plant. According to Night, they swore at him, "Get the fuck out of here, you fucking Indian" and removed the handcuffs. The cruiser then proceeded to drive away. When Night yelled, "I'm going to freeze out here," the officers stopped the car and yelled back, "That's your fucking problem" (Zakreski 2000). To that point the officers had not indicated on their car's mobile data terminal that they had left the scene of the house disturbance. It was only when they drove away from Night that they keyed "Available" into the terminal (Reber and Renaud 2005: 130). Contrary to police protocols, no record of their encounter with Night was made in their notebooks, and no report was filed with the Saskatoon Police Service. There was also no record of any attempt to check for outstanding warrants, criminal record, or other pertinent information about the man they had arrested (R. v. Munson and Hatchen 2003 at 4).

It took Darrel Night about twenty minutes to walk to the power plant from where the police officers had dropped him off in the minus-25-degree-Celsius weather. He hammered on the doors of the power plant in desperation, and it was another twenty minutes before he attracted the attention of a plant supervisor who was working the night shift. Despite his misgivings in seeing the poorly dressed man pounding on the door, the supervisor opened it to let him in. Night told him, "The police just dumped me out here" (Reber and Renaud 2005: 133). At Night's request, the supervisor called for a cab, which arrived shortly afterward to drive Night to his sister's place, less than one block from where he was arrested.

In addition to the plant supervisor and the cab driver, Night told his sister and other family members about what the police officers had done to him that night. But no official complaint was made. In Night's view, "Complaining was a waste of time" (Reber and Renaud 2005: 135). Some six days later, Night was driving with his uncle when they were stopped by a Saskatoon police officer for a seatbelt violation. While they were waiting for the officer to write up a ticket they heard the news over the radio that a frozen body had been discovered near the power station. Night's uncle ended up telling the police officer that the same thing had happened to his nephew. When the officer asked whether he talked to anyone about his experience, Night replied in the negative, saying "Nobody would listen to me anyway" (Reber and Renaud 2005: 155). The officer reported what he had learned to his superiors, and Night was brought to the police station to provide a statement. Several commentators suggested that if Darrel Night had not survived to tell about his experience, the phenomenon of Starlight Tours would never have come to public attention.

"Driving while Black"

Black people [also] stand a disproportionate chance of being charged and imprisoned in Ontario, and that this overrepresentation had skyrocketed within a period of six years, with 204 percent more Blacks jailed in 1994 than in 1986 (from 4,205 to 12,765 admissions), compared to an increase of 23 percent for whites (from 49,555 to 60,929 admissions) (Ontario 1995). Based on a survey of the general population, the Commission found a widespread perception among Black (58 percent), Chinese (31 percent), and white (36 percent) Torontonians that judges do not treat Black people the same as white people (Ontario 1995: i). While many judges and lawyers interviewed flatly rejected the possibility that systemic racism was a problem in the Ontario criminal justice system, others acknowledged differential treatment based on race as well as class or poverty: "Four in ten defence counsel (40 percent) and three in ten (33 percent) provincial division judges appointed since 1989 perceived differential treatment of white and racial minority people in the criminal justice system" (Ontario 1995: i–ii).

... A survey of 1,657 Metropolitan Toronto residents about their experiences of being stopped by police in the previous two years found that more Black (28 percent) than white (18 percent) or Chinese (15 percent) residents reported being stopped by the police in the last two years (Ontario 1995: 352). More Black (17 percent) than white (8 percent) or Chinese (5 percent) residents reported being stopped more than once in the past two years. Many more Black respondents (39 percent) than white (9 percent) or Chinese (14 percent) respondents believed that the officers who stopped them did not treat them fairly (Ontario 1995: 352).

When broken down by sex and race, the data showed that Black men were particularly vulnerable to being stopped by police. About 43 percent of Black male respondents, but only 25 percent of white male and 19 percent of Chinese male respondents, reported being stopped by the police in the past two years. Also, significantly more Black (29 percent) than white (12 percent) or Chinese (5 percent) men reported being stopped by the police two or more times in the past two years (Ontario 1995: 352).

Analysis of the male sample by age as well as race revealed distinctive patterns. Among men aged eighteen to twenty-four, Black (50 percent) and white (48 percent) men were equally likely to report being stopped by police in the past two years, while Chinese men (22 percent) were less likely to report being stopped. However, Black men (50 percent) aged eighteen to twenty-four were much more likely than both their white (24 percent) and Chinese (11 percent) counterparts to report two or more stops in the past two years. Every Black man aged eighteen to twenty-four who reported being stopped by the police said he was stopped more than once. By contrast, about half of the white or Chinese men in this age group who reported being stopped had experienced tat act on more than one occasion (Ontario 1995: 355). Similar patterns existed for older age groups, with Black men being most likely to have experienced a police stop in the past two years.

When the data on police stops were analyzed in a subsample of male university graduates, Black males (48 percent) with a university degree were much more likely than white (19 percent) or Chinese (11 percent) male university graduates to report being stopped by the police in the past two years. Black male graduates (39 percent) were also much more likely than white (11 percent) or Chinese (7 percent) male graduates to report two or more stops (Ontario 1995: 355). ...

Black respondents strongly believed that police stopped them partly or wholly because of their race. Reflecting the notion that police target African Canadians simply for "driving while Black," some of these respondents believed that they were stopped because they were driving an expensive car. One respondent, for example, said that police stopped him "because they saw a Lexus with a black driver. We were not speeding or anything. They had no real reason to stop us." Others believed that police suspected them of selling drugs. One man said he was stopped because "if you are black and you drive something good, the police pull you over to ask about drugs." In some cases, respondents believed they were stopped because they were accompanied by a white woman. Interestingly, some white people mentioned race as the reason for the police stopping them, but it was the race of their companion that was the factor. One young white male said that he was stopped "because my friend was driving my Mercedes and he's black" (Ontario 1995: 356).

"The 'Usual Suspects'"

[Similar themes emerged] from ... interviews [with] Aboriginal men who live in Winnipeg's inner city and are regularly stopped by police and asked to account for themselves. Officers often carry out warrant checks. When the men ask, "What did I do wrong?" the typical response is "You fit the description" because the police are looking for an Aboriginal man as a suspect in a crime. In other words, the men are stopped precisely because they are Aboriginal. For many of the men we interviewed, this experience has become an all too normal occurrence.

Twenty-year-old Frank said that he is accustomed to being stopped by police "once a week, guaranteed. I can't even, like, count the number of times where I've been stopped just for walking down the street wearing, like, all black or something." When asked what the police say when they stop him, Frank replied, "Nothing. Just, like, put some cuffs on me and say, 'Oh, we have a guy fitting your description. He's breaking into garages or throwing stuff at houses.'" Frank says, "It makes me mad. But, like, there's nothing you can do." ...

Chris, age thirty, reported similar experiences. When he had long hair, he said, "I'd get picked up like every other weekend, you know, just for questioning because I looked like somebody else. And so I figured if I cut my hair it'd be a little bit easier." The strategy helped somewhat. Chris said he now got stopped by police "maybe once a month." .... Owen, nineteen years old, talked about an experience that occurred on the night of his fifteenth birthday party. He was walking in West Broadway, an area in the most southerly part of the inner city, around midnight:

> I was leaving my place and I was walking my friend to his bus stop and when I was on my way back home after I'd left him — I was with three of my friends. We had all gone on this walk and we were at the end of my block. And five cop cars pulled up and all the cops jumped out with guns drawn to our heads and told us to "Get the fuck on the ground!" And they all — and they didn't really give us a chance to say much. If one of my friend's parents hadn't been driving by at the time — 'cause my friend's dad was picking her up, so he saw us all laid down on the ground with the cops drawing guns to our heads and he asked, like, what was going on and he vouched for us. So they eventually let us go.

The police told Owen that someone had been assaulted nearby. As he surmised, "I'm guessing we just fit a description." Owen had been pulled over by police "countless times" since then. The police, assuming he was dealing drugs for a street gang, would ask him: "Who are you selling for?" "Who are you banging for?" "Where's the shit?" ...

While Aboriginal men are presumed to be involved in the drug trade or affiliated with a street gang, Aboriginal women encounter a different kind of [racialized] stereotyping. Given the concerns with the street sex trade that operates in Winnipeg's inner-city neighbourhoods, police often assumed that Aboriginal women found in those spaces are sex workers. As one woman (and she does work in the street sex trade) noted: "They see a girl on a strip where prostitutes happen to roam, they automatically stereotype and think that they're, every girl is out there doing the same thing when, in reality, you know, half the girls that are out there aren't even working. They're just walking by or whatever."

Dianne, twenty-four years old, told us about an incident that happened in the winter of 2008. She had been visiting her uncle in the downtown area. On her way home to the North End, she walked across a bridge and stopped to use a pay phone to call her dad and ask for a ride the rest of the way. A police car pulled up, and the officers proceeded to charge her with a prostitution offence.

> They said I was standing around trying to work the streets.… They grabbed me and they handcuffed me and they took me.… I did get a lawyer and did get it dropped because there was no evidence or nobody saying that, like, no undercover cop saying that I was talking to them or anything. So they just said that they, the cops said that they saw me going to a car, which I wasn't. I was going to the pay phone. So if they don't know the difference between a pay phone and a car, then, I don't know, something's wrong with them.

Similarly, Christine, a thirty-three-year-old, told of being stopped by police on her way to the corner store. The police assumed that she was a sex-trade worker.

> I live in an area where there is prostitution happening there and, like, sometimes I go to the store and, like, right away they're driving by and then they slow down. Like, "I'm going to the store," and, like, "Oh, you're lying." Like what — a woman can't even walk the street today? Every woman that walks the street today is what, supposed to be a hooker?

Simply, then, … Aboriginal people are subject to the racialized and gendered stereotypes associated with the "usual suspects." Those of us who have never been the target of such stereotyping (especially by police officers) can only imagine how scary and unsettling that experience can be. Racialized policing, however, runs deeper than the use of stereotypes; it is also implicated in the particular cultural frames of reference or stocks of knowledge that officers adopt in the course of their work.

Where do these "cultural frames" about racialized young men and women as dangerous or sexually promiscuous come from? Naiman explains that culture organizes the social life of humans (norms, values, language, symbols) and helps us acquire what we need to survive (food, clothing, shelter, companionship). So, there is a profound connection between our social lives and the physical world. The criminalization of Aboriginal peoples' cultural practices (such as the potlatch or feasting) was a key strategy for the expansion of economic interests of colonialist Europeans who sought to control the land and its natural resources. Residential schools for Aboriginal children were strategies of cultural genocide that sought to exterminate "the Indian in the child" (Milloy 1999) and instill and promote European values and Christian beliefs. We need to consider contemporary policing practices such as "starlight tours" as cultural practices that are rooted in a colonial history.
    In the next chapter we continue to look at how the material and economic

dimensions of our society have produced dominant cultural values, norms, ways of talking and making meaning of tattoos, especially amongst women. Tattoos are symbolic of profound socio-economic change; their imagery and placement on our bodies play an important role in our culture as commodities and as acts of self-expression.

3 Culture, Society and History

"Resisting Conformity: Women Talk About Their Tattoos"

Jessica Antony, in Les Samuelson and Wayne Antony (eds.),
Power and Resistance, 5th ed. (Fernwood, 2012)

Historically, tattoos have had a negative image (Hawkes et al. 2004: 593). Tattooed bodies were thought to be monstrous — as examples of bodily excess, as sex objects or hypersexual beings, or as primitive, threatening, or circus-like spectacles. Tattoos were associated with undesirable class location and sexual behaviour — a "destructive decoration that flouts the possibility of untainted flesh" (Braunberger 2000: 1). Situated within a racist ideology, tattooing and body art were interpreted not as "the rational choice of an enlightened individual, but constitute[d] instead a primitive response more usually associated with the uncivilized behaviour of savages" (Widdicombe and Wooffitt 1995: 139). Lower class, marginalized people embodied the notion of tattooing — the sailor, military man, biker, gang member, or prisoner — and were seen as deviant and counter cultural. Today, however, what was once a practice reserved for the so-called "seedy underbelly"of society has become, in the eyes of some, just an appropriated marketing tool. In the last few years, the 7-Eleven convenience store chain has started selling an energy drink, called "Inked," to their young customers who are either tattooed or "those who want to think of themselves as the tattoo type" (Associated Press/ CBS News 2007). The drink's can features tribal-style designs, while the promotional posters include the outstretched, tattooed arm of a white male. This new marketing strategy ... was created to sell a drink "that appealed to men and women, and the tattoo culture has really become popular with both genders" (Antony 2012: 216). Tattooing can be used to sell products to the young or those who "think and act young" (Associated Press 2007). Other corporations are jumping on this marketing bandwagon as well, offering, for example, four free tires to anyone who has Dunlop's flying "D" logo tattooed on their body (MSNBC 2007). It would seem that tattooing's dubious past has all but disappeared. The Western history of tattooing, however, has posed a conundrum for contemporary North American capitalist culture: in order to create a tattoo market by commodifying tattoos in the pursuit of profit, a distance from this history had to be established. While tattoos were once a form of deviance, they are now much more embedded in mainstream culture — they are made normal through reality television shows, such as LA Ink and Miami Ink; through increasingly tattooed professional athletes and musicians, such as Allen Iverson, Mike Tyson, and John Mayer; or even simply through the proliferation of tattoo shops and parlours throughout North America. In order to enable their capitalist commodification, tattoos and body art required a social acceptability — especially for the middle-class consumer.

One way in which social acceptability has been accomplished is through appropriating Eastern culture (DeMello 1995, 2000) — a culture in which tattoos have had considerable significance and mark a rite of passage in the achievement of personal growth. This new generation of tattooing is one that has been defined both by rejecting the traditional working-class meanings and history associated with the practice and by appropriating and creating new meanings, a new history, and a new discourse surrounding tattooing practices. The focus of this new generation is on the tattoo as a means of personal and spiritual growth and the creation of individuality (DeMello 2000) — a set of meanings that differ significantly from the working-class meanings traditionally associated with tattooing, such as masculinity and patriotism. Furthermore, the creation of an entirely new history focuses on the roots of tattooing in Japanese and Polynesian cultures, rejecting the association of tattooing with the low-class and marginalized individuals that originally introduced the practice to Western society. As well, this new discourse surrounding tattooing borrows from the self-help discourse of the 1970s and 1980s, as tattoo enthusiasts now locate tattooing as an identity-altering practice. Nevertheless, the remnants of Western history have not been completely erased. There is still the association of tattoos as a sign of difference and resistance. In this regard, the mainstream acceptability and popularity of tattoos have proved problematic for women who want to use tattooing as a means of expressing their identities. The tattoo is particularly strange as it represents at once permanence and change. While in the physical it is permanent (tattoos are very difficult, almost impossible to remove from the skin), the meanings surrounding tattoos change over time. The problem for women, then, becomes two-fold: within our capitalist and patriarchal society, how do tattooed women negotiate the tension between tattoos as a sign of conformity (to mainstream consumer culture) and one of resistance or reinvention (as a challenge to patriarchal gender roles)? Given the increasingly commodified nature of tattooing in mainstream Western culture, are women's tattoos merely a reflection of that consumerist culture? Or, are women's tattoos a flouting of gender roles and resistance to a pa-triarchal culture that pushes women to act and carry themselves in certain, oppressive ways?

Are so-called "feminine" tattoos — butterflies and flowers, for example — considered not subversive enough to be seen as a resistance of patriarchy?

I am interested in addressing these questions not only as a fan of tattoos, but also as a tattooed woman myself. I acquired my first tattoo at the age of eighteen while on a trip to Australia, shortly after I graduated from high school. Since then I have become a collector, adding ten more tattoos to my body — the tenth being a piece, still in progress, that will cover my entire right arm. I became interested in the questions surrounding the problem of tattoos for women as I experienced some of these negotiations myself — feeling unfeminine with such large, prominent tattoos, or thinking about my own tattoos as a commodity in comparison to those whose skin has not been inked.

In order to explore the social and individual meaning of women's tattoos, I spoke with eighteen tattooed women. These women told me the stories of their tattoos: why they got them, how they decided on them, and how they feel about them. These "tattoo narratives" (cf. DeMello 2000) serve as a means of making connections between each tattoo project and a broader historical context, ultimately reconciling for these women the tension between conformity and resistance. Authenticity, a key theme in my analysis and the women's stories, has a number of meanings. It is used to refer to the desire, expressed by the women I spoke with, to create a legitimate, original self-identity through their tattoo projects; a sincere, long-term commitment to a tattoo; and the sense of uniqueness that comes from being marked as different. The women acknowledged the nuances of authenticity not overtly, but through the ways in which they explained and understood tattooing. DeMello argues that, in appropriating the Eastern history of tattooing, contemporary North American tattoo enthusiasts have created a new tattoo "text." This new tattoo text, in presenting tattoos as a symbol of individuality, allows for tattoos to become a part of the mainstream — it allows for them to be culturally commodified.

Cultural commodification, or the repackaging of once low-class cultural symbols into products for the consumption of the mainstream, is what bell hooks describes as "eating the Other" (hooks 1992). She argues that, through cultural commodification, the media inundate us with "messages of difference" that your sense of self-identity can be found in the Other or, in the case of tattoos, in a practice that was once reserved for the marginalized. The Other then becomes a product, commodified for the mainstream, as the media tell us that "the 'real fun' is to be had by bringing to the surface all those 'nasty' unconscious fantasies and longings about contact with the Other" (hooks 1992: 21) that are entrenched in Western culture.

Commodification is an integral process in capitalism. As Karl Marx and Friedrich Engels (1998) argued long ago, in capitalism there is an incessant, relentless search by capitalists for new markets, for constantly pushing the market into areas of human life that have not been turned into products to buy, sell, and consume. As they put it in The Communist Manifesto, over 160 years ago:

The bourgeoisie, wherever it has got the upper hand… has left no other nexus between man and man [sic] than naked self-interest, than callous "cash payment." It has drowned out the most heavenly ecstasies of religious fervour, of chivalrous enthusiasm, of philistine sentimentalism, in the icy water of egotistical calculation. It has resolved personal worth into exchange value, and in place of the numberless indefeasible chartered freedoms, has set up that single, unconscionable freedom — Free Trade. (Marx and Engels 1998: 3)

There are no bounds to the desire to turn everything into products for sale. … An example of commodification can be found all over Canada and the Western world. Che Guevera, an Argentinean revolutionary who is most famous for leading the Cuban Revolution with Fidel Castro in the late 1950s, was a Marxist who fought against the economic injustices in Latin America and the capitalist dictators that did nothing to alleviate their people's poverty. He fought specifically against the capitalist system of commodification — that is, the fruits of impoverished people's labour being exploited by those from wealthy countries. Now, we find T-shirts, mugs, hats, posters, and calendars emblazoned with Che's image, mass-produced — often by the labour of marginalized or impoverished people who are not paid a fair wage — and sold to the mainstream as an image of so-called rebellion, rebellion devoid of Che's original meaning. Elizabeth Hurley, a British movie star, was photographed a few years ago holding a Louis Vuitton handbag embroidered with an image of Che. In short, the image of a man who spent his life fighting the commodification of labour has now been commodified. This example points to the deep underlying dynamic of the commodification imperative: empty the meaning from anything and everything human and humane; reduce all to the essence of capitalism — things, people, emotions, and rights are only meaningful as products to be bought and sold as the basis for profit-making. Yet, is this process complete and all encompassing? Does everyone go along with the commodification imperative?

This new text, then, that is created when the practice of tattooing is appropriated from Eastern cultures is important in making sense of the ways in which the women I spoke with understand their tattoos. But to see this tattoo process as only commodification falls short because it does not recognize the constant shifting in the specific meaning of and narratives surrounding tattoos, political or otherwise. The ways in which we talk about tattoos has changed (as analysts like DeMello argue). I agree it has and must in order for tattoos to reach the place in mainstream culture where we see them today. However, I want to take the argument one step further in suggesting that, though tattoo discourse has changed as tattoos have become commodified, tattoo wearers — particularly women — are not merely marking themselves with a product devoid of any meaning except that of a popular commodity. That is, tattoos are not simply a commodification meant to represent a sense of false individuality — they are more complex than that, and they can represent genuine cultural connections made by women as they undertake their tattoo projects. More generally speaking, the sense of individuality and authenticity that tattoos represent for some women constitute one of the ways in which women negotiate conformity and resistance in a patriarchal, capitalist culture. In this sense, then, cultural commodification is nuanced and, in the case of tattoos as a form of self-identification, the struggle for self-identity is indeed one of the ways in which women confront and resist the ongoing capitalist effort to turn everything into a commodity, including permanent body modifications. Tattoos and tattooing are, then,

> a window on this process of commodification and the resistance to it in patriarchal capitalism.

However, in order to understand the contemporary problem of the tattooed woman

> — the negotiation between resistance and conformity — it is important to examine the historical context within which modern-day tattooing, and thus, tattooed women, is situated.

Historical Context

Tattooing reaches back thousands of years and can be found in nearly all parts of the world at some time (Caplan 2000: xi). Going back to colonial times, Westerners have had contact with cultures that revered tattooing. These practices eventually found their way into Canadian and U.S. culture. The commodification imperative — reduce all to the essence of capitalism: things, people, emotions, and rights are to be only meaningful as products to be bought and sold as the basis for profit-making. North American (co-lonial) tattooing is rooted in the sea voyages of early European travellers of the late eighteenth and early nineteenth centuries. Explorers to the South Pacific came into contact with the tattooed Other in Polynesia, Micronesia, and Melanesia. While Europeans had experienced tattooing as early as the 1600s, it was James Cook who first documented the "pervasiveness of 'tat-tooing' (a derivation of the Tahitian term *ta-tu* or *tatau*) among South Pacific cultures" (Atkinson 2003: 31).

European explorers' exposure to tattooed tribal natives had a profound effect — the explorers considered the tattooed natives to be savage and weird and saw tattooing as a frightening foreign ritual. Native peoples were cap-tured and transported back to Europe with the explorers as "living evidence of primitivism in the New World" (Atkinson 2003: 31). Sold and paraded through European museums and sideshows, these individuals — women especially — were seen by Europeans as the "radical self-expression, physical vanity, and exuberant sexuality they had denied themselves… in the service of their restrictive deity" (Atkinson 2003: 31). Many Natives were baptized and given new, Christian names in an attempt to liberate them "from their 'spiritual and physical slavery'" (Oettermann 2000: 195).

Many European sailors returned home decorated with tattoos, exposing the upper and middle classes of European society to the practice, and arguably "reaffirming [their] understanding of their own cultural advancement and progress, as the outwardly uncontrolled libidinal bodies of 'backward' tribal cultures of the world articulated a brutality long overcome in Western cultures" (Atkinson 2003: 31). The practice among South Pacific Islanders changed too as a result of colonizers' visits. Tattoo designs soon came to include images such as ships, flags, guns, cannons, and even portraits of European royalty. Their meanings shifted, as well. For example, Hawaiian tattoos were once thought to protect the person from harm, but after the introduction of guns and other weapons the significance of protective tattooing dwindled away. The Maori of New Zealand have traditionally tattooed their faces as a sign of status and lineage; however, after European explorers and colonizers began trading goods for the tattooed heads they found so fascinating, the Maori stopped tattooing their faces in fear of being decapitated (Govenar 2000: 213; Atkinson 2003: 32).

During this period, Europeans saw tattooing as both fascinating and deplorable a paradox of sorts — and interpreted the tattooed body as a source of exotic entertainment.

Sailors tattooed their bodies as both a keepsake of their overseas adventures and as a form of excitement, setting themselves apart from the majority in European society. With more and more sailors coming home with cultural inscriptions permanently marked on their bodies, tattooing started to creep into mainstream European culture and eventually (colonial) North American culture (Atkinson 2003: 33). In 1876 at the Centennial Exposition in Philadelphia, some of the first tattooed native people were put on display for the enjoyment and wonder of the audience. Even as members of the Navy were coming home adorned with tattoos, the majority of European and North American society had little to no knowledge of the practice.

Taking their cue from the success of tattooed sideshow performers, tattooed Navy servicemen coming back from overseas started to exhibit themselves in travelling circuses and sideshows. Part of the attraction, however, was the notion of a savage native from a foreign land covered in frightening markings. As the Navy men were obviously of European heritage, they concocted elaborate back-stories to accompany their exhibitions. Many would claim to have been captured by savages and tattooed against their will, thus perpetuating the notion of tattooing as the frightening ritual of an "uncivilized Other" (Atkinson 2003). The designs that were popular largely consisted of patriotic symbols, religious imagery, and erotic illustrations of women. These designs, Alan Govenar (2000: 217) argues, constituted a "folk art form" generated by word of mouth and imitation. This folk art provides, to some extent, insight into the cultural context of the time, as tattoo artists were necessarily aware of the demands of their audience. The social coercion that the designs adhered to promoted not only conformity, but tradition, thus serving as a visual representation of important symbols of the day. Primarily patriotic and religious, these designs communicated loyalty, devotion, and (oddly enough) conservative morals (Govenar 2000).

By the end of the 1930s tattoo exhibits were becoming less exciting and exotic as more and more people were becoming tattooed and exposed to tattoos. Tattooed performers then had to develop more elaborate back-stories to entice their audiences — such as the "abducted farmer's daughter," who was tattooed against her will — and women, in particular, found it necessary to dress more provocatively in order to maintain the interest of the audience (Govenar 2000: 225). As tattoos became more common, sideshow audiences turned to the circus for entertainment. To attract audiences, women took centre stage as tattooed attractions — women who were often the wives and girlfriends of tattooists or were simply lured into the profession with the promise of fame and fortune (Atkinson 2003: 35). The show then became somewhat pornographic, as women would take the stage and strip before the crowd, displaying their tattooed bodies. These shows became some of the most popular midway attractions through to the 1940s.

The introduction of tattoos into the carnival and sideshow exhibitions ultimately served as a means of exploring desires and emotions that were socially repressed at the time in a controlled way. Tattoos were seen as a form of deviance and tattooed bodies were considered savage and frightening. The sideshows provided the means for "North Americans to experience subversive pleasures with and tortures of the flesh without sacrificing commonly held cultural understandings of corporeal respectability" (Atkinson 2003: 36); that is, North Americans were able to enjoy these pleasures from a distance, without subjecting their own bodies to the taboo of marking the skin, which was seen as lacking respectability. This era firmly established the association between tattooing and social deviance, a particularly important connection to note as this association has carried through to the present. Returning home after the Second World War, servicemen found that their symbolically patriotic tattoos now held a great deal of negative social value. The significance and patriotism once associated with tattooing started to diminish, and by 1946 new recruits were no longer interested in becoming tattooed. Tattoos were even restricted in the military in the 1950s — if they limited the effectiveness of a man's ability to work (due to infection, for example), he would be prosecuted. In the context of the increasingly urban, family-centred nature of North American culture in the 1950s, tattoos were once again associated with disrepute and deviance. Societal values shifted toward material comfort and middle-class conformity, and tattoos were strongly identified with lower-class, criminal individuals and groups. Once a symbol of group expression and national pride, tattoos were now interpreted as a widespread sign of criminality (Govenar 2000).

Radical Shifts: Contemporary Commodification

The political upheaval of the 1960s and 1970s brought with it a great many cultural shifts, including the popular conception of tattooing. Women, in particular, began to question and fight normative notions of femininity and gender roles, resurrecting tattoos as a means of redefining themselves as women. Margot Mifflin explains:

> [Women] began casting off their bras as they had their corsets a half-century earlier, tattoos were rescued from ignominy and resurrected in the counterculture by women who were rethinking womanhood. The arrival of the Pill in 1961 had given women a new sexual freedom; a little over a decade later legalized abortion secured their reproductive rights. Not surprisingly, the breast became a popular spot for tattoos—it was here that many women inscribed symbols of their newfound sexual independence. (1997: 56)

With the swell of popularity — especially among women — in tattooing, the middle classes began to become involved in the historically marginalized practice. Cultural icons such as musicians and actors started to embrace the practice, thus enticing young, middle-class individuals to follow suit. While the popularity of the practice was already entrenched among the marginalized classes, the 1960s and 1970s saw an increase in its popularity among more privileged classes, thus introducing tattooing to the mainstream and drawing widespread attention to the practice. The designs that had held up since the early 1900s, however, were no longer of interest to young people. Not able to identify with the extremely patriotic imagery, they demanded more customized, personal images, which opened up the art to the appropriation of designs from other cultures. Tattoo artists as a whole also became a more educated, artistic group in keeping with the demand for more complicated, personalized designs. Young tattoo artists began to see tattooing as a representation of identity, "treating the body as less and less of a canvass to be filled with tattoos and more as an integral part of the self, the young middle-class insurgence into the tattoo artist profession redefined many of the old ideologies held strongly in the trade" (Atkinson 2003: 45). Artists experimented with different styles and shops moved from the urban ghetto to the youth centres of the city.

The 1970s and 1980s saw more people than ever before embrace tattooing as form of self-expression. Michael Atkinson explains this process:

> Influenced by political movements that shook conservative understandings of the body to the ground, interpretations of tattoos were more varied and subject to contextual construction. As women and more "respectable" social classes participated in tattooing it transformed into a practice of political identity construction. (2003: 46)

By the 1990s tattoos had become mainstream phenomena, with scores of tattoo shops cropping up in many major North American cities. In the present context, therefore, artists must now be able to adapt to new styles, designs, and needs of their customer base. New methods of communication, and thus, marketing, have brought a whole new dimension to the tattoo industry, with tattoo magazines, websites, message boards, and online communities developing and flourishing, bringing artists and enthusiasts alike together "into a information-rich community of social actors" (Atkinson 2003: 48). As people are now able to learn more about the process of tattooing via online resources, as well as communicate with tattoo enthusiasts around the world, more and more people are being drawn into the practice as both tattoo artists and tattooees.

As tattooing becomes more and more a mainstream phenomenon, the ability to decipher a tattooed body's authentic membership in a particular counter culture, while once quite apparent, now becomes not so easily done. Tattoos have become commodified — a trend, an immediate mark of individuality that can be bought and sold. Nevertheless, tattoos still serve as a means of communication. What they communicate, however, is indeed more difficult to determine.

4 The Basis of Modern Societies

Jessica Antony's chapter on women and tattooing makes clear how societies have changed over time and how our attitudes and behaviours are shaped by the social practices around us; tattoos have not always been commodified forms of self-expression commonly found amongst white, middle-class young men and women. What drives social change? Is it simply new ideas? Yes and no. Ideas are mobilized or made powerful when they are linked to material forces, such as capitalism. For example, in Chapter 4, Naiman (2012) explains how attitudes towards monogamy (which we take for granted today as common sense and indeed a natural expression of romantic love) emerged as the mode of production shifted away from subsistence level production to more complex forms of agricultural production that privileged men's productive labour. Through advancements in technology, families were able to amass surplus levels of wealth for the first time as fields produced large crops and weaponry enabled conquest of lands. In order to protect the landownership system, lineage or birthright was established to ensure that accumulated wealth was handed down to the male heir. The only way to protect the bloodline was to impose the cultural practice of monogamy, with a particular focus on restricting women's sexual liberty; indeed women could be executed for adultery. If the material world had not changed, would humans have decided monogamy was necessary? Perhaps not. We need to consider that some of our strongest beliefs and values are products of complex material change.

In this chapter we examine the predatory nature of capitalism as the basis of modern society. Capitalism requires socio-cultural practices (norms, beliefs, language and consequences) that ensure people go to work and pay their taxes so that profit continues to accumulate. As David McNally explains here, the practices of corporate power create the conditions for economic crises (overproduction, privatization, and commodification). The impacts of this profit-making system however are far reaching, as working-class and middle-class workers struggle with declining wages, inflation of costs for food and housing and higher taxes to fund multi-million-dollar corporate bailouts. But capitalism's own irrational practices are not the result of greedy corporate executives; rather the cyclical nature of economic crises is built into the very essence of capitalism as a mode of production. So, our everyday lives are structured by the material world of capitalism: our values and beliefs are formed in the shadow of capitalism. Part of the sociological imagination is acquiring the understanding of the context of our choices, so that we can begin to be critically engaged in the complex materiality of living in a capitalist society.

"Inequality, the Profit System and Global Crisis"

David McNally, in Julie Guard and Wayne Antony (eds.),
Bankruptcies and Bailouts (Fernwood, 2009)

Production for Profit

One of the key things about capitalism is that the economy is geared to produce goods for sale on the market. Societies throughout human history have used markets for the exchange of some goods, particularly luxuries. But only in capitalist society do people acquire the overwhelming bulk of all the goods they consume — their morning coffee and muffins, their accommodation, clothing, entertainment, transportation, the food for their daily meals — by purchasing them from a market seller. Prior to the rise of capitalism, most people worked the land and produced almost everything they consumed. They collected wood, straw, mud and rocks to build their dwellings. They grew crops and raised livestock. They made their own clothes, furniture, soap and candles. They gathered firewood, berries and herbs. They fished and drew water from the lakes, ponds, rivers and streams. In all these ways, they had direct access to the means of life. This is not to say that life was easy; nor is it to say they were free from exploitation; in fact, they generally had to pay rent and taxes to landlords and the state. But outside of periods of drought or warfare, most people could count on having food and shelter as a result of their possession of land (either as tenants or small owners).

Capitalism ended all that by privatizing land. Peasants were driven from their plots and forced to migrate to towns and cities in search of work for a wage. Land was concentrated into great farms worked by landless labourers hired to produce a "cash crop" for sale on the market, not for their own consumption. No longer able to produce for themselves, people had no option but to enter market exchange — transactions between buyers and sellers — in order to make ends meet. For the vast majority, this meant seeking a buyer for their labour so that they might earn wages with which to purchase the goods necessary for survival. In many parts of the world, perhaps most dramatically in China at the moment, we can see such processes at work today, as millions of peasants are dispossessed of land and transformed into propertyless labourers who migrate to urban areas in search of work.

With the rise of capitalism, people thus become "market dependent." Lacking economic self-sufficiency, the ability to produce the goods of life for themselves, their survival depends on the market — on whether they can sell their labour for a wage and thereby procure the money with which to buy food, shelter and clothing. This is what it means for a society to be "market regulated" — all basic economic activities take place in the market and must obey market pressures. For the majority of people, market pressure means coercion and insecurity; failure to find a buyer for their labour means they won't earn the cash necessary to buy the goods of life. Survival is no longer based on working the land but on buying and selling in the market.

The market thus becomes an ever-present part of their daily lives, rather than something they might attend once a month or so, as it was for people in peasant-based societies. Capitalism allows no other way of living.

But what drives such a market economy? What is the point of producing goods for exchange on the market? Why should business owners make investments that bring huge amounts of grain, cell phones, cars, steel and dvds to the market? First of all, business people produce commodities in order to make a profit. They have no particular attachment to loaves of bread or pairs of blue jeans or anything else. They produce these things if, and only if, they think they can make a profit on them. So, when they invest in a bakery, the real goal is not to produce bread [so there is healthy food for people to eat]; when they buy a garment factory, the objective is not to turn out jeans. For capitalists, the only purpose of bakeries and garment factories is to create profit. Capitalism is a system of production for exchange rather than for use (i.e., for direct consumption). Capitalists are indifferent to the concrete, useful qualities of what they produce. It is the saleability of the commodity, its capacity to generate sales and profits that matters.

Bread, steel, water, houses, blue jeans, books, computers and cars count for capitalist firms only as potential sums of money; the specific human needs they satisfy are ultimately irrelevant to the drive to accumulate wealth. For capital, all goods are thus interchangeable, merely potential sums of expandable wealth. They will invest in producing bombs or bread, cigarettes or vitamins — it doesn't matter which — as long as it will generate wealth. Whether their investment decisions are good for humankind is irrelevant. What matters is whether the investment, irrespective of its effects on humans or the natural environment, turns a profit. The question of food illustrates this particularly clearly. ...

But while capitalists are indifferent to the concrete goods being produced and their uses, the vast majority of people are not. It matters enormously whether the corn being grown will be used for food rather than as fuel for trucks or for heating factories. In 2007, for instance, less than half the grain produced in the world was eaten by people. The global grain harvest that year was 2.1 billion tons. But just one billion of that went to human consumption. The rest went to producing bio-fuels or animal feed. So, while a billion people teetered on the brink of starvation, most of the world's grain was diverted away from them — because that was the more profitable thing to do. This graphically illustrates how survival for millions can literally turn on the dictates of the market.

This example allows us to understand the perverse logic of an economy based upon production for profit. As a rule, when capitalists enter the market, their purpose is utterly foreign to the motivations of most people. For most of us, money is a means to get commodities that sustain life. We sell a commodity (usually our labour), get money in return and use that money to buy commodities (like bread and jeans) to consume. But the drive for profit is not a mere personal idiosyncrasy of an individual investor. Capitalists, after all, inhabit a competitive environment. Each owner of a bakery, every investor in a garment factory, is competing with many others. Each is trying to bring to market a product of roughly equal quality at less cost. That is the only way to be sure of sales and profits. This means that profits must regularly be ploughed back into the company in order to buy the latest technology. And that requires a continual flow of new investments to help the company become more efficient, capable of producing the same goods more quickly and cheaply. But such investments are not possible without making profits; they can only be paid for if the company makes more than it spends. As a result, the imperative to minimize costs and maximize profits is imposed on every capitalist by pressures of competition. .... This is why capitalism is an economy characterized by frenetic growth — at least until a crisis comes, which itself will have been caused by the very process of such growth. Since the company that stands still is the one that loses the competitive race, each is driven to expand incessantly ... So, while a person can treat land as a means of life, a capitalist must treat it as a means of growth, of profit-making. It is not enough that the land (or factories) provide survival; it must provide ever growing amounts of wealth. This constant drive to expand is at the very heart of economic crises of the sort the world is experiencing at the moment. As every capitalist firm invests in order to lower costs, boost sales and increase profits, they all build factories, offices, mines, mills, hotels and shopping centres at a manic pace, all the while retooling their factories, mines and offices with new equipment and technologies. This produces an economic boom in the early going. Then, if things start to falter, companies borrow to keep financing more investment, while pressing governments to lower interest rates so that consumers can keep borrowing and buying too. But a point comes at which there are simply too many factories and too much equipment producing the same thing, be it bread, jeans or cars, and too many companies opening restaurants or selling trips to the Caribbean. Some of these companies become entirely unprofitable. But they keep on producing in order to try to generate revenues in the hope of staying alive. This is the point at which capital has over-accumulated — more capacity to produce goods and services has been built than can profitably be utilized — and profit rates start to decline, as other authors in this volume explain. ... Indeed, the scandal of capitalism is that it produces the wealth necessary to feed, clothe, shelter and educate everyone, but it denies billions access to those goods. As a result, we witness the obscenity of people starving amid mountains of food. ...

In a crisis, all of this gets dramatically worse. As companies over-accumulate and profits decline, they lay off workers, close factories and stop investing. This lowers demand for goods and services, which in turn leads to further layoffs and plant closings, as a result of which more people are unable to buy the goods of life. Then all of this begins to hit banks, as many of their corporate and personal borrowers are no longer able to repay loans. Bank failures can then follow in quick order. The cumulative effect of all this is an economic recession, sometimes a very deep one.

Financial Instability and Social Inequality

A basic feature of a market economy is that it concentrates wealth in the hands of those who already have it. As the old saying goes, "it takes money to make money," and the history of capitalism proves the point: the market serves the rich. Sometimes public pressure forces governments to use taxation to redistribute wealth — although the effects are always much less significant than commentators usually suggest — but when states do so they act against market principles. Left to their own devices, markets transfer wealth to those who already have it.

... Let us look at this explosion in social inequality from two other angles. Viewed in relation to average incomes, we see that whereas the richest 1 percent in the U.S. earned 100 times the national average income in 1970, today they earn 560 times the average. The disparity between the pay of chief executive officers of U.S. corporations and the income of their average employees is equally instructive. In 1980 earned about 42 times more than their employees. By 2000, they were pulling in 525 times as much. While that ratio has declined somewhat since then, the gap between worker and CEO earnings remains obscenely high. While the disparities are not quite so large in Canada, they are huge — and growing. In 1995, for instance, the average compensation of the fifty highest paid CEOs in Canada was 85 times the average income of a worker. Twelve years later, in 2007, it was 259 times as high. That means that the top were earning the annual wage of the average worker in one day. ...

But does this mean that anyone who works hard will end up a CEO? Or that people who are working in low-paying manual labour jobs just do not aspire to more or are not smart enough to make it in the big leagues? In the next chapter, we look at the sociological answer to that question: advanced liberal democracies such as Canada and United States are structured intentionally to recreate poverty and protect the wealthy. So hard work is not enough.

5 Analyzing Social Class

In Chapter 4, David McNally explained the irrational mechanics of capitalist expansion through the endless pursuit of profit over usefulness and need. He provides us with an understandng of the foundation of social inequality: how capitalism as an economic and social system has resulted in both extreme poverty and extreme affluence. But the power of capitalism to organize social worlds does not lie exclusively in its structural arrangements. In this chapter, Robert Chernomas explores how social class as an outcome of a capitalist economic system is foundational to our social worlds: our relationships, our aspirations and personal goals, where we live, the food we eat and the music we listen to. As we learned in Jessica Antony's writing on tattooing, body modification itself has become a site of commodification and status marker of femininity and middle-class cool. We each possess a class consciousness that defines our values and beliefs and underpins our sense of place in society. For many working poor Canadians and Americans, however, class consciousness is not political; the working poor rarely vote for pro-worker parties, but rather are typically conservative in their political views — wanting to reduce taxes and cut social services like welfare benefits, criminalize the homeless and build more prisons — despite the deep connections between crime and poverty, lack of affordable housing and fewer social services. How do we explain the lack of working-class consciousness? And what are the implications of elite-class consciousness amongst the wealthy?

"The Economic Crisis: Class Warfare from Reagan to Obama"

Robert Chernomas, in Julie Guard and Wayne Antony (eds.), *Bankruptcies and Bailouts* (Fernwood, 2009)

[Working-class Americans] have paid a huge price over the past thirty years. And now, in 2009, millions of working Americans — and working people in most other industrialized countries — have lost their jobs and their homes, and all indicators suggest that things will get much worse in the months and years ahead. The entire capitalist system is in the midst of dramatic political and economic change resulting from its profitability problems. Right-wing U.S. politicians from Ronald Reagan to George W. Bush tried to solve these problems on the backs of working people.

Profit Is All That Matters

Profit is the lifeblood of the corporation and its owners. Profit enables them to own factories, mines, stores and banks. It is the reason they produce cars, bread, jeans, gasoline, insulin and homes; the reason they provide credit cards and home mortgages. It allows them to have power over the state and live better than everybody else. This power comes with a price. The capitalist rules of the game compel them to fight a war of competition with their rivals and a class war with their workers.[1] ... Capitalists are not in the business of producing goods and services. They are in the business of making profits using goods and services as the means. Without enough profits they shut down their factories, mines, stores, farms and banks, workers lose their jobs and production stops on cars, tvs and even food. Without profits capitalists will not, or more accurately cannot, invest in new machines to replace workers demanding higher wages, advertise their successes in production or bribe governments to give them what they need. By shutting down ("capital strike") or by leaving ("capital flight"), they coerce unions for concessions, stop environmentalists from making costly demands and warn citizens that social programs raise taxes and threaten their ability to compete with their foreign rivals. All the human and natural materials to produce what we need still exists, but if profits aren't being made owners shut things down.

I have often thought if extraterrestrial aliens had landed in the U.S. or Canada in 1929 and seen the mines overflowing with coal, farm land sprouting weeds and engineers selling pencils on the corner while children picked through garbage they would have been stunned by the sheer irrationality of it all. We may not want to be using much coal these days, but this current recession/depression is evolving in the midst of even more economic wherewithal, which would no doubt leave returning aliens even more perplexed.

The Traumatized Worker

If workers donate the lifeblood of the system to their employers and the state makes and enforces the rules for these transfusions, it is economists, as doctors, who provide both the prescriptions and public relations services required for a profitable and socially acceptable outcome. How do we know class warfare was policy option number one to restore profitability? For one, because the economists providing the policy advice admitted it, afterwards!

In the U.K., Alan Budd, professor of economics at the London Business School and chief economic advisor to Margaret Thatcher, describes, in astonishingly candid terms, what occurred during the 1980s, stating that conservative monetary and fiscal policy was seen by the Thatcher government as

> a very good way to raise unemployment. And raising unemployment was an extremely desirable way of reducing the strength of the working classes.... What was engineered — in Marxist terms — was a crisis

of capitalism which re-created the reserve army of labour, and has allowed the capitalist to make high profits ever since.[2]

The state deliberately created high unemployment so that the 80 percent or so of the population that depends on work for their livelihood would not defend their wages because of the threat of being replaced by the unemployed. And it worked. Alan Greenspan, the Chair of the Federal Reserve in the U.S. and the undisputed right-wing economist in charge during much of this period, acknowledges as much, albeit it more oblique language:

> Increases in hourly compensation... have continued to fall far short of what they would have been had historical relationships between compensation gains and the degree of labor market tightness held.... As I see it, heightened job insecurity explains a significant part of the restraint on compensation and the consequent muted price inflation.... The continued reluctance of workers to leave their jobs to seek other employment as the labor market has tightened provides further evidence of such concern, as does the tendency toward longer labor union contracts. The low level of work stoppages of recent years also attests to concern about job security.... The continued decline in the state of the private workforce in labor unions has likely made wages more responsive to market forces.... Owing in part to the subdued behavior of wages, profits and rates of return on capital have risen to high levels.[3]

Elsewhere Greenspan refers to these Americans as "traumatized workers." We also have evidence of what capitalists accomplished on behalf of profitability at the expense of wage earners. During the period from 1948 to the 1970s workers maintained more or less the same share of what they produced because labour productivity and wages grew together. They were being exploited, but at more or less a constant rate. Once the corporate sector and the state went to work on them, their wages fell for the next thirty years, while their productivity continued to grow (albeit at a slower pace), leaving the employers with ever more of what the workers produced. Karl Marx would have referred to this as a massive increase in exploitation. As Alan Budd explains, this was accomplished by the state, acting on the behalf of its capitalist class and using its taxing and spending power, its money and credit systems, its welfare and free trade regimes to fix the profitability problem on the backs of workers ....Unemployment, whether by corporate layoff or state design, was not the only weapon used in this class war. Trade agreements helped as well. Cheap overseas workers help the bottom line for those who employ them but not for those who compete with them for jobs.

The Traumatized Family

In its blind unrestrainable passion, its were-wolf hunger for surplus-labour, capital oversteps not only the moral but even the merely physical maximum bounds of the working-day. It usurps the time for growth, development, and healthy maintenance of the body. It steals the time required for the consumption of fresh air and sunlight (Karl Marx, Capital, Volume 1).

> You work three jobs?...Uniquely American, isn't it? I mean, that is fantastic that you're doing that. (President George W. Bush, to a divorced mother of three in Omaha, Nebraska, February 4, 2005)

According to the authors of The State of Working America, (SWA), employees in the U.S. work more hours per year than do workers in any of the other industrial countries. In contrast to the U.S., all of the other G7 countries have been reducing the work week, some substantially. In a dramatic turnaround, Americans now work longer hours than the Japanese, who during the 1980s were notorious for their commitment to their firms and whose intense work ethic was contrasted with Americans' less dutiful approach to their work lives. Between 1979 and 1995 the Japanese reduced their work year by 228 hours while the Americans increased theirs by 47. By 1995, Americans worked 215 more hours per year than Canadians.8 Europeans get four or five weeks of vacation by law, and the Japanese have two legally mandated vacation weeks, while the U.S. is the only industrialized nation with no minimum paid-leave law.

Much of the increase in hours is due to women working more. Between 1979 and 1989 in the U.S., the hours worked by "wives" increased by 270, adding six and half weeks of paid work per year to the family's income. This was made necessary by the fall in wages of husbands.[4] While some of these hours are certainly due to women's increasing desire for paid employment, it is also true that many families require two incomes to achieve the same lifestyle that one used to provide. ...

The only real increase in wages for a family has come from the second paycheque earned by a working wife. However, higher expenses have more than eroded that apparent financial advantage. With families facing falling wages, longer hours and increasing economic fragility, borrowing becomes an increasingly attractive option. The same corporations that fought tooth and nail against any attempts to raise wages and welcomed extended hours of exploitable work found it profitable to extend credit to anyone with a pulse. However, easy credit and ballooning debt created an inherently unstable system.

The Traumautized Consumer

To the possessor of money capital, the process of production appears merely as an unavoidable intermediate link, as a necessary evil for the sake of money-making. All nations with a capitalist mode of production are therefore seized periodically by a feverish attempt to make money without the intervention of the process of production (Karl Marx, Capital, Volume 2). The current crisis reveals the extent to which corporations rely on drawing profits from the personal income of working people. Falling wages, rising productivity and more hours working for corporations all helped improved profitability but not enough to restore it to the levels of the "golden age." And so capital turned to an additional source of profits, often referred to as "financialization." Profit-making occurs increasingly through financial channels rather than through production. Financialization means using credit cards, racking up mortgage debt and speculating on commodities like food or oil as means to increase profits.

The idea that we suffer from a shortage of confidence, that somehow if we just believe everything is okay, it will be, is the stuff of which fairytales are made. Debt obligations depend on everyone being able to pay — when one can't the chain is broken. Home prices, stock prices and credit card debt are never too high in and of themselves but rather in relation to the income and profits needed to pay them off. ... We are told over and over again that ours is an "ownership society," that is, we all have stocks and bonds, a stake in the capital market, thereby wiping out class as a way of understanding how capitalism works. All the talk of financialization and speculation suggests we created this mess together. So, we all need to share in the pain of getting out of it. We may well be sharing in the pain but the idea that we created this mess together and somehow shared in the bounty is preposterous.

Who is in debt and who is doing all that shopping? We know who made the money, the question that remains is who owed the money? Debt levels remained relatively constant at about 60 percent of GDP through the mid-1980s, when they began to rise rapidly. In 2007 the total value of all forms of household debt was at its all time high at 141 percent. Between 1989 and 2004 the middle 20 percent of households acquired 23.6 percent of all debt growth, while the next highest 20 percent acquired 28.8 percent of the total growth in debt over this period. The wealthiest 1 percent of households, on the other hand, acquired only 1.7 percent of all debt between 1989 and 2004. ...

The business class is likely badly shaken by the crisis and it is interested in some serious "change" from the Obama administration. Anxiety over the effects of the free market gone wild has led to demands for massive government intervention to save the business class from itself. So what can we expect these class warriors to do under the current circumstances? It must be said that this group is not made up of the right-wing economists who are ideological blind to the dramatically changing needs of their corporate masters and to the potential political dangers of a system not able to deliver the goods. These economists will be looking for solutions to restore conditions of profitability on the one hand and to try to ensure political stability on the other. To put it crudely Obama received half his $700 million of campaign contributions from small donors and half from mega donors (who contribute more than $25,000 each). Capitalism can work in social democratic regimes where access to healthcare is universal and minimum wages and employment benefits actually keep citizens out of poverty, just not in America up until now.

Chernomas's argument leads us to question why working-class people in advanced liberal democracies have been so reluctant to become politically engaged over the lack of accountability of corporate greed? Europeans in countries such as Greece have loudly condemned the austerity measures of their governments, yet Occupy Movements across North America have disappeared. According to Tony Simmons (forthcoming),

> Marx used the term "false consciousness" to describe the situation of those social classes in society which accept the ideology of the ruling class even when their own material interests are structurally opposed to those of the ruling class. Although this term can be used to analyze the distorted beliefs of any class, Marx focused on the case of the working class, which had accepted (and internalized) the values and beliefs of capital. For Marx, "false consciousness" refers to the inability on the part of individuals and social groups to correctly identify their position in society, and their relation to other social groups—especially to the dominant or ruling class. Marx believed that the study of history shows that many individuals have had illusions about their real place in society and their relationship to other social groups. Indeed, there is often a disjuncture, or a break, between what individuals, or social classes, think about themselves and what can be shown through a more dispassionate historical analysis. For example, even though the eighteenth-century French peasantry was severely exploited and oppressed by the land-owning nobility, many individual peasants saw themselves as independent and self-reliant farmers, and they distained to join with other peasants in any movement for social or political change. In much the same way, many poor white share-croppers (so-called "white trash") in the U.S. southern states saw themselves as superior to their Black counterparts, and therefore opposed any class-based movements for social, political or economic justice. Today, Marx would probably have seen the Tea Party in the U.S. — with its demand for corporate tax cuts, reduced government spending on health, education and social services — as yet another example of a working-class party that has fully embraced the propaganda of the ruling class.

Popular culture is key to the reproduction of false consciousness amongst young people. In the "reality" television show *Jersey Shore*, young adult viewers consume images of their peers engaged in endless outrageous hypersexualized antics, heavy drinking and shopping — a lifestyle supported by working three hours a day at a T-shirt shop for minimum wage. The likelihood of their eviction for not being able to pay the rent is a constant comedic theme. This wildly popular show has been mass-marketed, for example, with books of *Jersey Shore* quotes like this one: "those girls ain't hoes, it may take like a couple of times of hanging out before they'll get naked and get in the hot tub" and "lets get wastey pants tonight" (Fraser 2010). Media commentators claim that *Jersey Shore* "provides a healthy does of *schadenfreude* for the overburdened and unemployed masses. When we think things couldn't get worse, we only have to flip on the television" (Fraser 2010). But things have gotten worse for young adults today — stability of work and quality of work have all been undermined by corporate restructuring focused on a flexible workforce of contract and temporary workers who receive no pension or benefits. Real wages are falling and the cost of food and housing is rising. Is it any wonder that mass media content is saturated with antics of young adults that depict them self-absorbed, lazy and not very bright? Whose reality is depicted on reality television like *Jersey Shore*? Not the reality of millions of young men and women. As we examine in Chapter 8, popular culture is a powerful site of socialization that informs how we view the world and ourselves.

In Chapter 6 of *How Societies Work*, Naiman (2012) draws our attention to the way corporate power restructures the meaning of work, happiness and success. Mass-consumerism now defines our sense of leisure activity (think online shopping and family vacations to the West Edmonton Mall) and self worth (think about the importance of the size of a diamond on an engagement ring). Durkheim pointed to such cultural practices as threatening to social integration as we become enthralled by cultural expectations of selfishness and narcissism. As The Situation would say: "GTL baby, gym, tanning and laundry."

6 Living in Capitalist Societies

"Alienation and Discipline in High-Performance Sport"

Gamal Abdel-Shehid and Nathan Kalman-Lamb, in *Out of Left Field* (Fernwood, 2011)

When the topic of sports and economics is considered, the first thing that comes to mind for many fans and non-fans alike is the issue of high salaries. It has become commonplace to say that athletes are outrageously over-paid. After all, Sidney Crosby will earn $43.5 million over the course of his current five-year contract with the Pittsburgh Penguins of the National Hockey League (NHL) (cbcsports.ca 2007); Jose Bautista of Major League Baseball's Toronto Blue Jays will earn $65 million during his current five-year deal (Zwolinski 2011); and LeBron James of the Miami Heat in the National Basketball Association (NBA) will make $96 million over five years (Winderman 2010). It is easy to assume that these athletes are earning far more than their fair share. Who needs $96 million? Yet although athletes such as James earn more than anyone needs to, it is worth noting that, according to the logic of capitalism, they may not earn as much as they deserve. James' salary for the 2009-2010 season was $15.8 million (Van Riper 2010). In that year, the value of the team for which he played, the Cleveland Cavaliers, was $476 million (Forbes 2009). The next year, after James signed with the Miami Heat, the Cavaliers were valued at only $355 million (Forbes 2011). It is impossible to draw a perfectly straight line between James' departure and the decrease in the franchise's value, but it is clear that his leaving played a substantial role. We can certainly infer that James' value to the Cavaliers was closer to $121 million (the decrease in the franchise's value after he left) than the $15.8 million he was paid. As hard as it may be to believe, James was underpaid; his labour was exploited by the corporation that is the team.

Considering this, why is it that so many people complain that athletes are overpaid? One reason, we contend, is that athletes make money with their bodies. Western societies tend to privilege the mind over the body. Men who earn fortunes through technological innovation, like Bill Gates and Steve Jobs, tend to be championed as entrepreneurial geniuses even as athletes are indicted for their "bloated" salaries. Jobs earns only a $1 salary, but he holds $1.8 billion worth of Apple stock; by comparison, James' earnings seem pitiful (Babad 2011). It is also noteworthy that James is only allowed to be a salaried employee of his team, while Jobs is a shareholder, and thus owner, of his company. Clearly, power differences are at play here as well as earning discrepancies.

However, an even greater problem with the constant criticism of athletes' salaries is that the focus on the issue of over-payment deflects attention from the day-to-day struggles of the majority of working athletes who do not have the privilege of a million-dollar paycheque. Minor and independent league players in baseball and hockey in North America, for example, and college athletes in the United States, earn only a small fraction of what is earned by their professional peers, even though they generate revenue for teams. In fact, according to the official website of Minor League Baseball, first-year ball players can expect to make no more than $1,100 a month, which amounts to a potential maximum annual salary of $13,200, far below the poverty line (Minor League Baseball n.d.). Given that the minor leagues are staffed with far more players than the professional leagues — for instance, there are 228 official minor league baseball affiliates compared to the thirty major professional clubs, not including myriad independent leagues — the majority of those who play sport for a living in North America are significantly exploited (Minor League Baseball n.d). ...

Marxist perspectives on sport contend that sport is not at all a paradise where people work together in order to excel. Nor is sport something that allows those less fortunate an opportunity to rise up in society. Instead, the Marxist perspective suggests that sport is a reflection of the larger society — which is seen as fundamentally exploitative or unequal. The nature of this exploitation is not random; rather, it is based in the society's economic system. Before we explain the nature of the exploitation, let us recall how we define the term economy. Economics refers to the way in which goods and services are bought and sold in a given society and how the society organizes the production and distribution of these goods and services. Another phrase for economy, popularized by Marx and Engels, is mode of production.

Marx and his colleague Friedrich Engels argued that all societies over the course of human history have been defined by a struggle over various scarce resources. They noted that the nineteenth-century mode of production known as capitalism, which had emerged roughly around the sixteenth century, featured a struggle between two primary classes of people in society: the proletariat, or those who had to work or sell their labour to someone else for a living; and the bourgeoisie, who owned businesses and factories and thus did not need to sell their labour to someone else. In general, those who owned businesses (called the means of production) were in a different class or position in society than those who did not. According to Marx and Engels, the relation was not an equal one. Members of the bourgeoisie did not need to sell their labour to someone else because they received profits from the labour of their workers. They also had the privilege of deciding how to use those profits. Marx and Engels noted that the distinctive feature of capitalism was that labour had become a commodity, something that could be bought and sold. They also noted that all other goods and services produced in capitalism were commodities.

The position that sport in capitalist society is an exploitative enterprise, where workers are generally treated poorly at the expense of the owners, is the core of the Marxist view of high-performance sport. If we look at contemporary sport over the last thirty years, it is hard to disagree with this view. It is often the case that athletes have to play injured, or, if they don't play injured, they are treated as mere commodities often cast aside by their teams if they suffer injuries. We hear about these stories quite regularly from athletes; indeed, they seem to be more the rule than the exception in high-performance professional sport. Moreover, the increase in playoff games puts more and more strain on the bodies of athletes, increasing injuries. The widespread use of performance-enhancing drugs and drug scandals, such as those that have plagued the Tour de France in recent years, may also be seen in this light. It is clear that use of performance-enhancing drugs in high-performance sport is designed to maximize outputs, which is very much aligned with the trend towards the maximizing of profit within capitalist society.

Michael Robidoux's book *Men at Play* is a detailed explanation of the Marxist perspective on high-performance men's sport. Robidoux recounts the year that he spent traveling with the Troy Reds, a men's American Hockey League (AHL) franchise, an experience which provided him with a close look at the inner workings of a professional men's hockey team one level below the NHL (seen to be the premier men's hockey league in North America). Borrowing from Marx and Engels, Robidoux states that contrary to what we might think, professional sports are not all fun and games for the athletes. To the contrary, Robidoux says that professional athletes are, like most workers in capitalist society, alienated labourers, with little or no control over their conditions of work and thus separated from their product.

But Robidoux notes that there is a crucial difference between the labour of a professional athlete such as a hockey player and that of someone working in a teashop, hospital, or auto plant, for example. Although all are forms of alienated labour in capitalism, athletes are celebrities in a society that is, generally speaking, fascinated with celebrities. Hockey players are seen as larger than life; many people want to get close to them, hang out with them, and so on. The hockey players themselves are very seduced by this, as noted by the Reds athletic therapist:

> The guys [the athletes] they get a lot of stuff, and [people] want to give you stuff....You know, free meal, fifty-percent discount on clothing; they want to give you this, that, and the other thing. And the guys [athletes] eat it up. (Robidoux 2001: 151)

Robidoux argues that the desire to be a hero or celebrity has two main effects for the athletes. First, it makes them forget that they are workers and renders them almost completely ignorant of their rights as workers. As Robidoux explains, "because the opportunity to play professional hockey is, for most players, a childhood dream, few scrutinize their job and/or working environment" (2001: 153). Second, the power of the dream of playing in the NHL means that athletes may subject themselves to even more exploitation than other workers, because they can see a larger reward. A worker in a teashop, by contrast, will likely have fewer illusions than a hockey player about moving up within the company; and even if the teashop worker were to move up, to become a manager for example, she or he would know that there would be little reward in terms of celebrity. But professional hockey players have a desire to succeed and play in the NHL that is driven by the desire for celebrity. This, according to Robidoux, has severe consequences for the athlete; it "makes [them] much more vulnerable to exploitation, and thus, virtually powerless" (2001: 156).

So far, we have seen how Robidoux's interpretation of men's professional hockey mirrors the opinion held by Marx and Engels of labour in capitalism. The players are led to believe they will become stars, and for this they accept working conditions that are often harmful to their bodies and render them powerless in the labour process. In this sense their labour is indeed alienated. What's more, they are subject to what is called Taylorisation in that they work in very monotonous ways. Taylorisation refers to the manufacturing system developed by Frederick Taylor, one of the innovators of the assembly line in the United States. Taylor's aim in creating this assembly line system was to divide large jobs into very little tasks in order that one need not rely on one worker to do all the tasks. The previous system, called the artisanal system, relied on one highly skilled individual, sometimes working with an apprentice, to perform all the tasks required for the production of a commodity. This system still exists in many parts of the world. Examples of artisans are shoemakers, carpenters, carpet weavers, and bakers. Taylor wanted to break this system and make a job divisible so that no one needed a particular skill in order to complete a job. In Taylor's system, all a person needed to do the job was some brief training on a segment of the line. This, in Taylor's view, would greatly maximize output.

High-performance sport is also extremely regimented; it involves measuring drills, output, practice times, athlete's weight and height, statistics. Jean-Marie Brohm noted that the effect of all of these practices is that the body becomes like a robotic machine. He says that sport is a "mechanisation of the body, treated as an automaton, governed by the principle of maximizing output" (Brohm 1978: 56). For Brohm, the irony of high-performance sport is this: the very same thing that was supposed to be fun and games becomes just like another job — boring, repetitive, and unsatisfying. ...But as a result of this extreme control, athletes know almost nothing else outside of hockey.

Few athletes socialize with people outside of the hockey world because this is often seen as damaging to the health of the group. Robidoux argues that this process is indeed harmful to the athlete. He suggests that there is a "closed social environment of professional hockey [that] retards the players' ability to grow in almost every respect — except as hockey players" (Robidoux 2001: 181). In other words, the more that athletes are sheltered, the more they are subject to the team's discipline, and the more powerless they are in the social arena. The fact that athletes are often referred to as "boys" is another example of this. In Robidoux's view, the word is more than simply a nickname; it has deeper significance:

> Team officials treat the players as children both on and off the ice. It starts from the moment the players enter the dressing room, where their lives are not only ordered by their physical surroundings — from labelled seating to the two sticks of gum placed on their seats before and after games/practices — and continues through the rules and procedures players must follow, or suffer monetary fines. (2001: 181)

After reading Robidoux's study, we come to the conclusion that professional sport is very different from what we may see in the newspapers and on television. Most players, in search of a dream, receive little in the way of financial compensation and even less in the way of life skills to operate outside of hockey. In addition, they pay a very high price for the athletic excellence that so many of us dream about. Like all other forms of labour in capitalism, professional athletes are alienated form their work. They are made to repeat the same monotonous tasks over and over again. In short, contrary to the first impressions many people have, the rewards of professional athletes are an illusion, for the most part … fame is something other than power. Power is having control over one's life and having some financial reward for the work that one does. In that sense, those in power are clearly management or those who own sports teams. The professional hockey players are in control of very little, merely the details of the game itself, and almost nothing beyond that.

7 The Social Construction of Ideas and Knowledge

When considering the conditions of work, even for high performance professional athletes like NHL hockey players, it is important to ask why individuals continue to perform endless hours of physically demanding training or work long hours overtime, sometimes for a boss who sexually harasses us. Sociologists are interested in understanding our compliance or submission to authority that is not always in our best interest. Social order in advanced industrialized countries populated by millions of people from diverse cultural backgrounds is achieved through ideological domination. In Chapter 7, Naiman (2012) describes how ideology protects the interests of the power elites through the normalization of values and beliefs that justify the unequal distribution of resources and opportunities.

Ideological domination exists in the context of a dialectic — our submission is not complete or inevitable; rather we do engage in resistance and challenges to authority, but such acts are quickly countered by the state using a variety of techniques to regain control. These tactics can include coercive acts of power such as law-and-order policing and criminalization of dissent, but most often cultural institutions such as the media and the education system reinforce dominant ideologies to enforce our compliance. Viewing professional sports like the Stanley Cup playoffs or the Superbowl can function as a form of ideological domination that deflects our attention away from the drudgery and stress of our daily lives (and obscures the conditions of work for high performance athletes). But we also need to consider how the media protects the interests of the power elite through its story-telling strategies. The media reporting of the case of Robert Pickton in Vancouver, British Columbia, convicted in the gruesome murders of women on his pig farm, reproduces a dominant narrative of both Pickton and the women he killed that overshadows or deflects our attention away from the structural violence perpetrated by the state.

Missing Women, Missing News
David Hugill (Fernwood, 2010)

"Once We Became Aware" [Introduction]
Lillian O'Dare was thirty-four years old when she vanished from the streets of Vancouver's Downtown Eastside. Little is publicly known about her except for a few banal details. Newspaper reports tell us that she shared a birthday with

Elvis Presley, had "carefully waved" blond hair and was raised in Williams Lake. [Her disappearance] marked the dubious distinction of being the [first] episode in a pattern of predatory violence that would claim a long list of victims in this district. It was here — in [Vancouver's] oldest and poorest neighbourhood — that more than sixty local women, many of them street-level sex workers, were murdered or went missing between 1978 and 2002.

In Canada, where rates of violent crime remain comparatively low, murders and abductions can generate significant media attention and mobilize impressive deployments of the resources of law enforcement agencies. The recent disappearance of a Toronto teenager who vanished on her morning commute to school, for example, captivated local and national media for weeks and was the source of a wide-ranging investigation by police (Teotonio 2009). Events like these disrupt widely shared perceptions about what is to be expected in this country. Polling data in recent decades demonstrates that Canadians have a high degree of faith in the capacity of authorities to ensure both their own personal safety and the safety of the population in general (Gannon 2005; Statistics Canada 2005). Violent incidents, in the minds of many, constitute aberrational episodes in a continuum of otherwise orderly co-existence; rare and provocative disruptions of a prevailing peace. When they do occur, it is widely expected that they will be met with a swift and severe response by accountable and professional institutions.

The grisly series of events that unfolded in Vancouver's Downtown Eastside, however, can scarcely be considered aberrational. The disappearance of so many women — sustained over such a significant period — betrays a decidedly different reality; it demonstrates that brutality and predation had become a norm in the neighbourhood. Yet Vancouver's crisis of missing and murdered women generated very little formal interest before 1998, and few outside of the neighbourhood took notice as the crisis was spiraling out of control. O'Dare's disappearance in September of 1978 initiated a trend that would gain momentum rapidly in the years that followed. By the end of the 1980s, for example, an additional ten women had vanished from the neighbourhood. This pace quickened in the early 1990s as roughly a dozen more went missing by 1994. It spiked dramatically again after 1995 and more than thirty new disappearances had occurred by the end of 2001 (Missing Women Task Force 2007). But as the bulk of these crimes had unfolded, local authorities and journalists were missing in action; they made little acknowledgement of the genuine crisis that was taking place. At best, they had failed to notice. At worst, they had failed to care.

So what, then, was different about what happened in Vancouver? Why did the disappearance of a single teenager in Toronto — a tragic but definitively isolated incident — marshal vigorous police and media campaigns while a far more expansive series of tragedies in Vancouver was for a long time met with state inaction and media silence? The answers to these questions are complex and can only begin to be elucidated when we consider how an intersecting series of social and political practices operate to valorize certain lives while simultaneously disregarding others. What's clear is that the social and geographical location of the women that were taken from the Downtown Eastside operated to disqualify them from the protective assurance of authorities. As residents of a stigmatized inner city neighbourhood, sex workers in the bottoms rungs of Vancouver's street-level sex trade, drug users or poverty-stricken members of an increasingly stratified society and as racialized women, they were part of a social segment that was either rendered invisible to, or cast aside from, the core constituencies that are served by our collective institutions. As one politician asked: "do you think if 65 women went missing from Kerrisdale [an affluent Vancouver neighbourhood], we'd have ignored it so long?" (Wood 2004). ...

Carrie Kerr, whose sister Helen Hallmark disappeared in this period, recalls that police refused to open a missing persons file. "They told me 'No, go down to the needle exchange and leave her a message there,'" she recalls. Angela Jardine, who asked Vancouver police to follow up on her daughter's disappearance in late 1998, was told not to worry and that her daughter would likely turn up. Police delayed producing a missing persons poster for two months, assuming her disappearance was innocuous (Levitz 2007). Sandra Gagnon, who reported her sister missing in 1997, concedes that she encountered genuinely concerned police officers that were willing to pursue an investigation but was frustrated by their inability to connect individual disappearances to a larger pattern. "They never took the threat seriously... I can guarantee you that if it wasn't the Downtown Eastside, and they weren't hookers, something would have been done in an instant," she says (Amnesty International 2004). Police sustained the view that as "transient" sex workers and drug users, most of the missing had not actually disappeared; in most cases, they maintained that the women would soon show up again. They were, of course, devastatingly wrong. ...

A recent deluge of bureaucratic, journalistic and political interest in the case contrasts sharply with the prevailing culture of disinterest that had permeated police departments, news rooms and legislative chambers while women were disappearing with a marked frequency for two decades. In contrast to authorities, however, residents of the Downtown Eastside had long been aware that something horrific was unfolding in their midst. Since 1991 local activists have been organizing an annual Valentine's Day march as a public opportunity to honour the victims of violence and demand justice for the disappeared. But in spite of their efforts, few outside the neighbourhood's rugged twenty-one blocks — then as now Canada's "poorest postal code" — bothered to take much notice before a few local journalists began to do some probing.

The first media coverage of the crisis began to trickle out in the summer of 1998. Vancouver Sun reporter Lindsay Kines was the first mainstream journalist to catch wind of it. That July, he reported that police had begun to look for connections between ten disappearances of Downtown Eastside women that had been reported since 1996. Anne Drennan, a police liaison officer, assured readers that these files (and an additional six dating back to the late 1980s) were being given "the highest of priorities" (Kines 1998a). Kines' stories generated some initial public pressure. By September, he was reporting that the local force had moved to establish a "working group" to review cases dating back to 1971. As the public profile of the disappearances grew, speculation that they might be the work of a serial killer soon became widespread, but police were careful to play that down (Kines 1998b). By March of the next year, however, police had offered little indication that they were making any headway on the files and public concern had begun to morph into a growing "clamour" (Stall 1999b). Mounting public outrage crystallized in a series of well-attended demonstrations that spring, and local politicians were quickly losing the luxury of indifference. In an effort to demonstrate that they were taking the situation seriously, police officials soon assigned new officers to the investigation (Kines and Culbert 1999). But this alone was insufficient to appease the concerned. Frustrations were exacerbated after police issued two $100,000 rewards for information related to a series of home and garage invasions and allies of the missing women began to ask tough questions about official priorities. As the scale of the disappearances became more broadly known and anxieties about an un-apprehended serial killer built toward a crescendo, the case began to attract outside attention. In the wake of a visit from the television crime program America's Most Wanted — in town to do a segment on the disappearances — municipal officials finally acquiesced; in a last-minute effort to mitigate embarrassment, authorities announced that another $100,000 reward would be available to anyone who could provide information leading to an arrest related to the missing women. The initiative, funded and supported by municipal authorities, marked a stark reversal of Mayor Phillip Owen's initial position on the matter. Weeks earlier he had argued that it would be "inappropriate" to use public funds to provide a "location service" for prostitutes (Phillips 1999). When the America's Most Wanted segment aired, host John Walsh praised police efforts and spoke approvingly of the reward (Pitman 2002). … The day it was announced, police confirmed the severity of the situation; Drennan told reporters: "Once we became aware… that there was clearly something wrong here, something that we should be concerned about, we started to kick in additional resources" (Cameron 2007). …

Little hard evidence had been gathered by the fall of 2000 and the police department announced that they would scale back the review team that had been established. But even as police attention ebbed, the number of disappeared continued to mount: seventeen women went missing between 1999 and 2001. Concerned with the lack of progress, Kines and other Sun reporters launched a four-month investigation of the cases in 2001 and unveiled a damning series of revelations. They determined, among other things, that the official police figure of twenty-seven missing women was woefully inadequate and that at least forty-five cases should have been part of the investigation. They also concluded that while police had taken pains to maintain the appearance of an "aggressive, concerned investigation," their work had been devastatingly tainted by petty in-fighting, the absence of coherent leadership and a distinct lack of resources (Vancouver Sun 2002). It was now clear that, in spite of their protestations to the contrary, police could hardly claim to have made the investigation a real priority. Once again confronted with a spiraling public relations disaster — and an ever-expanding roster of missing women — Vancouver police were forced to take new action. Weeks later, they joined forces with the Royal Canadian Mounted Police to form the inter-jurisdictional Missing Women Joint Task Force.

The new unit raided a farm in suburban Port Coquitlam one year later. It soon became clear that the search was related to the missing women and the investigation quickly took on a robust media profile. Local and national media were captivated by speculation that Robert Pickton — one of the farm's owners who had been detained on a series of weapons charges — was being considered as a person of interest in the case. Pickton was well known in the area; he and his brother David operated a registered charity organization called Piggy Palace Good Times Society that was known for the large-scale parties and events it held on the farm. In the weeks that followed, journalistic digging and information that trickled out from investigators suggested that these events were often boisterous affairs that frequently included sex workers from the Downtown Eastside, often lured to the property with the promise of money and drugs. As early details became available, journalists anticipated that the dramatic prosecution of a serial killer would soon unfold and the story quickly soared to the top of news agendas.

Two weeks later, police confirmed media speculation and Pickton was charged with murdering two of the missing women. Within a year, ten additional murder charges were added to the indictment against him. By 2005, that number would climb to twenty-seven. If convicted, Pickton would become Canada's most prolific serial killer. Not surprisingly, media interest matched the magnitude of the accusations and the story generated prominent coverage for months.

That same interest would return again with a pronounced vigour in January 2007 when the trial phase of the proceedings against Pickton opened in New Westminster, British Columbia. The original indictment had been split in two during the voir-dire hearings and the Crown was instructed to proceed initially with six charges of first-degree murder. The lessened ambitions of the court did not dissuade the media, however, and a swarm of nearly four hundred media workers descended on the suburban courtroom to cover the story (Cameron 2007). It was a short-lived assignment for most; they were there to provide an initial context and then move on, not to return again until a verdict had been reached. For the Canadian print media, however, the trial seemed to merit a more thorough examination. Correspondents were enlisted to follow the minutia of trial developments but also to put the story in a larger socio-political context. In fact, this work had already begun for many newspapers. Since the initial raid of the Pickton farm nearly five years earlier, they had run stories that attempted to look beyond the particular modus operandi of the accused and examine what else could help to explain how dozens of women could be made to disappear from a densely populated urban neighbourhood. Many reporters looked to the Downtown Eastside for answers. Lurid portrayals suggested that the neighbourhood's "mean streets" and the social status of people on society's "fringes" offered part of the answer. Police negligence and bureaucratic inefficiency seemed to offer another. These early reports demonstrated that the case was bigger than being about a deranged killer; it was also about a criminal underworld, a dangerous part of town, [chronic] addictions, damaged and vulnerable individuals and indifferent or incompetent authorities.

Is a consideration of irresponsible policing, for example, sufficient to explain the state's complicity in the crisis? Do sympathetic portrayals of the victims disrupt the relentless stigmatization and demonization of street-involved women? Are audiences given enough information about the Downtown Eastside to adequately assess why social suffering and violence seem to have become so concentrated in this district?

Ideology as the Reproduction of Commonsense

… Are the press implicated in a grand conspiracy to conceal the *true* nature of this crisis? Are individual journalists beholden to a certain constellation of power and therefore compelled to distort? Do structural limits or editorial expectations somehow restrict a full telling of the story of the missing and murdered women? … In what follows, I adopt a particular conception of ideology as a way to approach this question….I theorize ideology not as a static or abstract set of propositions but as a series of representational and discursive practices that are embedded in commonsense or taken-for-granted assumptions about what our society is and how it works (Hall 1981). [P]ress reports operate to reproduce such assumptions by establishing particular "frameworks" through which audiences are given the opportunity to make sense of the crisis of missing and murdered women. Ideology, in this sense, is … a "field of power" … in which members of a society tend to formulate understandings of the world that they inhabit (Hackett and Carroll 2006)….

Ideology and News Discourses

Mass media institutions have access to striking concentrations of symbolic power. As such, they exist in a decisively ideological sphere; they are key sites where social meanings are produced and distributed (Hall 1981). Thus not surprisingly, communication researchers have long been interested in the relationship between mass media messages and social and political power.

Stuart Hall et al. (1978: 65), in their seminal consideration of a perceived mugging outbreak in the United Kingdom, consider why news narratives have tended to "reproduce and sustain … definitions of … situation[s] which favour the powerful." … [S]ome media scholars once considered (and, in some cases, continue to consider) mass media institutions as the exemplars of an engaged democratic citizenship. Mass media scholarship was once dominated by a series of liberal-pluralist assumptions that presented the institution of journalism as a "watchdog against the abuse of power, a righter of wrongs, a humbler of hubris and arrogance, a promoter of positive social change, [and] an agent to comfort the afflicted and afflict the comfortable" (Hackett and Carroll 2006: 21). … Social behaviorists like George Mead (1948: 326) argued that the proliferation of instruments of mass communication would provide a basis for social unity by providing individuals with the means to "identify themselves with each other." These approving assessments of the press were often sustained and reproduced by what media institutions said (and continue to say) about themselves. David Taras (1990), for example, suggests that the "mirror model" — which holds that mass media news discourses mirror reality and reflect issues and events as they truly are — is "widely accepted" among individuals working within news-generating organizations. Geneva Overholser and Kathleen Jamieson (2005) suggest that notions of media "mirroring" are still common among news institutions and animate professional pretensions of objectivity. Yet others have challenged this paradigm, suggesting that news [media] … holds up a "distorted mirror" which alters fundamentally the content it reflects (Taras 1990).

More prominently, a wide diversity of scholars have argued that the relationship between media outputs and political power hinges crucially on questions of ownership. Researchers have argued that the status of news-generating organizations as privately-owned corporations has engendered a near-seamless relationship between media messages and the interests of capital. Noam Chomsky and Edward Herman (1988) famously proposed that a "propaganda model" could be used to evaluate the extent of this relationship. … In this schema, the outputs of corporate media institutions will tend to reflect the interests of its owners, advertisers and those who fund its activities, as well as the opinions of those who are deemed appropriate sources and able to provide information quickly (well-financed and organized government and private institutions, including the military, for example). Media messages, they contend, are also tempered by the need to avoid flak from centres of power and by the prevailing ideologies of a society's most powerful interests (for Chomsky and Herman this included the "national religion of anti-communism"). Consistently, Michael Parenti (1993: 51) maintains that corporate ownership has had a decisive impact on media outputs. He argues that because corporate power permeates the "entire social fabric" of our societies, "opinions that support existing arrangements of economic and political power are more easily treated as facts." Prevailing notions of objectivity, therefore, necessarily reflect these particular biases and much of "what is reported as 'news' is little more than the uncritical transmission of official opinions." ...

Hall et al. (1978) stress that news messages are themselves a social product and insist that understanding their relationship to power requires understanding the "professional ideology" in which they are incubated and deployed. To this end, they examine the professional practices that shape news discourses, pointing to a series of structural necessities that influence news production to explain why media institutions tend to provide an "over-accessing" to people and institutions in positions of power. But perhaps more centrally for our present purposes, they also argue that media messages are articulated within "distinct ideological limits" and thus necessarily provide "frameworks" for evaluating issues that tend to tip in favour of established authority. Similarly, Ericson et al.'s (1991: 3–4) sprawling survey of media practices found that news discourses serve an inherently conservative function in that they perpetually "represent order" by installing particular views of "morality, procedural form, and social hierarchy" that promote particular "versions and visions" of social control....

"Defining the Boundaries of the Crisis"

Vancouver's crisis of missing and murdered women presents a potent challenge to liberal-pluralist claims about the essential fairness of governance in Canada. The absence of a dramatic official response as scores of women disappeared for two decades from a densely populated urban neighbourhood demonstrates the profound contradiction of the state's supposed capacity to provide a basic level of universal protection. [I]t reveals how a particular group of marginalized women were disqualified from the protective assurances of the state. ...

News narratives play a vital role in representing and maintaining this prevailing order. Media institutions have the ability to establish the "boundaries of public discourse," and it is within these boundaries that "priorities are set and public agendas are established" (Henry and Tator 2002: 235). Ericson et al. (1991) suggest that such narratives are important sites for state actors and institutions to win legitimacy for their political preferences by establishing their practices within broader definitions of order. As they put it:

> The news-media institution is pivotal to the ability of authorities to make convincing claims. It offers a pervasive and persuasive means by which authorities from various institutions can attempt to obtain wider consent for their moral preferences. Moral authority is always subject to *consent*, and legitimacy is always something that is *granted*. [emphasis in original]

Defining the Crisis: The Negligence Narrative

For media audiences in Vancouver, the view that police failure was complicit in the tragedy of missing and murdered women was already well established when authorities began their excavation of the Pickton farm in 2002. As Beverly Pitman (2002) observes, accusations that both the mayor and the police had bungled the cases began to emerge with the first local coverage of the disappearances in 1998 and 1999. She argues that a narrative of negligence — though secondary to other explanations — became part of the "media mill" for three reasons. First, it aligned with the stigmatization of the Downtown Eastside as a centre of criminality and vice, which had been privileged in dominant media discourses for nearly two decades. Second, friends and supporters of the missing women managed to make the case that the police operated on a double-standard and had avoided instigating a full investigation because the victims worked in the street-level sex trade. Third, for a brief period, the "representational work" of supporters, activists and sympathetic journalists had managed to generate an outpouring of sympathy that transcended well-established divisions between the Downtown Eastside and other parts of the city. And while Pitman (2002: 175–76) observes that this "uncommon kind of community" was eventually eroded by the inscription of fears that a serial killer was at work — the installation of a "Jack the Ripper" template — it is nevertheless important to acknowledge that these criticisms of police mismanagement did play a role in early local coverage. Jiwani and Young (2006) make similar observations in their survey of case-related content that appeared in the *Vancouver Sun*. They note that police negligence was sustained as a core element of these narratives but was profoundly overshadowed by a shift in media focus toward Pickton himself.

From February 8 to 22, 2002, nearly one third of all articles related to the case dealt directly with the failure of law enforcement. Friends and supporters of the missing women were central to this critique; their frequently quoted accounts of disinterested investigators, ignored information and a prevailing culture of unwillingness to take disappearances seriously established official negligence as a definitive explanation. Such claims were powerfully re-inscribed by the repeated invocation of authorized knowers, including criminologists and politicians, and legitimated by interviews with a former Vancouver detective who openly acknowledged that scant resources were dedicated to the disappearances and that tips, including one linking some of the missing women to the Pickton farm, were often not pursued vigorously or were ignored altogether (Matas 2002a).

By February 23, 2002, however, two first-degree murder charges had been issued and the focus of coverage shifted decisively away from the offences of the police and toward those of the accused himself. From February 23 to 27, 2002, the negligence narrative was consigned to the margins of the coverage and considered directly only once in a *Globe and Mail* editorial. Thus, from the arrest forward, the negligence narrative began to lose its central positioning ... [yet] the significance of this narrative should not be underestimated. ... The negligence narrative as more than a short-lived set of stories; we might consider it as one of the key paradigms through which the crisis of the missing women was rendered intelligible to national audiences. ... In other words, it operated to define negligent policing as a key problem and thus provided a framework through which the tragedy might become understandable. ... It is in the sixteen news stories, columns and editorials that consider the effects of police negligence that we find the vast majority of claims implicating the state in the violence of the crisis. The most critical recurring voices — family members Rick Frey and Maggie DeVries, and the prominent criminologist John Lowman — are largely confined to these articles. Frey's interventions — when not limited to narrations of grief — are primarily condemnations of selective policing. In one statement he laments what he perceives to be an official spirit of dismissal: "I'm sure the thought was 'it's another druggie, who cares'" (Girard 2002e). In another, he remarks "we felt ignored and brushed aside and we felt Marnie was being brushed aside because people just saw her as a drug addict and a prostitute" (*Toronto Star* 2007d). DeVries challenges this same culture of negligence. In one paradigmatic quotation, she asked of police performance: "if they're behaving like that with this case, then how is it with everything else? Everyone in Vancouver should be concerned about this" (Armstrong 2002b). Elsewhere she contends that if women from another part of Vancouver had gone missing with the same frequency, "there would be mayhem... there would be searches and media interest and rewards" (*Globe and Mail* 2002). Lowman echoes these sentiments. In one article, he argues: "clearly those responsible for the investigation did not show as much concern about the health and safety of the prostitutes than they should have" (Girard 2002e). And elsewhere: "the information out there gives the impression [the police] did not make this a priority the way it should have been" (Hume and Bailey 2002). ... I want to suggest that the negligence narrative constitutes such a framework and operates to limit the possibility of a broader analysis. By producing the sex worker as a subject fundamentally alienated from the protection of the police, these narratives lend themselves to a coherent ... way of explaining how so many women could be taken without eliciting an aggressive response by the state. To the degree that the state can be held accountable, negligence is defined as *the* problem. ...

The point here is not to deny the significance of police mismanagement. On the contrary, it is important to recognize the key role that this official disregard played in reproducing the conditions of endangerment in which the victims worked. Rather, I wish to underscore the limits of an analysis that explains this heinous set of crimes as a simple ... [as] irresponsible policing [and a] psychopathic ... serial killer. What both kinds of explanations have in common is that they produce a problem that is *manageable*. As long as this critique remains contained within the spheres of individual responsibility and bureaucratic bungling, it poses little threat to the legitimacy of the prevailing political order.

Hugill's analysis of the media coverage of the tragic deaths of sex trade workers in Vancouver's Downtown Eastside reveals how media reporting — despite its professionalism and national scope — reproduces narrowly defined explanations for tragic events that focus on personal troubles (addiction and prostitution). These narratives were woven together to create a dominate framing or commonsense understanding that absolved the state from systemic disregard for the women's safety for decades. Although Hugill uncovered that police were indifferent and negligent in the initial response to the cases of missing women, waiting several years before launching an investigation, in the next chapter we consider the overt use of police power through surveillance and arrest of homeless people to enforce public order. In both ways, the police work at the behest of the state to reproduce a particular social order.

8 The Role of the State

Many of us assume that social control is the result of self-control — how you and I choose to act or think determines crime rates, unemployment problems and the spread of infectious diseases. Through a sociological analysis, however, it is possible to see how our decisions are informed by social institutions like the media or the education system. These institutions are a part of what sociologists call "the state": "an organized political structure that carries out the tasks required by more complex societies" (Naiman 2012: 165). But how the state organizes and manages society oftentimes functions as social control, as the state "has monopoly on the legitimate use of violence" (Weber cited in Naiman 2012: 165). As Naiman explains, the state's primary role is to protect the capacity and the conditions necessary for the accumulation of wealth. However, the state must do so in the context of a liberal democracy wherein enshrined legal rights compel the state to provide its citizens certain protections from harm and disadvantage. This fine balance between the interests of the "1 percent" to amass and protect wealth, and the interests of the "99 percent," who work for the capitalist class, requires a powerful and sophisticated state that when necessary will govern through coercion: arrest, detention, incarceration, execution, occupation and genocide. As we shall see, the targets of coercive state power, however, are seldom corporate executives and are often homeless youth, squeegee-kids and prostitutes. The modern face of the coercive capacity of the state is "law-and-order policing": the militarization and weaponization of police forces, empowered through law with ominous powers of arrest, search and seizure, and detention. As increasing numbers of unemployed abandon their search for work and mentally ill people are without supportive housing, urban streets become spaces of survival through pan-handling, busking, squeegeying car windshields and prostitution. Outraged middle-class shoppers, restaurant-goers and business owners demand protection from the crime and disorder they see around them. As we learned in Chapter 3, there is a material basis to the social, political and cultural practices such as policing and criminalization of poverty. In this chapter, Les Samuelson examines the criminalization of poverty and the simultaneous disappearance of state regulation of corporate power.

"Crime as a Social Problem: From Definition to Reality"

Les Samuelson, in Les Samuelson and Wayne Antony (eds.),
Power and Resistance, 5th ed. (Fernwood, 2012)

In *The Rich Get Richer and the Poor Get Prison* (2010), Reiman and Leighton critically evaluate the implicit ideology of the criminal justice system, noting that any such system conveys a subtle yet powerful message in support of established institutions. It does this, they say, primarily by concentrating on individual wrongdoers, diverting our attention away from our institutions, away from considering whether our institutions themselves are wrong, unjust, or indeed "criminal" (Reiman and Leighton 2010: 179). Reiman and Leighton focus upon the "evils of the social order" that accrue from major inequalities of economic power in society — that is, they look at how working-class individuals are prosecuted differently than upper-class people or corporations for causing physical or economic harms.

However, as critical criminological analyses have repeatedly emphasized, our society is also characterized by massive inequalities of power based upon class, race, and gender. Thus, a range of these analyses focus on how legal practices reinforce class-based inequalities, the patriarchal subjugation of women and post-colonial social injustice for Aboriginal peoples. These inequalities generate differences of involvement and treatment within our criminal justice system, from the definition of crime to the responses of criminal justice personnel to offenders and victims. Certain individuals and groups are not born more "criminal" than any others, but the life conditions they may face vary greatly. Thus, for critical criminologists, a central "justice" concern is with how underlying social inequalities and processes operate to bring marginalized/oppressed people into the criminal justice system, while privileged individuals — if dealt with at all — tend to be treated leniently.

Class

There is no question that massive inequalities of wealth in Canada have been growing in the last two decades: Canada's richest people have amassed a record share of the nation's economic growth, according to a study by the Canadian Centre for Policy Alternatives. The top 1 percent earned almost a third of all income growth during the decade from 1997 to 2007, according to the study, which examines the wealth of Canada's richest citizens since the Second World War. "That's a bigger piece of the action than any other generation of rich Canadians has taken," said Armine Yalnizyan of the (Canadian Centre for Policy Alternatives). "The last time Canada's elite held so much of the nation's income in their hands was in the 1920s." Even then their incomes didn't soar as fast as they are today. (*Toronto Sun* 2010)

The class-biased nature of law has two basic dimensions. One dimension involves acts that are either defined in legislation as crime or are controlled through regulatory law. The second dimension involves the justice system's differential processing of working-class and professional-class individuals and corporations for "criminal acts." Critical criminologists hold that a relatively small group of individuals control much of the wealth and political power in our society. While not necessarily acting in unison, this elite is able to influence the political-legal process so that both criminal and regulatory law does not treat seriously the social, economic, and physical harms inflicted upon society by corporations. By contrast, the crimes committed by working-class people, which are frequently a result of their life circumstances, are prosecuted more severely under the law; incarceration is often the end product. Put simply and bluntly: "Corporate actors regularly and repeatedly violate... standards of moral and legal behaviour, do much more physical and economic harm than any other violators of these standards, and continue to be treated as upright members of our society, giving meaning to Clarence Darrow's aphorism that most people classified as criminals are 'persons with predatory instincts without sufficient capital to form a corporation'" (Glasbeek (2002: 118).

On the one hand, the Canadian state has failed to define as "crime" much corporate behaviour that has economic and physical costs, to individuals, society, and the environment, far exceeding the costs of street crime (Gordon and Coneybeer 1995; Snider 1994). Corporate crime, or "suite crime," is defined as "crime" committed by a corporate official in the pursuit of organizational goals, usually profit. Some of these acts are illegal under either criminal or civil law; yet many such acts that are economically and physically harmful to society are not. This criterion is ostensibly the core element in the prohibitions and punishments of the Canadian Criminal Code.

The costs to society of actual corporate crime far exceed those of street crime. Colin Goff (2011) tackles this issue via a related, but not identical, concept, white-collar crime — crimes of fraud and injury that are carried out during the course of a (seemingly) legitimate occupation. Gomme (2007: 304–06) notes that business crime that is known and makes its way into official records represents only the tip of the iceberg. Still, the annual Canadian losses due to embezzlement, computer crime, commercial fraud, unnecessary auto repairs, unneeded home improvements, price fixing, illegal corporate mergers, false advertising, and other business crimes are staggering. The accounting firm Ernst and Young estimates the costs of white-collar crime in Canada at $20 billion (Gomme 2007: 306). "The federal government estimates that in 1998, economic crimes such as securities and telemarketing fraud [alone] cost Canadians $5 billion" (Goff 2011: 125). Using early 1990s U.S. data, Laureen Snider (1994: 276) puts the issue into focus: "all the street crime in the U.S. in a given year is estimated to cost around $4 billion, much less than 5 percent of the average take from corporate crime."

Consider the Enron $63 billion investors fraud orchestrated by CEO Kenneth Lay. Enron started as a profitable pipeline company delivering natural gas. But CEO Hay and his senior executives wanted much greater, and quick profits (Hagan and Linden 2009: 514–15). To keep the company growing, Enron executives began to use illegal financial measures to make it appear that profits were continuing to increase. The "culture of greed" at Enron (Hagan and Linden 2009: 514) was enormous and had help from many of Wall Street's big "respectable" players: Executives were not content with the millions of dollars they had taken from the company. As the illegal schemes began to unravel and the company began to slide into bankruptcy, Enron paid $681 million to 140 top executives, including $67 million to CEO Kenneth Lay, who continued to encourage employees and members of the public to buy Enron stock even as he and his executives stripped the company of much of its remaining capital.... While Enron executives must take most of the blame for the company's demise, they had help from the managers of other large corporations. The Arthur Andersen accounting firm, one of the world's largest, allowed Enron's many lapses of legal and ethical standards to slip by its auditors in order to help it obtain lucrative consulting contracts with Enron. Many of Wall Street's largest banks and brokerage firms collaborated with Enron in order to profit from stock commissions, consulting contracts, and interest from loans. (Hagan 2009: 515) Enron apparently got help from one of Canada's biggest banks, CIBC. "While not admitting any wrong doing, in 2005 CIBC paid $2.4 billion to settle a lawsuit in which CIBC was accused of helping Enron to hide its financial dealings" (Hagan and Linden 2009: 515, emphasis added).

Too often such corporate greed is dismissed as entirely economic and thus less a problem than street crime that is violent. Yet, as Gomme (2007: 306) notes:

> This is a grave misperception — business crime is frequently violent. The volume of assaults and murders in Canada pales in comparison with the number of injuries, debilating and life-threatening diseases, and deaths attributable to business enterprises and professions engaging in unsafe practices, marketing dangerous products, violating workplace safety regulations, and polluting the air, the water, and the land. Death in the workplace ranks third, after heart disease and cancer, as a major killer of Canadians.

Schmalleger (2007: 42) calculated a ratio of 2:1 workers killed by jobs versus murder for the U.S. in 2004. This is likely true in Canada. Even these figures likely underestimate the seriousness of corporate violence. Beirne and Messerchmidt (2006: 204) conclude: "We are actually safer in the street than indoors; the evidence presented here suggests that we are safer almost anywhere than in the workplace."

Is all this physical violence and injury just accidental? It is estimated that 40 percent of industrial "accidents" are a result of working conditions that are both unsafe and prohibited under existing law. About 25 percent, while not illegal, are dangerous nonetheless (Gomme 2007: 306). Yet, these violations and harms are not pursued with the same vigour as street crime injuries.

To classify these industrial deaths as "accidents," as is generally the case, completely obscures the context within which they occur. The 1982 Ocean Ranger oil-rig tragedy, which cost eighty-four lives, puts the case more clearly. According to the conclusions of the official investigation itself, "Intervention could have offset design flaws and overcome lax shipping classifications, inadequate seaworthy standards and poor marine training of staff and prevented the disaster" (quoted in McMullan and Smith 1997: 62). I grew up in St. John's, the supply depot for this rig. Local people working on the rig had nicknamed the rig the "Ocean Danger" because of its poor safety standards and operation.

In 1992 the Westray mine explosion in Nova Scotia, one of Canada's worst, claimed twenty-six lives and was also no accident. "Initial investigations suggest the existence of careless management, unsafe working conditions that included explosively high levels of methane and coal dust, outdated equipment and a remarkably lax and inept regulations and enforcement system" (McMullan and Smith 1997: 62). Glasbeek (2002: 121) notes that, by the time of the explosion at the Westray mine, a staggering record of fifty-two breaches of the health and safety standards had been compiled. With fifty-two non-criminal charges under the Occupational Health and Safety Act, thirty-four were stayed by Crown prosecutors, who expressed fears they might interfere with criminal prosecutions. Subsequent to a final Supreme Court of Canada March 2007 decision, prosecution against two mine managers charged with twenty-six accounts of manslaughter and criminal negligence causing death was abandoned. They decided not to pursue the charges because there was not enough evidence to secure convictions.

Importantly, on March 31, 2004, Bill C-45, also known as the "Westray Bill," amended the Criminal Code to establish new legal duties and imposed serious penalties for workplace injuries or death. A Canadian Centre for Occupational Health and Safety (CCOHS 2011) report notes that to date there have only been four charges laid, with one conviction, one dropped, and two still before the courts.

Even when convicted of similar misbehaviour, the well-to-do are often treated more leniently by the criminal justice system. Consider these two cases of fraud. In June 2001 a medical practitioner convicted of fraud for overbilling the publicly funded health-care system by just under a million dollars — money used to take luxury trips to Germany, Italy, California, and New Zealand and stay in five-star hotels with his partner — was sentenced to a conditional sentence of two years, to be served, not in jail, but in the community. The medical disciplinary board added to the sentence by suspending his ability to bill the healthcare system for a short length of time. The "harshly dealt-with" practitioner appealed the medical disciplinary board's decision. Next, consider the case of college student Kimberly Rogers. She was convicted of welfare fraud for collecting it and student loans to help finance four years of community college:

> Kimberly Rogers had died alone and eight months pregnant, in her sweltering apartment in Sudbury, Ontario, while under house arrest for welfare fraud. What many do not realize is that the policies and conditions that set the stage for this tragedy are still in place and in some respects have actually worsened.
>
> Kimberly Rogers was charged with welfare fraud after collecting both social assistance and students loans to help cover the costs of attending four years of community college. She was convicted in April 2001 and the penalty was six months under house arrest (with the right to be allowed out of her hot apartment three hours per week); a requirement to repay more than $13 thousand dollars in benefits; eighteen months probation and loss of the right to have part of her student loan forgiven. At the time of Roger's conviction, Ontario Works regulations specified that anyone convicted of welfare fraud would be automatically suspended from receiving benefits for three months. This stipulation has since been made tougher. Anyone convicted of welfare fraud in the province of Ontario will be banned for life from ever being able to collect social assistance. (Keck 2002)

After her May 2001 launch of the first Ontario citizen Charter of Rights and Freedoms challenge to Ontario's Welfare (Ontario Works Benefits) laws:

> Rogers' benefits were reinstated for the interim, but this was not the end of her problems. Even with Ontario Works benefits, she was unable to support herself and her unborn child. After a deduction of 10 percent (towards repayment to Ontario Works) Rogers received $468 per month. With $450 going towards paying the rent. Rogers was left with $18 to cover all other necessities.... "I ran out of food this weekend. I am unable to sleep and I cry all the time (Kimberly Rogers, affidavit to court May 2001). Tragically, while still under house arrest, Kimberly Rogers died just weeks after the Ontario Superior Court of Justice released its exceptional decision. (Keck 2002)

Glasbeek (2002: 123) notes: "A study of welfare fraud documented that 80 percent of all persons convicted of welfare fraud of this type were given jail sentences. In contrast, another study shows that "prison" is imposed in 4 percent of all tax evasion cases, even though the amount stolen vastly exceeds that stolen by welfare abusers. Unemployment benefit frauds reveal the same pattern: the rate of incarceration is twice that by tax evaders." Corporations, even government "corporations," and the privileged can apparently kill, maim and rob with relative impunity while the poor get prison — or worse, in the case of Kimberly Rogers. This is one form of the class bias of criminal law.

Another form lies in the fact that corporate harmfulness is often not even defined as criminal. Most often, costly and harmful corporate behaviour, when classified as illegal, falls within regulatory law rather than the Criminal Code, where most street crime is placed. This distinction is often made on the basis of legal notions of culpability, which were established to prosecute individual offenders for street crime but not corporations or corporate officials for industry-related killings. In Canada prior to 1941, corporations were immune to any criminal liability because they were deemed to have no minds of their own (McMullan 1992: 80). There was little progress in this area until the late 1970s and early 1980s when cases heard before the Supreme Court of Canada began to fit corporate offenders into an individualist model of liability, evidence, procedure, and sanction (McMullan 1992: 80).

But there is dispute and confusion over whether the Canadian Charter of Rights and Freedoms under sections 7 and 1(d) is meant to enforce relatively rigid mens rea (guilty mind) requirements for the prosecution of corporate offenders. In Canada, the Crown must prove "blameworthiness" to get a Criminal Code conviction. It refers to "the guilty mind, the wrongful intention" — a necessary element in establishing criminal conduct (Verdun-Jones 2007: 66).

McMullan (1992: 80–81) also states that in the Irwin Toy Ltd. case the Supreme Court of Canada ruled that a corporation's economic rights were not protected by section 7 of the Charter, as are the "life, liberty or security of the person." While the matter is still up in the air, Canadian judicial history suggests that Canadian courts have not been inclined to extend the scope of corporate criminal proceedings to include the illegal acts or omissions of a corporation's agents or employees. In addition to the problem of mens rea, corporations have been almost exclusively prosecuted for regulatory violations — such as those governing health and safety — and not for the consequences of those violations (Reasons, Ross, and Patterson 1986; McMullan 1992). For example, a company would be fined for not installing safety bolts in a construction crane, but not prosecuted for the death of several workers who were below the crane when it collapsed.

Corporations have frequent and vociferous input into the regulations governing them, generally under the guise of being enlisted to co-operate in creating "workable laws." The result is a lax system of regulation. Corporations are often able to avoid prosecution for illegal activity, but when they are prosecuted, the penalty is usually an inconsequential fine levied against the corporation, and the ruling does not usually single out individual corporate decision makers legally or publicly. Even when the court does name individual corporate offenders, the penalties, both legal and social, are usually only nominal.

Snider (2002) notes that the 1999 investigation of insider stock trading in Canada was carried out by a newspaper, not the securities commission. "Some (corporate) insiders were making fortunes ... (but) until this was publicized, neither the Ontario Securities commission nor the Toronto Stock Exchange had taken any... action" (Snider 2002: 224). Unfortunately, even with much public fanfare about tightening regulations around corporate governance and stock trading, the Canadian government "crackdown" on corporate misbehaviour has followed the lead of the U.S. Sarbanes-Oxley Act — the main concern is not with the losses suffered by "the proverbial average citizen" but with the threat to the markets that these misdemeanours pose (*National Post* 2002).

These conditions reflect a major class bias in the application of criminal and regulatory law. It should not be hard to understand why, in the 1970s, 90 percent of the seventy largest U.S. corporations were habitual offenders, with an average of fourteen convictions per corporation (Edwin Sutherland 1977; see also Clinard and Yeager 1980). John Hagan (1992: 465) reports that more than half of Canada's largest corporations have been recidivists, with an average of 3.2 decisions against them.

Perhaps we need corporate "three strikes and you're out" legislation. The federal Conservative government is "getting tough" on street crime with its 2011 omnibus crime bill, with mandatory sentences, no consideration for time served while waiting for trial and so on. Forthcoming are tough amendments to the Criminal Code and sentencing practices.

The lenient attitude towards corporate crime and white-collar criminals might be hardening. Opinion polls reveal that popular thinking and sentiment are in favour of tougher laws, regulations, and sanctions regarding corporate misconduct. In some instances judicial decisions have emphasized corporate responsibility for harmful acts. For example, the operations manager of a waterfront oil recycling company was jailed for ninety days when he admitted that the company, knowingly and fraudulently, spilled hazardous chemical waste into the Toronto harbour (Gomme, 2007: 327). Finally, there have been proposals to break down both the individual and organizational inducements to corporate crime and the traditional defences for it, through the creation of a culture that does not tolerate corporate crime. The proposed solutions include: "shaming and positive repentance, new legal tools and controls, corporate accountability and restructuring, new forms of penalty and criminal sanctioning, and the application of countervailing force against corporate crime" (McMullan 1992: 118).

In the mid 1990s, it appeared that, at least in some respects, the rich won't always get richer while the poor get prison. Snider (1994: 278) stated, "Pro-regulatory pressure groups (for example, environmental activities, 'green' politicians trying to eliminate chemicals from farmers' fields, unionists working to secure stronger health and safety laws in the workplace, and feminists working to control the pharmaceutical industry) are absolutely central to the regulatory process." A few years later, Snider (2002: 231) was much more pessimistic about what she termed the "corporate counter-revolution," whereby corporate marauding is receiving very little attention and political-legal action:

> Government obligation to help the marginalized and desperate has disappeared, but its obligation to punish the powerless has been reinforced.... By decriminalizing and deregulating profitable corporate acts that were once seen as corporate crime, and by downsizing regulatory agencies and cutting regulatory staff, governments at all levels have been quick to shed their historic responsibility to protect citizens from corporate excess, fraud, and abuse of power.

A recent event in Canada highlights these concerns. In the "wake" of the Gomery inquiry, Paul Coffin, a Montreal ad executive, pleaded guilty to defrauding Canadian taxpayers of $1.5 million in the Quebec sponsorship scandal. The Crown asked for a thirtyfour- month federal prison term. The judge, in line with Coffin's views, ordered a speaking tour to lecture business students on "ethics." This was part of his two years less a day conditional sentence with no jail time (National Post 2005). The Crown later appealed Coffin's sentence, and he was eventually sentenced to eighteen months in prison. ...

By decriminalizing and deregulating profitable corporate acts... governments at all levels have been quick to shed their historic responsibility to protect citizens from corporate excess, fraud, and abuse of power. [Yet] ... on October 17, 2006, Stephen Harper's Conservative government introduced its "three strikes legislation" in the House of Commons. Under this law, third-time violent/sexual offenders would automatically be categorized as "dangerous offenders" and be liable to indefinite prison sentences. The Crown would not have to prove the case; the onus would be on the accused to prove otherwise. Many observers thought that this bill would hit Aboriginal offenders the hardest, leaving them with "no hope" (*StarPhoenix* 2006). The news was appropriately juxtaposed with a report from Canada's correctional investigator released just a day earlier. Correctional investigator Howard Sapers called the treatment of Aboriginal Peoples in the federal justice system a "national disgrace." Overall the federal inmate population went down 12.5 percent between 1996 and 2004; during the same period our national crime rate in general also went down. But during the same period the number of First Nations people in federal institutions increased by 21.7 percent, a 34 percent difference between non-Aboriginal and Aboriginal inmates. The numbers of Aboriginal women in prison increased by "a staggering 74.2 percent." (Canada 1996). The *StarPhoenix* (2006) article ended by noting, with some conscience and historical clarity: "It is a world where a population that the Canadian government institutionalized and traumatized through the residential school system would be further disadvantaged." ...

The Harper federal government has been working obtusely, often with misinformation and in denial of academic and community protests, to "fill more prisons." Representing virtually every major religious group in Canada, the Canadian Church Council on Justice and Corrections sent a letter to Prime Minister Stephen Harper (CCJC 2011):

> December 17, 2010
>
> Dear Mr. Prime Minister
>
> The Church Council on Justice and Corrections (CCJC) is most concerned that in this time of financial cuts to important services you and the government of Canada are prepared to significantly increase investment in the building of new prisons.... Increasing levels of incarceration of marginalized people is counter-productive and undermines human dignity in our society. By contrast, well-supervised probation or release, bail options, reporting centres, practical assistance, supportive housing, programs that promote accountability, respect and reparation: these measures have all been well-established, but they are underfunded. Their outcomes have proven to be the same or better in terms of re-offence rates, at a fraction of the cost with much less human damage....
>
> Sincerely, The Church Council on Justice and Corrections

... As Jeffrey Reiman (2007) states, in order for a real "society" to exist there must be two-way-street social justice. Harry Glasbeek (2002: 283) puts this very well at the end of his book *Wealth by Stealth*:

> To be a democrat is not an abstraction. It is a state of being: "Democracy is a world that joins Demos — the people with Krakia — power.... It describes an ideal, not a method for achieving it. ... It is a historical project ... as people take it up as such and struggle for it." These proposals take up what we have learned in the previous pages about the enemy of this historical project, and they are intended to help fuel the spirit of would-be democrats as they engage in their struggles to bring together people and power, break down the corporate shield, and lay the groundwork for a humanizing transformation of our polity. Only if we recover, and enrich our political lives as democratic citizens, will we be able to be effective participants in local and worldwide movements to tackle the enormous human problems we face.

9 Neoliberalism and Globalization

In the previous readings, it is a clear that the state plays a somewhat contradictory role in society: on the one hand it increasingly polices and punishes those who fall between the cracks, for example, those on welfare or those who demand change, such as the G20 protestors in Toronto in June 2010. On the other hand, the state appears to have disappeared from constraining the power of corporate elites to pursue profit regardless of environmental and human cost. As Samuelson sets out, this simultaneous ratcheting up and unravelling of policing is a precondition of how central class is to how society is organized and managed. Yet, for many students sitting in a university classroom, the state does not appear particularly coercive or oppressive. After all, university tuitions are partially subsidized by provincial governments; we have universal health care and the Charter of Rights and Freedoms which protects us from discrimination, and we have legal rights such as "innocent until proven guilty." So why do sociologists claim that the state is a coercive apparatus of power that protects the powerful? Naiman provides a sociological analysis of how the role of governments has changed over the past few decades, highlighting that much of the benefits of living in Canada today were achieved decades ago under the welfare, or Keynesian, state, named after John Maynard Keynes, an economist whose theory of how the state could best manage the economy through the management of labour (workers) revolutionized how advanced democracies were governed. In short, the welfare state appeared to be "a protector and provider of citizen well-being and security" (Naiman 2012: 193). However, these protections are now under threat as the welfare state is dismantled and a neoliberal state is established. Why is the welfare state disappearing? As sociologists, to answer this question we need to examine the changing material or economic conditions of globalization. Todd Gordon argues that policing is a form of class control not crime control; the criminalization of street work and street life (prostitution, squeegeying and homelessness) disciplines the poor through compulsory workfare programs or incarceration. But the state also governs at a distance through its domestic economic and foreign policy policies and its military industry complex. Gary Teeple lays out for us how the War on Terror has been used by advanced Western democracies such as the United States, Canada and the United Kingdom as a tactic to weaken democratic rights and protections of citizens to obscure what he calls "terrorism by the markets" and "terrorism by the state." Our sociological imagination forces us to confront a different set of truths about the War on Terror.

Cops, Crime and Capitalism:
The Law-and-Order Agenda in Canada
Todd Gordon (Fernwood, 2006)

"Contemporary Law-and-Order Policies"
Since the 1970s governments in advanced capitalist countries have undergone significant changes. These came about in reaction to the global economic crisis, which began in the 1970s [much like what we experienced in 2008]

The Keynesian State Form
Keynesian policies[1] were partly based on the global strength of the American and Canadian economies at the end of the Second World War. It took several years for Europe and Asia to recover from the devastation of the war. In the absence of serious competition, the North American economy, already technologically more advanced, was able to bolster its competitive strength and long-term profitability. The policies were fostered, too, by a recognition of the strength of the working class in terms of organization. In Canada, for example, a significant strike wave occurred during the 1940s. The period also saw a rapid growth in industrial unionism.[2]

In Western Europe and Japan, meanwhile, Communist-led trade unions gained in strength, providing an incentive for companies to promote collaboration. Meanwhile, the war had wiped out weak industries, and into this vacuum came industries with more advanced American production methods. Large pools of labour reserves kept excessive wage increases in check. The internationally coordinated monetary regime under the leadership of the U.S. economy and the dollar provided a firm foundation for the strong renewal of accumulation and the introduction of Keynesianism.

"Keynesianism," Bonefeld (1993: 69) suggests, "was an attempt to integrate labour into the capital relation on the basis of full employment growth policies and institutionalized forms of redistribution of wealth." The organized working class won, among other things, the right to bargain collectively and a commitment to monetary policies conducive to low levels of unemployment. It also won a significant increase in wages via various entitlements from the state such as unemployment and welfare benefits, health care and pension programs. Capital and the state, absorbing working-class struggle through the formalized administration of the union movement, achieved greater social peace with the working class. This helped guarantee that wage increases were kept at the same level (or below) as increases in productivity. It also established the ability to contribute to "the partial nationalization of social reproduction" of the working population, and thus to a healthy and stable workforce, by means of more standardized social policies (Sears 1999: 92).

All of these new measures helped to establish the welfare state. In Canada, a series of social-welfare measures laid the foundation for this welfare state: universal health care, introduced under the Health Care Act; unemployment insurance benefits; and old-age pensions available to all seniors at the age of sixty-five. Still other measures improved the health and safety of workers. For example, workers injured at a job site could file for benefits under the Workers' Compensation Program. Labour laws were revised to regulate working conditions under the provincial employee standards acts, which contained important definitions of a working week, a working day, overtime, and vacation pay. As a result, paid work increased in value beyond the actual pay cheques. Unionized workers were more amply rewarded than non-unionized workers, given the new fringe benefits: private pension plans, medical and dental plans, paid sick days, etc.

All of these things, together with the spread of U.S. technologies and production methods and the coordination of the international economy under U.S. leadership (Bonefeld 1993: 70–71, see also Clarke 1988: 244 ff.), helped contribute to a period of historic levels of economic growth for most advanced capitalist economies, sustained by unprecedented secular profit rates and productivity increases, leading to the long-term prosperity, and thus stability, of capitalist economies.[3] However, specific groups in Canada, including women, people of colour, Aboriginals, gays and lesbians, and Francophones, were in many different ways excluded partially or totally from these gains (Sears 2003).

Emergence of the Crisis

By the late 1960s cracks in the Keynesian foundation of many of the advanced capitalist economies began to appear. The mechanisms designed to keep capital's tendency to overaccumulation from expressing itself and thus to ensure long-term profitability had run their course. Overaccumulation of capital, driven by "the unfettered development of the productive power of labour" (Bonefeld 1993: 72), continued to worsen, contributing to a decline in the rate of profit. This increased the dependence on relatively cheap and easily accessible credit to sustain economic growth and thus contributed to growing inflation. In other words, the conditions that had paved the way for the period of unprecedented economic growth now led to structural imbalances in the advanced capitalist economies. The boom times — expressed in the growing markets for capital and consumer goods, high profits and easy access to cheap credit — had encouraged employers to invest in production (in technologies, tools and machinery) at a rate at which, eventually, they could no longer be employed profitably. The growth in the productive capacity of capital had far outpaced the growth of the market, putting downward pressure on prices and profits. The Keynesian regime of cheap credit enabled capital to sustain accumulation despite the weakened profits without restructuring or triggering a recession. The cost was increasing inflation and mounting debt. ... By the mid-1970s, governments in much of the advanced capitalist world began to abandon Keynesian policies and take more coercive measures against what they viewed as a dangerously rebellious working class.

In the 1980s, the federal government in Canada began cutting its direct spending on social programs and its social transfers to the provinces. It also reorganized the criteria for getting social assistance (Russell 2000: 39). The result has been twofold: the amount a recipient can receive for unemployment benefits has dropped considerably over a twenty-year period. To receive payments, recipients have to attend job-training programs. These programs, however, do not provide any of the particular hard skills that are touted as crucial for success in today's labour market. Instead, they stress the importance of assuming greater responsibility for one's lack of work and making more effort to find whatever work is available.[4] These conditions apply only for those who meet today's Employment Insurance eligibility requirements. In 1989, 87 percent of unemployed Canadians qualified for unemployment benefits. By 1996 that number had dropped dramatically to 42 percent (Gabriel 2001: 136).

A similar, if not harsher, trend has taken place with respect to welfare benefits. Before the federal government axed the Canada Assistance Plan in 1996 and replaced it with the Canada Health and Social Transfer, mandatory work programs connected to welfare programs were prohibited by federal law, though this did not prevent entirely "workfare-style experimentation" (Peck 2001: 218). Since 1996, not only have the transfers decreased substantially: the conditions imposed by the federal government on the provinces have also been eliminated, opening the door for workfare. Thus, while welfare benefits have decreased dramatically, in most cases falling well below minimum wage levels, at least seven provinces have now made mandatory participation in employment programs an eligibility requirement. As an Alberta Tory social services minister stated bluntly, welfare "has to be uncomfortable enough that people will try to find an alternative way of living" (quoted in Peck 2001: 218). This ... is the central aim of governments' cuts to and reorganization of benefits programs.

Despite sharp cuts to welfare in Ontario under the Harris government, administrative costs have remained high as a result of attempts to implement workfare. The costs have had to cover the hiring of more welfare spies, officially called Eligibility Review Officers (Mosher 2002: 47), and Andersen Consulting to find more ways of throwing people off the rolls. One Ontario welfare official, interviewed by Peck, made this comment on the Tory's costly welfare strategy: "I don't think costs even enter the equation. It's more [concerned with] having people behave properly" (quoted in Peck 2001: 244). This also suggests, contrary to commonly espoused opinions in both academia and popular media, that the restructuring of the state in recent years "does not simply require the reduction of state power." Rather, as Sears (2003: 12) argues, "The 'free' market is not produced by the elimination of the state, but rather the mobilization of state power to reduce barriers to commodification." Social programs are being actively used to reorganize the labour force in a manner suitable to lean production.

Of course, this strategy has been accompanied by an ideological assault on benefits recipients. Governments and mainstream media have pushed the idea that those on welfare or unemployment benefits are lazy, undeserving and starving the government and public of much-needed funds; and that most recipients are cheating the system or generally criminally inclined. But the problem for the state and other neoliberal boosters, to be clear, is not the poor per se. Like the nineteenth-century moral reformers and those administering the New Poor Laws, poverty in and of itself is not a concern … officials saw poverty as the appropriate condition of the working class, for it would compel people to seek a wage for subsistence.

This attitude clearly informs welfare reform today. What cannot be tolerated is indigence: the condition of the able-bodied poor collecting social assistance or avoiding wage labour. It does not matter what kinds of jobs exist in today's labour market; we never hear government officials or reporters talk about how badly paid, insecure or alienating such jobs may be. Instead, we get stories of the slothful and vice-ridden character of welfare recipients or panhandlers, and how work, often couched in very moralist terms, is the only appropriate thing to improve their character; … "the best social assistance program ever created is a real job" (quoted in Peck 2001: 236).

The result of neoliberal restructuring in Canada, as elsewhere, has been an increase in non-standard or flexible employment and a corresponding decline in income and wages for significant sections of the working class. "Despite the decline in official unemployment," Burke and Shields (2000: 98) note, "levels of economic marginalization continue to climb." This marginalization gets expressed in the increasing prominence since the 1980s of what they refer to as "vulnerable forms of work such as part-time, contract and other types of 'flexible' and inherently volatile employment" (Burke and Shields 2000: 105). By 1998, well over one-third of the adult labour force in Canada was stuck in such flexible or insecure work (Burke and Shields 2000: 112). While wages for most full-time and more secure work stagnated through the 1990s, the wages for "vulnerable" work have remained significantly less. In 1998, the median wage for workers under the age of thirty in vulnerable work was only twelve dollars an hour, and workers in this type of employment can only expect very marginal increases in their wages as they get older (Burke and Shields 2000: 112).

"Towards a Theory of Terrorism"

Gary Teeple, in Sandra Rollings-Manusson (ed.), *Anti-Terrorism: Security and Insecurity after 9/11* (Fernwood, 2009)

Throughout the twentieth century, Western governments have applied the epithet "terrorist" to actions or groups that challenged the established order. The term was often used after the 1918 Russian Revolution as synonymous with "communist" or "socialist" and implying an association with the Soviet Union. During World War II, the Nazis branded internal resistance to occupation as "terrorist"; and after the war, the allied nations gave the same label to national liberation movements in colonial countries. Following the disintegration of the Soviet Bloc and the events of September 11, 2001, use of the word acquired a new importance. In 2002, Washington made "terrorism" the defining characteristic of the present era and the foreseeable future. "The enemy is terrorism," it declared, and the "war" against it would be indefinite (White House 2002).

Enormous political pressure was applied and massive military resources were marshalled to prosecute this war. In the United States, new security laws were pushed through Congress or promulgated by executive fiat, and government departments were reorganized to reflect these new priorities. Under U.N. Security Council Resolution 1373, Washington promoted "counter-terrorist" emergency laws for every member country, undermining the rule of law everywhere. The invasion of Afghanistan in 2001 and then Iraq in 2003 took place with fabricated justifications and little regard for international law (Parry 2006; Corn 2003; Rampton and Stauber 2003). In other countries, such as Canada and the U.K., anti-terrorist laws were passed quickly and without significant public debate. The world order, as reflected in the U.N. Charter and Universal Declaration of Human Rights and other international agreements, was turned on its head.

The Antilogies of the "War On Terrorism"
The rationale for such a transformation, however, has been less than convincing. Statistical data on terrorist acts reveal a striking discord between the purported threat, on the one hand, and the resources marshalled and extraordinary legislative changes made, on the other, to fight terrorism. According to the U.S. State Department's (2000) annual survey of terror, the number of reported deaths from terrorist acts show an irregular but steady decline from the late 1980s. Although the year 2001 was anomalous, with an estimated 3,000 fatalities on 9/11, the loss of life appears to rise after the U.S. declared its "war" (Enders and Sandler 2002; Tilly 2005). In 2002 the report listed 725 people killed and 625 in 2003 — both higher than in 2000 or throughout the 1990s.

There are other seeming disjunctions. Former U.S. Secretary of Defense Donald Rumsfeld, for instance, admitted that "we lack the metrics to see if we are winning or losing the war on terror" (Krueger and Laitin 2004). If data on the nature of the "enemy" appear unimportant, so too do data on how many innocents have been killed and injured by U.S. military and allied forces. Whatever their faults, reasoned estimates of the number of deaths in Iraq do exist. Within the first two years of the invasion, they ranged from about 30,000 to over 100,000 (Iraq Body Count; BBC News 2004, 2006). In the fall of 2007, the highest estimate had risen to over one million and the lowest to about 75,000 (*LA Times* 2007; Iraq Body Count 2007; Media Lens 2007). This is not to mention the civilian casualties caused by the U.S. military attack on Afghanistan, or the loss of life caused by years of sanctions in Iraq before the invasion, during which the death toll is estimated to be between 500,000 and 1.8 million (Gordon 2002; Rubin 2001; Campaign Against Sanctions on Iraq 1999). In short, U.S., British, and other military forces have killed vastly more innocent people in the "war on terrorism" than have officially designated terrorist acts.

Some argue that the threat of terrorism is not to be found so much in property damage and the number of victims as in the destabilization of democratic politics or a "way of life" (Laqueur 1986). It can safely be said, however, that since 9/11, the "war on terrorism" has dramatically undermined the principles of liberal democracy, overridden the rule of law, … held thousands in secret detention without the right of habeas corpus or representation or trial, opened the door to torture as acceptable, … and killed tens of thousands of civilians. The principles of the U.N. Charter and the Universal Declaration of Human Rights and associated covenants and conventions, moreover, have all been trumped by declarations of unilateralism and preemptive intervention. As for Western freedoms, the anti-terrorist laws passed by the majority of states since 9/11 allow for more executive arbitrariness.

Compared to other causes of death and property damage around the world, the losses due to terrorist acts make the enormous "counter-terror" efforts seem patently illogical. The annual murder rate in the U.S. over the past few decades, for example, exceeds the cumulative death total due to terrorism over the whole decade preceding 9/11. In the U.S., each year since 2000, the number of road deaths has exceeded 40,000, while fatalities related to smoking and alcohol consumption number well over 100,000 annually. Globally, since 1981 over 25 million people have died from the HIV/AIDS (UNAIDS 2008; Avert 2008). The effects of HIV/AIDS and other diseases, such as tuberculosis, malaria, measles, dysentery, and cholera, are so great that the economies of some developing countries are "crippled by these diseases" (BBC 1999; WHO 1996). Such a list could easily be extended, but it suffices to indicate that, in light of all the issues that threaten humankind and actually destabilize social systems, the threat of terror is insignificant.

Even the official explanation for the "war on terrorism" does not correspond well with what we actually know. Despite U.S. assertions about Al Qaeda, for example, knowledge of the supposed architects of September 11 remains indefinite (Griffin 2004; Tarpley 2005; Ahmed 2002, 2005; Marrs 2004). The nature, size, and significance of al Qaeda remain unknown, although we do know it was created by intelligence services, mainly the CIA and the Pakistani ISI, to confront the Soviet military in Afghanistan (Ahmed 2002).

A major part of the "war," moreover, was launched in Afghanistan in 2001 and Iraq in 2003 without any evidence that either government was involved in the terror of 9/11. U.S. and British government officials repeatedly blamed al Qaeda for the bombings in Madrid in March 2004 and London in July 2005, but these pronouncements have been difficult to prove in subsequent investigations and trials (Porteous 2006; Ahmed 2007).

There is, furthermore, no evidence that all the military actions and expenditures since 9/11 have increased the security of the world. The loss of life and property in Afghanistan and Iraq has had little effect other than to destabilize the region. The war on Iraq has led to much death and destruction and has left the country without the infrastructure, food and industrial production, and security that it had under the dictatorship of Saddam Hussein. There is no evidence that the anti-terrorist measures introduced throughout the Western world have prevented any terrorist attacks. We know very little, moreover, of the alleged terrorists who have been incarcerated, interrogated, and tortured, because their detention and treatment have been carried out outside national and international law. Across three U.S. prisons in Iraq, for instance, there were about 18,000 detainees in 2007, with an expected 20,000 by the end of 2008. Few have been formally charged; arrests and detentions have been arbitrary and beyond the reach of international law. The question of guilt or innocence has appeared to be irrelevant, and the effect is to create terror in the subject population and, by extension, across the world (*Washington Post* 2007; *Guardian* 2005).

The military and economic power of the industrial states, it cannot be overstated, greatly outweighs all the officially designated terrorist groups and "state sponsors" put together. Any one of the industrial states has repressive apparatus vastly more powerful than even the largest sub-state organizations accused of terrorism. The industrial nations have extensive police and military forces and bureaucratic machinery at their disposal, access to a vast global surveillance system, the use of global institutions.

All these points suggest that the threat of terror is not as significant as the authorities claim. Even this cursory examination of the evidence makes it clear that the reaction to the declared threat is far out of proportion to what we know of "terrorist" activities and their effects. If the rationale for the "war on terrorism" appears to be wanting, it is not immediately clear what would explain the monumental commitment of state resources to fighting it and the systematic undermining of the political principles of liberal democracy. ...

If terror is a tactic and not a goal, what does a "war on terrorism" mean? What does it mean to have a war on a tactic, especially one that has been used so pervasively? The answer lies in who uses the label and why. Employed by the state, it can embrace all those who oppose or resist the status quo or its expansion. It can serve as an umbrella slogan for opportunistic use, justifying repression against whomever or whatever may stand in the way of foreign or domestic policy, including other governments, political parties, separatists, nationalists, critics of any sort, and religious factions. ... However incomplete, this brief examination of definitions reveals terrorism to be in essence a tactic, not a thing in itself, open to use by states, organizations, and individuals alike, for a variety of ends. All are terrorists if they commit acts of terror; what they have in common, their motives being different, is the nature of the act they have committed. The explanations of why this kind of attack is employed and by whom remains to be examined. ...

In mainstream political science (McCamant 1984), most theories of terrorism ignore the state as perpetrator (unless it is "socialist" or defined as a "sponsor") because the discipline assumes liberal democracy to be legitimate and to possess formal mechanisms for expressing dissent and achieving change. No political system, in any event, willingly admits that its principles are open to challenge that is simultaneously justifiable and unlawful. If liberal democratic states commit terrorist acts at home or abroad, conventional political science sees them as committed in the defence of the realm or for the worthy spread of its principles, and therefore as legitimate acts (Ignatieff 2004). For this reason, most theories in political science see terrorism as strictly a non-state form of illegal opposition to rightful principles. In general, the opposition — whether based on class conflict, political conviction, or religious belief — is seen as arising not from the system itself but from alien systems, beliefs, or personal pathologies. There is little appreciation that contradictions, conflicts, and inequalities in the system itself may give rise to resistance from sectors of civil society, not to mention that these sectors or the state may use terrorism in repressing opposition (Stohl and Lopez 1986).

In many of these theories, insurgencies and guerrilla armies are often conflated with or reduced to terrorist groups. Although such opposition forces may employ terror, there is no necessary link between the two. A cursory knowledge of U.S. interventions around the world makes it clear that there are many countries in which opposition is spawned by the brutality, amorality, and illegality of these and other state interventions (Blum 1998; Chomsky 1992). Resistance in itself has nothing to do with terrorism.

There are also socio-economic theories that focus on the grievances of certain sub-national entities (the poverty, chronic unemployment, political frustration, hopelessness, or humiliation of strata, classes, aspiring "nations," or occupied peoples) that are said to provide the rationale for terrorism as a means of countering an oppressive system. While these factors may well underlie some non-state terror, how they transform their victims into terrorists is left unexplained. The weakness of such theories becomes evident in light of the many hundreds of millions who suffer such conditions and do not turn to terror. These grievances may point to a partial rationale, but they are insufficient to explain why some turn to terrorism and others not, and they completely ignore the issue of state terrorism and the terror embedded in the system itself.

None of the conventional theories of terrorism should be dismissed out of hand; where they do focus on one or other proximate cause, they offer partial explanations. They are not, however, sufficient accounts.

Many studies (George 1991, Sluka 2000; Stohl and Lopez 1986, 1988; Blackstock 1975; Chester 1985; Davis 1997; Gelbspan 1991; Nutter 2000) provide an abundance of empirical evidence and argumentation pointing to the state as terrorist. Nevertheless, the explanations remain tied to a proximate cause — the need to maintain the conditions for capital accumulation and to create quiescent intellectual and working classes. These causes might well be considered sufficient if the argument is that state terrorism is a policy instrument of ruling that can be changed or corrected with a change of government, increased legitimacy, or pacification of opposition, as often these studies assume. They constitute demonstrable explanations for state terror, but they do not address the underlying cause. If the position is that the use of terrorism is inherent in the state, moreover, the question remains about the nature of a system that makes terrorism intrinsic to its operation.

... As the unity of capitalists grows and expands globally, the role of the state becomes less concerned with managing inter-capitalist relations and more with restraining the growth of a monolithic power and interest in the working class, the main systemic challenge to the capitalist class. A system defined by class contradictions and exploitation in civil society, a system overseen and maintained by a not-disinterested state, is also defined by terror — of the market and the state.[5]

Terrorism of the Markets

It is difficult to grasp marketplace society as intrinsically terrorist because it is the normal state of affairs. For the citizens of modern industrial societies, the markets in capital and labour create a chronic but implicit state of intimidation that coerces them to act and think in certain defined ways. Because this fear is immanent and systemic, it is experienced as ordinary and natural. To understand this terrorism, then, one has to "problematize" normalcy.

In civil society, terror is an inherent characteristic of the labour and capital markets. Competitive mechanisms, they are defined by supply and demand, over which there is only limited control, and allocate social resources while providing the main avenue for the accumulation of wealth, always unequally. Markets are by definition "imperfect," that is, they always present unequal access and offer unequal advantages for some over others; there is no such thing as a market of equal competitors, and there are always winners and losers. Conceptualizing the market as terrorist means recognizing that participation in society for workers and corporations is through competitive processes over jobs and other contracts, more or less outside individual or political control. The uncertain outcome for workers translates into greater or lesser access to the means of life, and for corporations more or less accumulation of capital. Failure in the market can mean bankruptcy or mergers for corporations, and for workers the denial of the very means of life. It can mean the end of participation in society as marketplace with all the implications of unemployment. To avoid these fates, both workers and corporations often feel obliged to compete without morality, compelled to advance the accumulation process at any cost.

Terrorism is implied not only in the very operation of a market, but also in the fact that markets follow cyclical patterns. They are always in flux, developing through periodic economic booms and slumps that provide a backdrop of intimidation to the system as a whole. The inevitability of recurring economic crises in a market system, with the attendant bankruptcies and unemployment, creates a permanent sense of insecurity and uncertainty about sources of revenue and future prospects. The terror of the possible loss of livelihood on all sides hangs over the whole system. Again, the effect is compulsion to work harder to accumulate and to act unscrupulously in an effort to avoid becoming a victim of economic crisis.

The labour market, moreover, has never provided full employment; it has always precluded a certain percentage of the labour force from work, whatever the trend in the business cycle. The terrorism here lies in the chronic failure to provide for some, and the periodic inability to provide for many, that stand as warnings for all. The one constant in the labour market is the possibility of being excluded from access to the means of life. For the worker the threat of joining the unemployed is always present, and the effect of this threat is to modify behaviour, producing compliance with the goals of the system.

Because it is defined in part by competition between workers, the labour market becomes the breeding ground for all sorts of attempts to establish preferential treatment. The working class turns on itself, or is turned on itself, with individuals, groups, strata, or regions searching for means to gain advantages over another. Racism, bigotry, sexism, ethnocentrism, nationalism, and individual disparagement all become instruments to create a privileged status in the market. They all result in increased market terror for the targets of discrimination who, by virtue of skin colour, religion, gender, ethnicity, strata, and so on face a socially constructed disadvantage in competition, a disadvantage often confirmed in discriminatory laws (Vann Woodward 1974; Allen 1994; Myers 1960).

The corporation alone, moreover, possesses the right to work in that it owns the means of production and distribution. Management controls who works and when and at what. The worker has some control at the point of production, through knowledge, skill, and experience, but these character-istics are not generally peculiar to an individual or group, and only when controlled by a union of some sort do they usually become an advantage to labour. If the right to work is a prerogative of capital, the worker has the right not to work, but this is less a right than a prescription for poverty and deprivation. The terrorism implicit in corporate control over the right to work lies in the consequent managerial power to dismiss individuals, control pensions, impose mass layoffs and plant closures, and the threat to the worker of unemployment, potential social death, and impoverishment.

If subordinating access to the means of life to markets is intrinsically a framework of terror, then any use of the market carries similar implications. Access to the justice system in capitalist nations, for example, is for the most part dependent on legal representation as private property. This places access beyond the reach of many and always subject to one's financial status — not to mention its subversion of the purported equity of the legal system itself. Similarly, a medical system that is subordinated to private property makes access to health care dependent on individual financial resources, with the attendant fear of personal bankruptcy and impoverishment as a result of a medical condition. Without state assistance, moreover, old age, illness, accidents, pregnancy, handicaps, and so on, all can subject individuals to the terror of the markets.

Increasingly, global labour markets operate without the restrictions of trade union representation or the protection of enforced social reforms. The terrorism implicit in labour markets is being given new life in the era of global accumulation (Giroux 2004).

Terrorism by the State

From the sixteenth to the eighteenth centuries, before modern industrial capitalism, European mercantilist states played a significant economic role in providing the foundation of the capitalist mode of production. Acts of violence on a colossal scale were perpetrated in order to transform the wealth of "national" as well as "foreign" lands into capital and the inhabitants into workers. From the domestic enclosure movements or "clearances" and related work and vagrancy laws to the violence of the colonization process and its forced labour, the state played a largely terrorist role (Polanyi 1944; Rodney 1981; Davis 2001; Elkins 2005; Hochschild 1999). Such activities of the state continue today wherever the capitalist mode of production has not yet been fully established.

Once industrial capitalism and the modern liberal democratic state had been established, different forms of state terror were developed. These states are defined by the principle of the rule of law. It not only guards market relations and so perpetuates the instability of competition, but it also has brought a degree of security from state arbitrariness. All such states, however, possess the constitutional right of exception to this principle in the form of so-called "official secrets," "reasons of state," "state of emergency," "national interests," forms of "constitutional dictatorship" (Rossiter 1963; Galnoor 1977), and more recently, "anti-terrorist laws" (Cole and Dempsey 2002; Chang 2002; Brown 2003). State arbitrariness is itself intimidating, but in the form of legal exceptions, police impunity, or emergency statutes, it carries the element of fear to the whole system.

Even the normal functioning of the law has a terrorizing effect. Criminal law, for instance, by and large stands as a bulwark for the economic inequalities that result from a system of private property. In fact, the legal system as a whole presents itself as a coercive force in defence of unequal access to the necessities of life. Many other laws are intended to keep the working classes from combining to challenge the system. The existence of such constraining laws intimidate those who would seek to organize or protest even within the constraints set out within the law (Panitch and Swartz 1993; Moody 1999).

Besides the law itself, there is the legal and illegal use of police in harassment, assassinations, beatings, unwarranted searches, arrests and incarcerations, espionage, sabotage, infiltration, blackmail, and so on. Most groups or individuals who have dared to offer a serious critique of the status quo or worked to unite parts of civil society and possibly challenge the prevailing property relations have met with various levels of intimidation by law enforcement officials striving to maintain the divisiveness of civil society (Mackenzie 1997; Blackstock 1975; Chester 1985; Gelbspan 1991; Goldstein 1978; Davis 1997; Johnson 1989; Nutter 2000; Wise and Ross 1964; Wise 1976).

The conscious non-enforcement of law or the non-prosecution of certain criminals also serves as a means to keep civil society divided against itself, allowing its component parts to sort themselves out according to what might be termed "the law of the jungle" (Jacobs 2006; Fitch 2006; Chavez and Gray 2004). Some laws promote the divisiveness of civil society, most obviously the gun ownership laws of the United States, which constitute one of the foundations of pervasive fear in U.S. civil society and a powerful mechanism by itself to control the working class. On a global scale, the vast sales of small military weapons perform a similar role.

The state can also manipulate the degree to which the markets affect the working class. By increasing or decreasing the extent of social reforms, the state can raise or lower the disciplinary impact of the market on the working class. In other words, the state can manipulate the degree of terrorism of the market in order to achieve certain desired effects. The limits on unemployment insurance, for instance, are managed for this purpose; immigration policy can be manipulated to increase competition and lower wages; and the promotion of a private medical system, subordinating health care to the market, to the demands of profit maximization, creates employee passivity where medical insurance is attached to a job and chronic fear where it is not affordable (Moynihan and Cassels 2005; Griffith, Iliffe and Rayner 1987; Andrews 1995; Doyal 1979).

The Great Depression of the 1930s plunged capitalist nations into one of the longest and most serious periods of market terror yet experienced. To contain social unrest, all the industrial states attempted to further institutionalize class conflict, to restrict civil liberties, to introduce extra-market reforms, to launch anti-communist fear campaigns, and to employ the police and the courts in more systematic oppression. In Italy and Germany, where the effects of World War I created social upheaval, the growing power of the socialist and communist parties was kept in check by the corporate financing of political parties and leaders that employed terrorism as their stock in trade (Guerin 1973; Salvemini 1973; Brady 1937).

No controlling agency or institution can ignore the importance of ideas in maintaining power — and in instilling terror. The state must promote a set of ideas that fashions a common understanding and acceptance of the prevailing form of property relations, their reproduction, and consequences. Unquestioning obedience to secular authority, a belief in a spiritual power, the notion of predestination, the idea of meritocracy, and the belief in a genetic basis to ethnic differences are some of the ideas that support the hierarchical and authoritarian relations necessary to maintain the status quo. Implicit in these ideas are elements of intimidation; they are beliefs that constrain behaviour by means of real or imagined fears of one sort or another or acceptance of what is deemed to be ordained.

The ideas of socialism and communism have always been a threat to the ideas that complement capitalism. After World War II, the Cold War, in part a war of ideas, was employed to challenge the promise of socialism and its reality abroad. In the U.S., a wave of anti-communism was given free rein by Congress and the courts in the late 1940s and 1950s. This propaganda was aimed at bringing critical intellectuals and the working classes, living with the terror of an unpredictable labour market and the memory of its failure in the 1930s, into line with U.S. postwar ambitions. Anti-communist sophistry had several purposes: to demonize the U.S.S.R. and the Peoples' Republic of China as possible alternative economic models, to mask U.S. interventions around the world (countering either struggles for socialism or liberal democratic governments espousing nationalism or reformism), to provide the rationale for the military-industrial complex, and to undermine state intervention designed to regulate or de-commodify the markets.[6] For their ideas and principles, scores of U.S. citizens were sent to jail, some committed suicide, thousands lost their jobs and were socially ostracized and harassed, and many more thousands lived in fear of arbitrary dismissal and ostracism. More than a decade of anti-communist witch-hunts went a long way to instilling fear over one's beliefs and undermining the credibility of socialism, not to mention associated organizations (Caute 1978; Schrecher 1986, 1998; Price 2004).[7]

Terrorism has not been confined to systems of market capitalism. The coming of the first socialist state in 1918 expanded the necessity for using terror. The Bolsheviks employed revolutionary terror in their first couple of years of existence to ensure their survival in the face of civil war and intervening Western armies (Trotsky 1961). They also used terror to consolidate their rule and collectivize property over the first decade, and from the late 1920s until his death in 1953, Stalin used terror as a means of maintaining his personal power over the regime. A state capitalist system, parading as socialist, without the chronic pervasive terror of the markets, must lean towards other mechanisms for social control. Given the lack of workers' control and the monopoly of capital by the state, the police state is one of the few answers to questions of legitimacy.

During World War II, the use of terror was widespread, in particular by the Nazis and Japanese military. Slave labour, concentration (and death) camps, widespread indiscriminate summary executions, collective punishment, "medical" experiments, systematic rape and prostitution of women and massive bombing of civilian targets were all part of their rule and methods of war. In certain measure, the Allied forces replied in kind with the bombing of non-military targets, particularly Dresden, Hamburg, Tokyo, and then Hiroshima and Nagasaki (Garrett 2004; Lackey 2004). Historical comparisons are always problematic, but it is probably accurate to say that there were more innocent victims systematically annihilated in the six years of this war for the purpose of terrorizing one or the other side into capitulation than any comparable period in history.

Part of the explanation lies in the unprecedented degree to which science and technology were applied to the production of weaponry in this war. Applied science and technology also made possible the colossal acts of terror that ended the war — two bombs that levelled two cities and killed tens of thousands of civilians in an instant. The threat of atomic and later nuclear bombing with ballistic missiles became a terrorist tactic employed many times over by the United States — in Eastern Europe, Korea, Vietnam, and Cuba — and a significant part of the general backdrop to the Cold War (Morgan 1996). It was one of the main pillars of the policy to contain socialism. The strategy of nuclear deterrence soon led to a nuclear arms' race, culminating in the policy of "mutually assured destruction" — mad. The whole world was held in the grip of the possibility of nuclear annihilation; the civilian populations of the Soviet Union and the West were the stakes in this exercise in terror. Fear was palpable throughout the industrial world and systematically maintained lest any doubts be raised about the need for military expenditures (Prins 1983; Cox 1981; Lifton and Falk 1982).

Another significant use of terrorism after World War II was in the building of the "new world order," which included the process of de-colonization. In 1945, the largest part of humanity lived in European or American colonies or spheres of influence, but such nation-based structures had to be dismantled to accommodate U.S. designs for expansion and the globalization of capital (Fann and Hodges 1971; Magdoff 1969). The problem was how to allow for independence from colonial or imperial rule while keeping the newly independent countries within the orbit of global capital. This dilemma was addressed with military coups, fomented civil wars, mass arrests, assassinations, the outlawing of socialist, communist, and even nationalist parties, the suppression of human rights even as they were being declared by the U.N., the development of counterinsurgency warfare, coercive diplomacy, the expansion of torture, the creation of death squads, the promotion of arms sales, and Western-created secret police forces and sponsored military and police training programs throughout the non-industrial world. In little more than two decades after World War II, many millions were killed throughout Asia, Africa, and Latin America by the United States and European colonial powers in an attempt to forestall the struggle for independent national development or socialism in these countries (Blum 1998, 2000).

More indirect means were also applied to keep these nations tied to the emerging global capitalist system, in the form of economic terrorism. Although many forms of coercion fall into this category, the main instruments have been the policies of the IMF and World Bank. Through a variety of mechanisms, dependent countries were indebted to these institutions and quickly found that increasing indebtedness carried obligations that led, in effect, to the near-suspension of their capacity to determine economic development independently. The policies imposed called for the reduction of state activities, including subsidized health care, education, social reforms, assistance to agriculture and national industries, and the building of infrastructure for civilian benefit. All the policies implied a set of broader objectives: the use of the national state to prevent national or "mixed-economy" policies, to reduce wages, to provide open access to foreign investment, and to promote commodity exports. No longer were there colonial or imperial administrations; now global institutions, the IMF and World Bank, GATT and then the World Trade Organization, were to enforce the rules of a skewed market in the new world order. The consequences included a reduction in standards of living, food riots, the loss of a self-sufficient national agricultural base, the denial of national aspirations, the perpetuation of illiteracy and poor health, the destruction of pre-capitalist modes of production and the consequent displacement of millions, and a constant "brain drain" to the metropolitan countries (Perkins 2004; Payer 1974; Hayter 1971; Walton and Seddon 1994). The terror of a highly skewed global market was imposed by the IMF and World Bank.

... Globalization

As long as the state and civil society remained national, unemployment limited, and material betterment a hope, the legitimacy of national governments could be maintained. As the site of capital accumulation shifted progressively to regional and global levels, however, national markets have been increasingly subordinated to the transnational. As a consequence, the role of the national state has been subverted by the creation of supranational quasi-state structures and agencies designed to regulate larger markets. Not only do these markets operate largely beyond the jurisdiction of national governments, but they also require policies to facilitate the increasingly supranational accumulation of capital.

These neoliberal policies have an impact on the legitimacy of liberal democracy, which is invariably national. If the traditional powers and roles of the national state are increasingly usurped or overshadowed by these supranational policies and institutions, it gradually becomes evident to the citizenry that the electoral process is losing its meaning. When national policies are broadly determined at other levels, national officials find it ever more difficult to pretend that government policies are representative of popular or national interests. Legitimacy, grounded in the supposed consent of the governed, begins to be exposed for what it is.

Legitimacy also begins to falter for another reason. Neoliberal policies are designed to maximize corporate control of social reproduction, in part through the process of privatization and de-regulation of the public sector. The expansion of the market, a euphemism for increased control by private corporations, is made the principle and practice of state policy, and thus pressure builds to retrench social reforms, to undermine the policies and programs that alleviate the worst consequences of the market. The terror of the market and of corporate monopoly over the right to work is promoted vigorously in practice and as ideal. Legitimacy, based on social reforms, increasingly comes into question.

Conclusions

In all social formations resting on systemic inequality, terror is an integral part of the system. In a capitalist society, the main source of terror lies in the operation of the markets. Here, terror is by and large implicit, an entrenched and largely unseen aspect of everyday life. Similarly, private corporate ownership of the means of production and distribution places the power of terror in the hands of those who manage and control the system. Terror, it follows, is not a deviation from the norm, but an inherent part of society as marketplace.

... The "war on terrorism" can credibly be understood as a "war of terrorism" (Herman 2004), a pretext to justify the undermining of national liberal democracy in a world that can no longer pretend to operate according to its former principles and practices. It can be seen as a "war" to help transform governance so that the limited control of a liberal democratic state is subordinated to the principles and practices of global markets. It can also be taken as the terrorism of a system needing to parade as if under threat, a perpetrator disguised as victim, in order to advance its interests. It can be understood as the terror of the global markets in search of an excuse to coerce the world into giving up what limited democratic controls exist in favour of submission to one freedom alone, the freedom of corporate private property.

Since 9/11, almost all the actions of the U.S. administration point to such a conclusion. In its domestic policies, it has systematically moved to protect corporations from prosecution, to grant them increased tax benefits, to boost military spending, to dismantle health and safety regulations, to reduce state welfare benefits, and to encourage market principles and practice wherever possible. In order to police the world, Washington has proclaimed a unilateral foreign policy, threatened pre-emptive strikes against countries or groups it deems a threat, intimidated the world with nuclear weapons, and declared its opposition to international rule of law by rejecting many international treaties and agreements. It has set up prisons around the world out of the reach of international law for the purposes of holding unknown numbers of unnamed detainees for indefinite periods and for undisclosed reasons — a fate beyond the rule of law and a warning to us all (Van Bergen 2005; *Washington Post* 2005).

Capital has moved beyond the stage of development that required governance in the form of liberal democracy; there can be no return to the twentieth century and the nation-state as the political shell of national capital. Increasingly, global and regional markets and their regulatory agencies prevail, without civil legitimacy. In their defence, Washington has declared a "global war" without an apparent end — a "long war" whose objectives and enemies are not identified. It is difficult to imagine a clearer example of global state terrorism to establish and maintain the hegemony of global markets.

Much of what we have read so far has delved into the historical and structural foundations of human society, so as to map out the connections between our social worlds of what we watch on television, purchase in the mall and learn in school. For most of us, the coercive and repressive forms of state terrorism discussed by Gary Teeple seem abstract and someone else's problem, not our own. Recall from earlier chapters the ways in which ideology is conveyed through mass media, popular culture and education curriculum so as to distract us or obscure from view, how interests of the power elite are reproduced and normalized. Yet, as he has explained, the War on Terror is a rhetorical tactic — used to enable repressive practices within advanced liberal democracies such as Canada and the United States that have curtailed our civil liberties. Indeed, neoliberal governments engage in "terrorism of the markets," which produces the human suffering of poverty and social isolation even within the most affluent countries. As we will read next, living in these neoliberal times has a devastating impact on the bodies of the poor. Jeff Shantz's experience of homelessness reminds us that structural power is experienced by many people as violence.

10 Inequality of Wealth and Income

"On the Streets There's No Forgetting Your Body"

Jeff Shantz, in Diane Crocker and Val Marie Johnson (eds.),
Poverty, Regulation, and Social Justice (Fernwood, 2010)

On the streets there's no forgetting your body. Its hunger gnaws at you constantly. Tired bones suffer regular reminders that pavement makes a rotten mattress. Skin burns from the heat of sun and the lash of wind. The wet cold of rain ... the entire body shivers from the marrow outward. My homeless body is the low-end site of biopoltics. It is in the low-rent district in which postmodern struggles are engaged. The street is the prime example of what Mary Louise Pratt (1991) calls a "contact zone," those spaces in which cultures meet, clash, and wrestle with each other. ... These contacts are often quite brutal and vicious. Poor people are subjected to ongoing violence simply because of the poverty that we embody.

I have overhead many times from allegedly respectable citizens that I am not worthy of living. My body is expendable. In a popular series of ads for a Toronto radio station a homeless person is depicted sitting on a garbage can; emblazoned on the photo is the word PEST. A middle-class tourist is overheard to say about those of us who rest outside his hotel: "The kindest thing would be to get them all drunk and just put them to sleep. Nobody would know the difference. Nobody knows them. They'd never be missed." Graffiti screaming "Kill the poor" has shown up around town over the last few years.

The threatened violence is too often played out for real. There has been an increase recently in the number of physical attacks on homeless people.... We are reminded of the vulnerability of our bodies when a friend is killed while sleeping in a park or dines from the winter nights or her body turns up in an alley near the streets where she worked. Not long ago a self styled vigilante attacked me screaming that he was "cleaning the garbage off the streets." My inferior position was made clear when he identified me as a "faggot" and my partner as a "whore" by virtue of us being on the streets. ... My body when it is living on the streets is painfully exposed. I have no shelter and few defences. Our life expectancy in Canada is six and half years shorter than for wealthier housed people. My body simply stands less of chance of being around than yours. ... This is a naked life. As Giorgio Agamben (2000) notes in his discussion of naked life, we are the ones whose lives are considered worthless. We are the exception to the human subject of modern sovereignty. We are the lives who are deemed not part of the citizenry. Being labeled criminals, deviants, thugs, and pests as homeless people often are, erases my humanity; it places me in the realm of post human. I was human once, but that was before I allegedly abandoned civil society and its work ethic and became the despised "street youth" the mere echo of a person. Naked life: a condition of violence.

These politics of exclusion remove our poor bodies from civil society and the realm of citizenship. Governments do not invite us to take part in discussions on the issues that affect our lives. Poor people do not fill the comfortable chairs at summits on living and working opportunities. We are not asked to tell our own stories. We are treated as objects rather than as subjects. We do not design the experiment, and we are not invited to present the findings: "poor people have as much control over government initiatives or think tank theorizing about their future as lab rats have in a cancer drug experiment" (Swanson 2001:77-78). Bell hooks notes that while it is now fashionable to talk about overcoming racism and sexism, class remains the "uncool subject" that makes people tense. Despite being such a pressing issue class is not talked about in a society in which the poor have no public voice; breaking this silence is crucial. As hooks notes, however, "we are afraid to have a dialogue about class even through the ever widening gap between rich and poor has already set the state for ongoing and sustained class warfare (hooks 2009:5).

...Despite the images conjured up by names like vagabond, drifter, or hobo, being homeless is an experience of bodily and spatial confinement: "Poor bashing is being told you aren't free to go where you choose" (Swanson 2001:19). More and more poor bodies are constrained bodies. We cannot avoid each other's bodies the way middle class suburbanites can. Our notions of property and privacy are vastly different from those of you who have plenty of living space. In hostels and shelters our bodies are crammed together in small spaces. Going to shelters can leave us beaten up, having our few belongings stolen, or contracting tuberculosis, supposedly a disease of the past that is rampant in contemporary shelters. Ironically given our immobility our bodies are time travelers picking up ancient illnesses that the rest of the population only reads about in history books.

The ticket to mobility is the capacity to spend. As hooks notes, "no matter your class, no matter your race, if you have access to credit, to cash, every store is open to you" (2004:82). If you lack the possibility of being a consumer, doors are slammed in your face. Nowhere is this clearer than in the criminalization of poverty, when the body ends up in cells and courtrooms. Our bodies are public sites of struggle, matters of great contest. My poor body is beaten by police and vigilantes "cleaning up the streets" insulted by professionals, and dragged in courts; it endures days in welfare and legal aid offices.

Still, my body is also a site of strength, standing in solidarity withstanding blows. When you have lived on the streets and dealt with various abuses the body becomes resilient. To survive I struggle over perceptions of my body and the meanings attached to it. Opposing poor-bashing is a good way to confront the internalized messages of shame and blame over our situation. This opposition can stop the bashers, deconstruct the messages about poverty and its causes, and provide a starting point for organizing with other poor people to fight poverty. Part of that struggle involves recounting our stories providing glimpses into the many "contact zones" — the streets, struggles, and courts — in which our bodies live. Sometimes telling our stories, raising our voices is enough to be heard beyond the streets, requires a good old-fashioned riot. We are hungry let us eat. We are weary, let us rest.

11 Race and Ethnicity

While many of the readings so far have emphasized the central role of class — as a social structure, as an economic necessity, as an identity and as a form of power — we need to understand how class intersects with race and gender; the power and powerlessness is experienced by different people differently. In this chapter, racism is theorized as a social determinant of health; that is, experiencing oppression can make you sick and limit your access to health care. Poverty and racism collide in the lives of millions of people everyday, rendering them more likely live with chronic illness or face barriers when seeking help.

"Race and Racism as Determinants of Health"

Josephine B. Etowa and Elizabeth A. McGibbon, in Elizabeth McGibbon *Oppression: A Social Determinant of Health* (Fernwood, 2012)

Inscribing Racism on Body and Mind

There is little doubt that race, more accurately racism, determines health. The compromised mental and physical health outcomes of Indigenous peoples and peoples subject to translocation and slavery is well documented. First Nations people living on reserves have reported rates of heart disease that are 16 percent higher than the overall Canadian rate, and First Nations women and men have life expectancies that are 5.3 and 7.4 years shorter, respectively (Statistics Canada 2001). Statistics also show that African American lung and cancer patients are less likely to receive chemotherapy (Earle, Venditti, Neuman, et. al. 2000) and unlikely to receive treatment for prostate cancer (Hoffman, Harlan and Klabunde 2003). Black women are significantly less likely than White women to receive minimum expected therapy for breast cancer (Breen, Wesley, Merril, and Johnson 2004). Evidence also suggests that Black women in Canada face similar barriers to appropriate care and experience health deficits that are similar to those of African American women. Although most available race-related population health and epidemiological research is from the United States, there is little reason to believe that these inequities are not present in Canada and elsewhere. Table 1 provides evidence of how oppression becomes inscribed on the body, mind and spirit to create sustained health difficulties.

Table 1 Racism as a Social Determinant of Health: Health Outcomes and Access to Care*

Cancer: Breast and Cervical

- A Canadian study found that Aboriginal women who have experienced breast cancer must be made visible within health-care in a way that recognizes that their experiences are situated within the structural context of marginalization through colonial oppression (Poudrier and Mac-Lean, 2009).
- Among Black women aged less than 50 years, those who reported frequent everyday discrimination (e.g., being treated as dishonest) and major experiences of unfair treatment due to race (e.g., job, housing and police) were at statistically significantly higher risk for developing breast cancer than were women who reported infrequent experiences (Taylor, Williams, Makambi, et al., 2007).
- Ethnic minority women are diagnosed with more advanced disease and experience greater morbidity and mortality (Kim, Ashing-Giwa, Kagawa-Singer, et al., 2006).
- Black women are less likely than White women to be screened or to present with asymptomatic disease (Merkin, Stevenson, and Powe, 2002).

Cancer: Prostate

- African American men have higher morbidity, mortality and risk than Caucasians (Maliski, Connor, Fink, et al., 2006).
- African Americans with prostate cancer present with more advanced disease, and they have poorer survival rates than U.S. White men, even when diagnosed at the same stage (Oakley-Girvan, Kolonel, Gallagher, et al. 2003).

Cancer: Other

- First Nations adults in Canada have a 20.8% higher rate of cancer than the general Canadian population (Assembly of First Nations, 2007).
- African Americans are significantly less likely to receive major colorectal treatment for their cancer, follow-up treatment and chemotherapy (Cooper, Yuan, and Rimm, 2000).
- Members of visible minorities were less likely than White people to have been admitted to hospital, tested for prostate-specific antigen, administered a mammogram or given a pap test (Quan, Fong, De Coster, et al. 2006).

Cardio-Vascular

- Racism may increase risk for hypertension; these effects emerge more clearly for institutional racism than for individual level racism. All levels of racism may influence the prevalence of hypertension via stress exposure and reactivity and by fostering conditions that undermine health behaviours (Brondolo, Love, Pencille, et al., 2011).

Table 1 Racism as a Social Determinant of Health: Health Outcomes and Access to Care*
Pain (Chronic and Acute)
• African-Americans were more likely than Whites to report that they felt discriminated against in their ability to obtain care or treatment for their pain (Whites 9%, African-Americans 15%, Hispanics 13%). African-Americans males with low income were almost 3 times as likely as Whites to feel discriminated against in their efforts to obtain treatment for pain (27% vs 10%, respectively) (Nguyenlo, Ugarte, Fuller, et al. 2005).   • In geographic settings with predominantly racial and ethnic minority patients, 62% of patients were undertreated by who standards, and they were three times more likely to be under-medicated than patients seen in non-minority settings (Green, Anderson, Baker, et al., 2003);   • African American patients in nursing homes had a 63% greater probability of no pain treatment than non-Hispanic White patients. African American and Hispanic patients were less likely than non-Hispanic White patients to have pain reports documented in their charts (Green, Anderson, Baker, et al., 2003).
Diabetes
• First Nations adults have almost four times the rate of diabetes than the general population (Assembly of First Nations, 2007).   • Black women have more than twice the risk of developing adult-onset diabetes than White women. Black men have more than one and a half times the risk of developing diabetes (Brancati, Kao, Folsom, et al. 2000).
Sickle Cell Anemia
• Although sickle cell disease is not curable, early diagnosis would ensure appropriate management strategies, thereby reducing the number of deaths cause by the disease. Routine screening of Black newborns is an unrealized dream in Canada (Enang, 2002).
* Please note: This table cites the terms used by the authors of the studies (I.E., Black, African American, Hispanic, Aboriginal, Ethnic Minority, Visible Minority, White, Caucasian, etc).

How Do Race and Racism Determine Health?

Although race is universally applied as a stratification variable, race has absolutely no scientific meaning. Like national boundaries, the definitions of human races are strictly social constructions, evolving over time and space to accommodate the flow of human history. Our beliefs about race and its relationship to health and disease are influenced by the myth of innate racial differences that has evolved within our society (Kauffman and Cooper, 1996). Williams (1999: 176) defines race as "an ideology of inferiority that is used to justify unequal treatment (discrimination) of members of groups defined as inferior, by both individuals and societal institutions." Race has also been described as a social construction involving the classification of individuals into arbitrary groups and the assignment of disparate meaning and value to these constructed groups (Houston and Wood, 1996). Witzig (1996) confirms that race is a social construction created from prevailing social perceptions and without scientific evidence.

Racial classifications affect the personal, social, political and material circumstances of people's lives and consequently shape how they view themselves and others as well as their personal and societal relationships (Houston and Wood, 1996). Begley (1996: 68) states that the term race "can have a biological significance only when a race represents a uniform, closely inbred group, in which all family lines are alike — as in pure breeds of domesticated animals. These conditions are never realized in human types and impossible in large populations." Mosby's Medical, Nursing and Allied Health Dictionary defines race as "a vague unscientific term for a group of genetically related people who share some physical traits" (Glaze, Anderson and Anderson 1994: 657). According to Witzig, only 0.012 percent of the variation between humans in total genetic material can be attributed to differences in race.

Yet race is an emotionally laden word which evokes deep feelings and triggers stereotypical images about certain groups of people (Logan, Freeman and McRoy, 1990). Physical identity and social categorization, the essence of race, determine the predominant perceptions of people of colour in the Western world. For example, when people think of Black families, they immediately think of a racial group (Logan, Freeman, and McRoy 1990). Although scientific evidence rejects the use of the social construct of race, it is still used in the health literature. Authors have even employed race "to attribute not only to physical characteristics, but also psychological and moral ones to members of given categories, thus justifying or naturalizing a discriminatory system" (Begley 1996: 68). Systemic racism is common in society and arbitrary race groupings are part of this kind of racism (Witzig 1996).

Shifting perspectives on the meaning of race notwithstanding, we cannot ignore the concept because we live in a society where race is one of the fundamental means of social categorization. Researchers cannot transcend these categories because there are no objective criteria for racial categorization other than "official" ones such as those used in the Canadian Census (e.g., visible minorities). It is equally important not to abandon these categories altogether because they capture important information about differences in disease risk and etiology. In addition, they help us to recognize the social reality of the associations between race and inequities in health and health care. The pathways through which racism affects health are shown in Figure 1, which illustrates how biased information, stereotyping, prejudice and discrimination interact within complex systemic webs to create and sustain oppressions such as racism, sexism, and classism.

We all hold stereotypical views about individuals and groups of people.

Figure 1 Ruling Power Relations and the Cycle of Oppression

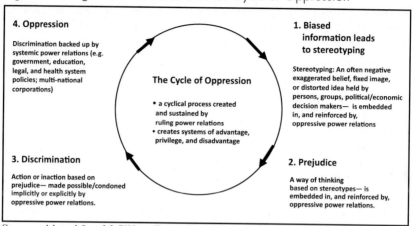

Source: Adapted from McGibbon, Etowa & McPherson, 2008a.

These stereotypes can lead to thinking in a particular way, which demonstrates prejudice. Henry, Tater and Mattis, et al. (2000) explicate common negative stereotypes of people of colour: Aboriginal people (savages, alcoholics, uncivilized, uncultured, murderers, noble, needing a White saviour, victim; Blacks (drug addicts, pimps, prostitutes, entertainers, athletes, drug dealers, murderers, gangsters, butlers and maids, simple-minded, savages, primitive, needing a White saviour); and Asians (untrustworthy, menacing, unscrupulous, submissive, maiming, quaint, gangsters, prostitutes, cooks, store vendors). These stereotypes lead to prejudicial thinking. When we then act or fail to act in a particular way, based on our prejudice, we participate in discrimination. For example, health care professionals are also immersed in these well known stereotypes. This stereotyping leads to inaction in the form of fewer specialist referrals for people of colour and disproportionately less follow-up treatment, as documented in this chapter.

When our discriminatory actions or inactions are supported or condoned by the health care system or other institutional structures, this process constitutes oppression. Although racism is demonstrated in individual and systemic actions or inactions, it is more deeply rooted at the systemic level because the power to make decisions, to take collective action and to allocate resources resides at this level (Enang 2002). Systemic oppression is supported by policy action and inaction regarding persistently compromised health outcomes of people of color.

Racism at the systemic level manifests in material conditions and in access to power, including differential access to educational opportunities, health care and research resources (Etowa, Weins, Bernard, et al. 2007). Racism also includes interconnected factors of economic, environmental, psychosocial and iatrogenic (caused by hospitals and clinicians) conditions

(Krieger 2003). Table 2, which includes evidence from two qualitative studies in Canada, illustrates how systemic racism is articulated in everyday life.

Racism and Health: A Social Determinants Perspective

The concept of "determinants of health" provides a foundation for analysis of health and health care and the discovery of points for social action to address individual and systemic racism. Included in determinants of health are aspects of biologic and genetic endowment and social determinants. The social determinants of health, as laid out in the Toronto Charter (Raphael 2009a) and as revised by Mikkonen and Raphael (2010), include early childhood development, employment and working conditions, income and its equitable distribution, food security, health care services, housing shortages, education, social exclusion, social safety nets, gender, age, race and Aboriginal status.

Table 2: Racism as a Social Determinant of Health: Voices from the Margins
Racism as Poison: "Racism in Canada is like slow poison… I see it as poison that invades the Black psyche, the Black experience… and unless we can get rid of that poison, we're not going to be totally healthy… It's insidious. It's slow. It's sly… It doesn't get you right away" (Etowa 2005).
Racism as a Stress: "It [racism] causes certain amount of pressure and certain amount of stress… I used to suffer with severe migraine headaches." (Etowa 2005).
Racism and Workplace Stress: "I was really close to suicide… I remember thinking to myself if I should take something, they'd probably revive me and I don't think I want to hang around here. It's just too stressful… I wasn't sleeping… I remember thinking… if I'm desperate to do this I'll just walk on the bridge and jump over it… That was what, we knew that's a real suicide, when you feel as if you really don't want to be revived. And because my head nurse was in psychiatry, I went to her and said, look, I am so desperate, I just feel like going down and jumping off the bridge… It was killing me. It was killing me" (Etowa 2005).
The Impact of Racism: "They wanted to break me. They really wanted to break me. And they're very close to it, very, very close… I wasn't sleeping… And I found myself talking to myself when I was giving out pills… I was so stressed out.… I remember going on down the ward and… I would double check everything, because I was sort of spaced out. Somebody would tell me something, I'd have to go back over the phone number… it was stress 12 hours a day. I was sort of talking to myself to keep on doing things right" (Etowa 2005).

Table 2: Racism as a Social Determinant of Health: Voices from the Margins
Stereotypes and Quality of Care: "They were taking my blood. She got the student nurse to take my blood. But she couldn't find my vein. And she kept plucking around on me, and it was hurting me. So I told her, 'No, you can't keep doing this.' And the nurse said, 'No just try it one more time.' I said 'No, you're not trying it no more. Why can't you do it?' She said, 'Well, it's known that Black people have tougher skin than White people'" (Enang 1999).
Curriculum Content and Lack of Diversity: "We need more of our people in the health care professions. And if it means we're going to have to start fighting to allow our young people into medical school, then we'll have to start doing that. I think that we need to attack some of the training institutions for change in their curriculum and in their approach. Then we need to attack our school, especially high schools and elementary schools, to get some mentors into the schools to encourage children to go into health care professions" (Enang 1999).

Historically, it has largely been assumed that differences in the health of people of colour were due to differences in biologic and genetic endowment — the biophysical attributes which are inherited from our parents or acquired throughout our lifespan. It is now well recognized that biologic and genetic endowment, although very important in determining health, are not the major determinants of the health of individuals, families, communities and nations (Raphael 2004). Rather, health inequities have been closely linked with differences in social, economic, cultural and political circumstances. Economic inequities, in particular, have been implicated in poor health: people with fewer economic resources are at much greater risk of illness and are much less likely to have timely access to health and social services (Galabuzi 2006). Differences in income levels and socioeconomic status (SES) demonstrate the continued primacy of material influences on health (Wilkinson and Marmot 2005). Inadequate household income for securing healthy food creates nutritional deficits, which greatly impact health and development across the lifespan. When families lack access to basic essentials, such as food, education and safe shelter, their health is compromised.

Health inequities along racial lines have been created and reinforced by limited access to educational and employment opportunities for minority groups through processes such as segregation (McGibbon and Etowa 2009). Racial differences in SES have been well documented in the literature, and health researchers examining the association between race and health routinely adjust for this variable (Krieger 2003; Williams 1999). Thus, SES is not only considered a cofounder of racial differences in health but "part of the causal pathways by which race affects health" (Williams 1999: 177). Race is therefore an antecedent and a determinant of SES, and racial differences in SES are to some degree a reflection of the implementation of discriminatory policies and practices premised on the inferiority of certain racial groups (Williams 1999). Krieger (1987) argues that the poorer health of Black people relative to the White population is the result of White privilege, enforced through slavery and other forms of racial discrimination, rather than innate inferiority. Furthermore, Krieger (2003: 195) states that "health is harmed not only by heinous crimes against humanity, such as slavery, lynching and genocide, but also by the grinding economic and social realities of what Essed (1991) has aptly termed, 'everyday racism.'"

[The social determinants of health] intersect with identities such as race, social class and gender to produce a powerful synergy of disadvantage for racialized peoples. For example, gender intersects with race to cause a higher rate of unemployment among immigrant, Indigenous and African Canadian women (Galabuzi 2006; Statistics Canada 2006b, 2006c). Poverty has been directly linked to decreased access to health care and decreased health outcomes. Here the intersections of age, race, gender and [social determinants of health] such as employment and income combine to limit health care access. Immigrant women of colour, who earn less than the Canadian average for women, face additional barriers related to geography, since their extended families are often far away and many immigrant individuals and families lack the resources to maintain connections with their country of origin. Senior Canadians are at particular risk, regardless of gender, race or ethnicity, since home care, or family care, is becoming medical support "on the cheap." Family members, usually women, have taken on the additional burden of home care. Pan American Health Organization director Mirta Periago (2004) asked the following question at an international gathering in Washington: "What would happen if all the women of the world decided to go on strike and for just one day refused to provide health care in their homes and communities? What would be the catastrophic implications for global well-being?"

Most women of colour experience all the major forms of oppression, including classism, racism and sexism. A close examination of the United States 1990 census revealed that 34 percent of Black women were living below poverty line compared to 11 percent of White women (Krieger, Rowley, Herman et al. 1993). More than fifteen years later, these figures were mirrored in a Canadian study of Black women in rural communities. Among the participants who responded to the income question, a significant 72 percent earned less than $15,000 in average annual personal income and 45 percent earned less than $15,000 in average annual household income, which is well below the national and provincial poverty lines. These statistics revealed that a considerable proportion of Black families in these communities were very low-income earners. Income remains an important measure and an integral determinant of the SES of individuals, families and communities, and there is a strong relationship among income, other health determinants and health status (Etowa, Weins, Bernard, et al. 2007)

Galabuzi (2006) has written extensively about the interconnections among racism, social exclusion, unemployment, underemployment, individual and family income, and education. As Canada enters a new century, racialized people continue to experience stark inequities related to each of these SDH. The income gap between racialized and non-racialized earners continues to be an important indicator of racial inequality in Canada, as demonstrated by unemployment, labour-market participation and employment income (2006). Galabuzi reports that employment income for racialized people was 15 percent lower than the national average, for racialized women, the inequity is even greater — their average earnings in 1996 were $16,621, compared to $23,635 for racialized men, $19,495 for other women and $31,951 for other men. In terms of education, the proportion of racialized group members achieving post-secondary degrees is growing at a higher rate than in the general population. Yet there has not been a corresponding Race and Racism as Determinants of Health increase in employment or income. So what factors cause this discrepancy? As Galabuzi (2006: 111) points out, the discrepancy suggests an 'x,' or unknown, factor: "We suggest that this 'x' factor is the devaluation of the human capital of racialized group members, resulting from racial discrimination in the labor market."

Inequities in the SDH combine to amplify systemic threats to the health of people of colour. The gap in the low-income rate between recent immigrants and Canadian-born individuals has widened significantly in recent decades. In 1980, low-income rates among immigrants who had arrived between 1975 and 1980 were 1.4 times those of people born in Canada. In 1990, low-income rates among immigrants who arrived between 1985 and 1990 were 2.1 times those of the Canadian-born, and by 2000, low-income rates among recent immigrants were 2.5 times those of the Canadian-born (Statistics Canada 2003). Statistics Canada defines recent immigrants as those who arrived in Canada during the five years before the census in question. Immigrants of colour have the compounding burden of racism, which makes their incomes even less, on average, than the general population of immigrants in Canada.

Racism and Barriers in Access to Care

An increase in acute care health services does not necessarily improve population health. However, in the debate about the salience of health care as an SDH, there is often a failure to analyze barriers in access. When individuals and families access health care they arrive with more than their immediate physical and mental health concerns. The intersections of their identities (e.g., age, gender, race, social class) and intersections of their social determinants of health (e.g., early childhood development, employment) are inextricably linked to their health concerns. Statistics in the previous section provide foundational evidence for the direct and often devastating relationship between these intersectionalities and inequities in access to health care. For example, the vast majority of health care in Canada is provided with the assumption that individuals and families can afford costs currently considered peripheral: transportation, prescription medications, over-the-counter antibiotics and anti-inflammatory drugs, orthopedic braces, time away from work, child care and so on. Adequate employment and income has thus become a prerequisite for full health care access and optimal health, particularly for rural, remote and northern Canadians (McGibbon 2009).

Health care access then becomes a powerful determinant of health by virtue of its policy-based neutrality, or the presumptuousness regarding the hidden costs of full access, and its employment-neutral stance regarding which Canadians can, or cannot, afford access and health maintenance costs. When individuals and families cannot afford to follow up on recommended treatments due to lack of money, they are at risk of being labelled "non-compliant" and thus having their health problems blamed on their lack of initiative. As evidenced in this chapter, lack of affordability is related to age, gender, race and social class. Canada now has 15.5 percent of children living in relative poverty, defined as households with incomes below 50 percent of the national median, thus ranking seventeenth out of twenty-three developed countries (Unicef 2005).

Barriers in access are woven into the health care system, which is itself grounded in medical imperialism. For example, Black people are subjected to insensitive or inappropriate care when their illnesses are interpreted as the consequence of inherent predispositions to violence or sexual promiscuity (Bernard 2002; Utsey, Ponterotto, Reynolds, et al. 2000) or from subtler assumptions embedded in the health care system, particularly the tendency to embrace White, middle-class, male experience as normative. The health indicators assessed in the Apgar test, used to assess health of newborn babies, for example, is derived from assessment of White newborns. This process makes the Apgar assessment of the skin color of the Black newborn much less useful (Enang 2002).

In the health fields, cultural competence is the main approach to addressing these individual and systemic barriers in access for racialized persons and groups. Although initiatives related to cultural competence have fostered cross-cultural health care and created a mutual ground to initiate a dialogue about issues of difference, a critical analysis of racial issues and an understanding of the macro-level workings of the health care system are necessary to design and implement much needed policy changes to ensure truly accessible health services for racialized and marginalized peoples. Although health literature suggests that there is a need for health care professionals to understand and adapt to cultural diversity through culturally competent care, proponents of anti-racism have argued that professionals must challenge racism, rather than opting for the politically soft option that merely reifies culture (Alleyne, Papadopoulos, and Tilki 1994). These authors further note that such an approach denies the centrality or existence of racism and pays "superficial attention to cultural rites and rituals" (583).

Models of cultural competence fall short on a number of counts. Following years of efforts to implement such models in health care, there remains minimal evidence to demonstrate its effectiveness in improving health outcomes or reducing health inequities (McGibbon and Etowa 2009). Drevdahl, Canales and Dorcy (2008: 20) illustrate the problem with cultural competence with an analogy: "Cultural competence is like a goldfish tank in the centre of the hospital waiting room. It improves the atmosphere and helps patients relax; however, it does not eliminate the actual problem that brought the patients into the hospital in the first place."

In contrast, the term "cultural safety" is now in common usage among anti-racist health and social services practitioners. The concept of cultural safety (*kawa whakaruruhau*) appeared in a formal sense in New Zealand in the early 1990s, when it was used to describe a more focused cultural response to power imbalances between health professionals and the recipients of health care, and Maori recipients in particular (Woods 2010). Cultural safety has subsequently been perceived as a guide for responding to the health problems of many of the world's most vulnerable or marginalized ethnic groups (Woods). Cultural safety is distinguished from cultural competence in its explicit attention to oppression, imperialism, post-colonialism and White privilege (McGibbon, Didham, Smith, et al. 2009)

A cultural safety approach holds great promise for disrupting racism in the health fields and elsewhere, even with the complex challenge of integrating this way of being and thinking into practice, research, education and policymaking. Racism has been increasingly implicated in known disparities in the health and health care of racial, ethnic and cultural minorities groups. Despite the obvious ethical implications of this observation, racism as an ethical issue per se has been relatively neglected in health care ethics discourse (Johnstone and Kanitsaki 2010). In a society that is increasingly multicultural, there is now a movement, albeit small, among health practitioners, educators, researchers and policymakers to reframe racism as a moral issue in health care:

Such changes demand a greater awareness and responsiveness towards the cultural differences between each individual and/or groups of individuals, and especially the shared beliefs and practices of various minority social, ethnic, religious and gender groups in society, such as young people, elderly people, and those who are mentally ill or disabled. However, the values, ideals and basic rights of such groups have often been overlooked, ignored or minimized because, as is common in western or postcolonial countries, any arguments from a cultural or ethically relativist perspective are often overridden to favour those of the more prevalent views of western ethnocentrism and moral universality. (Woods 2010: 718)

Conclusions

The evidence of racism as a social determinant of health requires not only an understanding of biology and genetics, but a consistent focus on the threat of racism. Racism as a process and an outcome overlays all other health determinants for people of colour. The way forward lies in sustained attention to the foundations of racism, including White privilege, Eurocentric biomedical hegemony and modern-day post-colonial repetitions of historical imperialism. In Canada we have barely begun a truth and reconciliation process about Canada's legacy of slavery and genocide. This chapter focuses on some of these antecedents of the markedly different health outcomes of people of colour, compared to White people. We provide core ideas for understanding the how and the why of these health inequities. Although there has been little attention to post-colonial theory in the health fields (Anderson 2000), a sustained focus on oppression and structural power is surely the path to reducing the human and financial costs of continued racism.

12 Gender Issues

Social inequality is a key dimension of how human society is organized; the classification of people into categories of deserving and undeserving of freedom, human rights, employment, medical care, even housing. As we read about racial profiling by police and the disparate medical treatment of racialized men and women, another dimension of power in human societies is gender. The case of Kimberly Rogers, discussed in Chapter 8, reveals the gendered consequences of welfare reforms: Rogers was a single mother and full time university student collecting welfare; she died of heat stroke while living under house arrest for a welfare fraud conviction. As David Hugill explained in his writing about the missing women cases in Vancouver, it was clear how gender intersected with how police responded to reports of missing prostituted and drug addicted women; gender informed how the media told the story about the crisis of the missing and murdered women. In contrast with the social construction of women as undeserving of protection from predatorial violence, in this chapter we examine how girls and women have long been viewed as threatening or dangerous.

"The Social Construction of 'Dangerous' Girls and Women"

Karlene Faith and Yasmin Jiwani, in Carolyn Brooks and Bernard Schissel (eds.), *Marginality and Condemnation*, 2nd edition (Fernwood, 2008)

Most criminalized women do not come from middle-class families. The crimes committed by women tend to be the result of poverty, privation, and past experiences of abuse. When women kill, their victims are most often family members, particularly abusive spouses (Boritch 1997: 219–20), and these women cannot readily be characterized as "violent." Rather, these criminalized women are the "underclass," generally not the stuff of which big news is made.

Instead the news focuses on another class: the "dangerous" woman, a figure who appears regularly on our newspaper pages and television screens. Intensive media attention targets in particular women who commit crimes of fatal violence against strangers. Print and television journalists and traditionalist criminologists are mutually reinforcing in their attention to sensational, anomalous violent offences by girls and women. Indeed, popular and academic theories of girls' and women's "dangerousness" in this regard abound. The general effect is to place disproportionate attention in the least representative cases of the women who come into contact with the criminal justice system — and to draw generalizing conclusions from those atypical cases. The dangerous, violent women become the ones whose media images extend in the public imagination to all "criminal" women. The result is the skewing of the public's perception of girls and women convicted of illegal behaviour.

The decontextualized nature of news reporting results in misrepresentations of social reality. A one-year study (1992–1993) of Saturday news stories in five regional papers concerning crime by women found that more than 50 percent of the stories focused on the issue of women committing serious violence. Such crimes represent less than 0.5 percent of all charges laid against women for violent crimes (Boritch 1997: 16). (Most violence-related charges are for common assault.) The majority of the articles, aside from those that dealt with Karla Homolka, were stories about women who had killed their spouse or a child (Gordon, Faith and Currie 1995). This press coverage is a serious overrepresentation of violent crimes by women. There was not a single article in any of the papers on shoplifting, which is the predominant crime committed by both men and women. Ultimately, this phenomenon prompts fear, outcry, more aggressive prosecution of girls and women, harsher punishments for all women convicted of crime, and a backlash against feminist ... movements.

Prison is a junction in which social inequities converge. In Canada it is primarily Aboriginal people and Blacks who are overrepresented in jails and prisons and this is because of structured racism. But media accounts of crimes by girls or women seldom acknowledge structural factors. Focusing on uncommon crimes of violence, the accounts individualize and pathologize the accused with little or no reference to social context. The accounts tend not to stress another fact: that recidivism among women who have served sentences for murder is extremely rare (which is also the case for men).

In the following pages, as examples of media-saturated crimes involving girls or women, we discuss three cases: Leslie Van Houten, who was involved in one of the 1969 "Manson murders" in California; Karla Homolka, who in the early 1990s assisted Paul Bernardo in the sexual-torture killings of three young women, including her own sister, in Ontario; and Kelly Ellard, convicted of the brutal 1997 murder of classmate Reena Virk, in British Columbia. In each instance, the offender was a pretty, middle-class white girl, which not only distinguishes her from most criminalized women but also exacerbates the horror of the white majority — because, after all, "she's one of us." In other words, people seem to expect violent behaviour from people who are "not like themselves," people who are different. They do not expect it from themselves or their own. As it seems to go: when "we" (whoever "we" is) commit behaviour that shocks "our own kind," we are appalled, unlike when "they" misbehave, to which "we" respond with "Well, what can you expect?"

The three young women in our cases exuded danger because they broke gender codes in the most extreme ways possible. Their crimes are not comprehensible to the white middle class that bred them. Although the crimes seemed senseless, all three cases are indicative of power abuses — either because of having social power or reacting to others who have it.

The stigma of dangerousness, as applied selectively to individuals and to entire marginalized populations, is rooted in tradition. We begin, then, by setting the historical context in which the social divisions of "us" (good) and "them" (bad) became firmly entrenched in Western societies.

The Construction of "Dangerous Classes" in Western History

According to the Christian Bible, the first woman on Earth, Eve, committed the first human sin by eating an apple from the tree of knowledge, thus losing her innocence. She exacerbated her sin by seducing Adam; the snake signified the sexualized evil that now contaminated God's first human creatures. Women were by nature either evil or saints: whores or madonnas. It was about their sex. The dangers of women's sexuality is a recurrent theme in religion and in the history of theoretical criminology (Lombroso and Ferrero 1895; Pollak 1950). The theme reflects attitudes that feminists generally refer to as misogyny. The evil of women as sexual beings has also been a dominant theme in modern Western practices of criminal (in)justice.

The witchhunts of the fifteenth to eighteenth centuries are a conspicuous example of traditional fears of women, and of the uses of the church, law, and public hysteria to construct the idea of a dangerous woman (Klaits 1985; Marwick 1975; Trevor-Roper 1975; McFarlane 1970; Parrinder 1963). The Bible declared that witches, as allies of Satan, were to be killed (Exodus 22: 18). The churches conducted the witchhunts, generating rumours, distrust, accusations, and social panic. They turned suspects over to the state for trial in a court of law followed by execution (burned at the stake; drowned in boiling oil; hanged; beheaded). About 15 percent of the executed witches were men; often they had the choice of testifying against their wives or being themselves convicted of witchcraft (Wilson 1993).

Understanding that the best defence is a good offence, a woman afraid of being accused would lay blame on a neighbour for causing a misfortune: a miscarriage, illness or death, a cow drying up or a chicken that stopped laying, a storm damaging the barn, or some other calamity. The accused were charged with fornicating with the Devil, as his servant. Since witches committed havoc unseen by mortal eyes, no witnesses were necessary. Married women, rich as well as poor, and mothers together with their daughters were executed indiscriminately. Disproportionate numbers of single women and widows were executed — women without men, women who by choice or circumstance lived independently of men's supervision. If they kept small, domesticated animals as companions, as many did, they were de facto suspects. These were women who did not satisfy gender-role expectations, and they were thus perceived as dangerous women. As many as nine million women and girls may have been executed over three centuries, contributing to one of Europe's greatest holocausts (Ehrenreich and English 1973).

Women were censored and silenced in all realms of public life, and it was up to the men to keep their wives in line. For one thing they would not tolerate abusive language (Sharpe 1984). In accordance with Blackstone's British legal commentaries in the eighteenth century, men had a responsibility to discipline women, with the caveat that the stick the man used to beat his wife should not be thicker than his own thumb (from whence tradition came the expression "rule of thumb"). When women scolded, both men and women were breaching gender codes. It was a crime for women to nag their husbands or harangue others in public. The punishment for this crime was public humiliation of both the woman and the man. The harshest punishments fell on women, who were often whipped, confined in a pillory in the town square, dunked in water, or forced to wear a brank, also known as a "scold's bridle" — a helmet with a mouthpiece with small metal spikes inserted into the woman's mouth; if she attempted to speak, it would cut into her tongue (Underdown 1985: 123). Men were humiliated in noisy public rituals, subject to intensive ridicule for failing at manhood.

The formal tradition of criminology, the study of crime and punishment, commenced in nineteenth-century Europe in concert with the Industrial Revolution and the emergence of modern capitalism. In England, masses of people migrated to the newly urbanized centres, particularly London, where the lure of factory jobs supplanted agrarian culture (Thompson 1963). The promise of urban comforts, however, was not fulfiled for many of these unskilled migrants, and high unemployment produced rashes of what we now call street crime. These crimes, primarily related to the theft or destruction of property, were indicative of class divisions that separated the emerging capitalist class from people who were relegated to bare-survival wages or no paid work at all. The more affluent members of society, a distinct minority of the population, correctly perceived the antipathy of the unruly masses upon whose labour they depended for their affluence. Thus was born the political notion of "the dangerous classes."

The writings of Karl Marx were unequivocally focused on the work and social conditions of working-class men, whom he identified as the proletariat who would ultimately overthrow the capitalist class and establish communal, profit-sharing, worker-owned industry. He failed to recognize the significance of the chronically unemployed, the lowly riff-raff, whom he labelled the lumpenproletariat. In his estimation, they were social pariahs and parasites who contributed nothing to society. In his glib dismissal of the least resourceful victims of capitalism, Marx, in effect, was colluding with the bourgeois notion of the dangerous classes.

Women who failed to find legitimate employment, however dubious the benefits of such labour, often found themselves in brothels or working as street prostitutes and petty thieves. In Marx's terms, they, too, were relegated to the despised lumpenproletariat. More seriously, they were stigmatized as the dangerous carriers of sin and disease, which justified England's Contagious Diseases Acts (1860–83). This Act gave police the power to stop any woman on the street and send her off for an invasive medical examination. By the late nineteenth century the nuclear family, with parents and children living as an insulated unit and the patriarchal father at the head, had replaced the extended family in which women had held more decision-making power. This familial arrangement was "naturalized" through social ritual and legal regulation, effectively domesticating middle-class Western women. Rather than being described by male authors as evil, they were now idealized as the heart of the family, virtue personified. Their "natural" compliance and nurturing ways would earn them the protection of their husbands and, by their example and adherence to Christian teachings, instill morality in their children. As Kathleen Kendall (1999: 111) puts it, "Convict women were perceived as either more morally corrupt than criminal men because they violated natural law, or as innocent victims of circumstance."

Canada's first separate jail for women, Toronto's Mercer Reformatory, which opened in 1880, was built on the premise that women and men require different approaches to confinement (Strange 1985–86). Incarcerated women were perceived as being more rowdy than the men, requiring strict discipline to develop good work habits, self-control over passions, and a cessation of drunken or violent behaviours (Goff 1999: 165). With its emphasis on instruction in the domestic arts and religion, the reformation of imprisoned women in Canada was inspired by the work of Elizabeth Fry in England. Her goal was to reform women who, upon release, could attract a husband and manage a household, and who would give up drinking, prostituting, gambling, yelling, and cursing. With sufficient religious and domestic instruction, and with discipline and patience, she believed, these rebellious, ill-kempt, mean-tempered women would metamorphose into quiet, respectable homemakers.

Like women in jail, women at large required instruction in the arts of compliance and subordination — the need for which contradicted the ideology of women's natural submission to men (Faith 1993a). In European criminal courts, men could be held responsible for crimes committed by their wives, because women (notwithstanding their "natural" evil) were now thought to be "naturally" passive, and therefore incapable of conceiving and carrying out a crime. If a middle-class woman became unruly, that behaviour was blamed on the father or husband. These attitudes culminated in the Victorian age.

When ill-paid workers engaged in strikes and protests against those who exploited their labour, they were perceived not only as a threat to the smooth running of a profit-driven market economy but also as a danger to the safety and comfort of those upon whom they were dependent for their meagre livelihoods. Women were often active as "Luddites," weavers who smashed mechanical looms in protest against losing jobs to technology (Thompson 1963: 216–19). They protested food prices and scarcities and chased after the middleman, taking the grain from him and paying him a fair market price (Stevenson 1979). Women who aggressively and collectively protested on the streets and in the factories were de facto dangerous because they were behaving like men.

Cesare Lombroso (with his son-in-law, William Ferrero) was the first "scholar" to write about women who broke the law (1895). The "father of criminology," he formally established the myth that, when out of (men's) control, women at large were more vicious, dangerous, and monstrous than any man. In 1950 criminologist Otto Pollak published a speculative essay on "female criminality" in which he asserted that women were more deceptive than men, due to having both to hide their monthly period and to fake orgasm. Biology thus equips women with the skill of deception. He speculated that nurses and caretakers often kill the ill or elderly with poison, but get away with it.

Men have taken a great deal of effort over the centuries to teach women to stay in their place, and to restrict their opportunities for immoral or illegal behaviour. In this postmodern age, gender-bending is commonplace, and gendered hierarchies are legally challenged, often successfully, everywhere in the Western world. Women themselves are now in social-control positions, as policy-makers, practitioners, and professionals in every field. And yet, half a century later, Pollak's concerns with women's dangerousness, apparently based on fear of women's sex, have by no means abated in society (Hudson 1989), despite and consistent with the preponderance of male sexual violence.

The Twentieth Century

The popularization of psychology in the mid-twentieth century caused a shift from generalizing women as inherently bad to seeing them as inherently mad. In the 1950s new pharmaceutical industries promoted mood-changing and tranquilizing pills specifically targeted for depressed housewives and prisoners. Women were more likely to be sent to a mental hospital than to a prison. Because the numbers of women in the criminal justice system were so low, relative to men, and because men dominated the academic world, very little was published that shed any light on women in the system. When they weren't fictionalized as masculine and violent, they were seen, as by the Gluecks in the 1930s, as a pathetic but dangerous class who transmitted sexual diseases and bred inferior offspring (Glueck and Glueck 1934/1965). "Bad seed" theories have proliferated in Western history, literature, and entertainment: the simple idea that some people are born bad — supernaturally cursed or genetically unfortunate.

Beginning in the late 1960s, the interdisciplinary field of criminology came under the strong influence of critical sociologists and historians, some of whom were examining criminal justice systems as implicated in widespread social injustice and material disparity. Others, particularly feminist scholars, began to rectify the absence of women in the criminology literature (Heidensohn 1968; Bertrand 1969; Klein 1973). By the end of the 1970s, an abundance of new research had produced a rapidly growing literature in the areas of women, crime, and punishment. Two of the most prominent books, Freda Adler's Sisters in Crime (1975) and Carol Smart's Women, Crime and Criminology: A Feminist Critique (1976), were to have significant international influence on the direction of new scholarship. By the 1980s, gender was an exponentially expanding area in criminological research, as well as in every other discipline.

Adler's work stimulated a shift from thinking of criminalized women as monstrous, pathetic, and/or pathological to thinking of women as independent agents, in a process of "gender convergence" with men in society as a consequence of the "freedoms" gained by the women's movement. These new freedoms, as Adler saw it, included women's increased opportunities to break the law. This "liberation thesis" was unsupportable, but the media were unrelenting in associating a fictional rise in violent crime by women with the women's movement. In fact, women have been charged with approximately 10–15 percent of all violent crimes since the beginning of record-keeping, but to make their point the media offered skewed percentage increases. For example, if one jurisdiction had zero murders by women in 1974, but two murders by women the following year, the homicide rate for women would increase by 200 percent, as a blip. The press would headline the percentage increase but omit the low base numbers in their reports. When in the following year there were again zero murders by women, the press did not issue headlines declaring that women's homicide rate had decreased by 200 percent. Women killing people is far more titillating and newsworthy than women behaving themselves.

Adler (1975) was strenuously criticized for suggesting that women's liberation would result in increased crimes by women, and Smart (1976) demonstrated otherwise. Women's theft rates did go up in the late 1970s, but the robberies were not committed by women who had been influenced by women's liberation, nor by serious crooks. They were primarily the work of young single mothers who were experiencing the "feminization of poverty." They bore no resemblance to news reporters' fictionalized versions of wild, violent women running amok, as was propagated through the 1970s and again in the 1990s (Chesney-Lind 1997). At all periods of history, when women have organized for women's rights, they have met with fierce resistance from men and women who represent the status quo. In exploiting Adler's study, the media played directly into the hands of male supremacists. However, Adler's work as a sociologist also invited challenges from feminist scholars, and much research was catalyzed by her theory.

While the media continued to falsely report a rising degree of violence by girls and women, the actual rates of violence, and rates of most other crimes (by both men and women), were on the decline through the 1990s (CCJS 1999: 188–226), and continue to decline (Alvi 2000: 56–57). Marge Reitsma-Street (1999) thoroughly examined the data, arguing that it conclusively proved that over the past twenty years charges for murder and attempted murder by girls had been constant and infrequent. The work of Walter DeKeseredy and his colleagues (1997) demonstrates that when girls and women are violent they are most commonly defending themselves or fighting back, with a man initiating the violence. Assault rates have gone up for girls in some locations, but this has less to do with more violence by girls than with social responses to those behaviours (DeKeseredy 2000: 45-46; Pate 1999: 39; Schramm 1998), including official reporting and prosecution. The kind of schoolyard bullying or scuffles with parents that would formerly have been resolved privately has now, with "zero tolerance," become a matter for criminal justice.

In 1998 the Canadian journalist Patricia Pearson revived and capitalized on the recurrent myth of women's dangerousness. Recycling an old theory, Pearson asserted that the feminist movement bears some responsibility in this (fictional) crime wave by violent women. Her basic argument, which is much like Pollak's earlier theory, is that our "politically correct" society is in denial about female aggression; in the feminist tradition of identifying girls' and women's victimizations and systemic powerlessness, feminists rob women of the need to accept responsibility and to be accountable for their actions, such as husband-beating (Pearson 1998: 30). Feminists, in Pearson's critique, have failed to recognize women as "rational" decision-makers with personal agency, who commit aggressive and/or violent crime as a calculated individual choice. The news media again, predictably, exploited the provocation that women's liberation was making excuses for violence by women.

Meda Chesney-Lind (1999: 114) points out, though, that feminists do not campaign for the right to be violent. She criticizes Pearson's "conflation of aggression and violence" and her false assertions of increases in women's serious crime. As Chesney-Lind (1999: 116) notes, "Troublesome facts rarely disrupt Pearson's flow." Given that men commit up to 90 percent of violent aggression, rather than vie for equality in this area it would make more sense, as Chesney-Lind observes, to focus on theorizing about the "consistent, powerful sex difference" in men's and women's crime rates. Moreover, Pearson "minimizes and dismisses women's victimization and its clear connection to women's violence, and then argues that such violence should be punished without regard to gender" (Chesney-Lind 1999: 117–18).

Chesney-Lind (1997) uncovers how the media and criminal justice tend to label a group of girls a "gang" if they are not white. Bernard Schissel (1997: 51) refers to the exaggerated press coverage accorded to youth gangs as hate crimes perpetrated by the media. Journalists quote academics who haven't studied gangs but offer expert opinions (DeKeseredy 2000: 55). Media reports about gangs take on a tone of moral panic even though, as Sandra Bell (1999: 157–63) observes, most so-called youth gangs are involved neither in violent crime nor in claiming turf. In support, Bell cites Karen Joe and Chesney-Lind (1993), who found that girl gangs are primarily social support groups for marginalized girls.

Critical scholars recognize how the media skew reality by focusing on statistically insignificant but culturally sensational crimes, such as school shootings or a girl beating another girl to death. Contrived imagery of a rising tide of delinquency sets up destructive misrepresentations about young people and crime (Alvi 2000: 15–18; Bell 1999: 84–85; Schissel 1997). Shahid Alvi (2000: 18) reports that 94 percent of Toronto newspaper stories on youth crime involve violence, even though most crimes by youth, such as theft, are non-violent (Bell 1999: 80). Girls are rarely aggressors in these stories, and they more often appear as victims.

A study of girl violence in Western Canada (Artz 1998) was based on interviews with just six adolescent girls who were involved in assaultive behaviours. The media colluded with the author's emphasis of girl-on-girl violence as signifying a rising trend, with the attendant theme of family dysfunction. In a study of girl's "dope gangs" in Detroit (Taylor 1993), the author emphasizes the factor of violence as an element in the drug use, but does not suggest that girl gangs signify a trend. Certainly the evidence is lacking for establishing a trend of violent girl gangs in Canada, but the media insist on it with an explicit anti-feminist stance. For example, in Alberta Report, under the headline "Killer Girls," the author states: "The latest crop of teenage girls can be as violent, malicious and downright evil as the boys. In fact, they're leading the explosion in youth crime. It's an unexpected by-product of the feminist push for equality" (quoted in DeKeseredy 2000: 38). By contrast, the Detroit study includes an analysis of poverty, racism, and criminal (in)justice, and a discussion of a steady stream of resourceless Black girls who are processed through the system unheard and unseen, as if they were dangerous (Taylor 1993).

In establishing various levels of security, Correctional Services of Canada (csc) classifies prisoners: those who are not deemed a risk (for escape, or to cause harm to others) are classified minimum or medium security; maximum security is reserved for those perceived as a threat to the good order of the institution, whatever their crime. In 2000, about 18 percent of the 357 federally sentenced women incarcerated in Canada were classified as "maximum," and they were disproportionately Aboriginal women. Through the 1990s women labelled "maximum" were sent to men's psychiatric prisons around Canada, where they were placed in solitary and drugged. In committing millions of dollars to new segregation buildings at four women's prisons, csc is implying that these units are needed for the safety of the public (Hayman 2000). In fact, very few women are criminally "dangerous," or even perceived to be. The women so labelled would be more accurately generalized as "uncooperative" with the prison regime.

Even more restricted than prisoners labelled "maximum security" have been those officially declared by the court as a "dangerous offender." Following from the Habitual Offenders Act of 1947 and the Criminal Sexual-Psychopath Act of 1948, the dangerous offender designation was first proposed by the Ouimet Committee, a 1969 government commission for prison reform. The commission reasoned that the distinction, and tight control over those so labelled, would encourage communities to be more accepting of the vast majority of prisoners and those newly released, who pose no threat.

... Only two women in Canada, Marlene Moore and Lisa Neve, have been designated dangerous offenders. Critics observe that men require much more serious criminal histories, usually involving rape and/or murder, before being designated a dangerous offender, and that Moore and Neve were victims of a double standard. Neither of them had killed anyone, but the net-widening law permits use of the designation with just one violent offence, which can be assault, as in the case of both Neve and Moore. Both were chronically abused, in trouble from a young age, and in and out of prison from their teens. Marlene Moore robbed a woman on the street at knifepoint. Lisa Neve, who worked in the sex trade, assaulted a co-worker with a knife, and issued threats. Moore, after spending much of her life in prison, committed suicide at the Prison for Women in 1988 at age twenty-eight (Kershaw and Lasovich 1991). After five years with the label, Neve's super-maximum dangerous offender classification was overturned in 1999, when she was twenty-six, and she was immediately released from prison. By all accounts, she has been "reformed."

Facing the Contradictions

For half a century, from Caged in 1950 to the prison-porn flicks of the 1990s, Hollywood movies set in women's prisons have consistently presented a pat set of stereotypes: evil, masculine women, both prisoners and matrons, presented as violent lesbians, often as women of colour; the sweet, innocent, blonde white girl who is imprisoned due to a mistake, often wrongly convicted for a crime committed by her boyfriend; the psychotic criminal who goes berserk; the super-sexy bad girls who cheerfully do the dirty work for a controlling, sadistic dominatrix. The most common stereotypes are devil women; lesbians as villains; teenage predators and super-bitch killer beauties (Faith 1993a, 1993b; Birch 1993).

The fictions of Hollywood rarely coincide with the truths of women's lives. It is neither monsters nor pathetic victims who get locked up. Rather, upon first entering a woman's prison, one is struck both by the diversity of the women, in terms of age, appearance, and demeanour, and by their ordinariness and approachability. The same "types" of women one finds in prison would be found in an urban department store. They do not look dangerous, and indeed few are. Certainly women of colour are vastly over-represented (Monture-Angus 2000a; Gilbert 1999; Neugebauer-Visano 1996), and the white women are not middle class. Race, class, and gender are both distinct and conjoined, each dynamically influencing the other in criminal justice processes.

Women on death row are not usually conventionally feminine in appearance (Farr 2000). An exception was the softly appealing Karla Faye Tucker, who was executed in Texas in 2000 after winning the hearts of Christians throughout the United States through national television interviews. Tucker was not a feminine woman when she was sentenced; she was softened by her conversion to Christianity, following the crime. Women with masculine characteristics are not more likely to kill than feminine women. They are, however, perceived as more dangerous, and if convicted they are more likely than feminine women to receive the death penalty, especially if they are lesbians and most especially if they are women of colour (Farr 2000).

The closer a woman is to the ideals of femininity, the more shocking it is when she violently betrays her gender role. Because the offence defies "common sense," particularly when the victims are strangers, the accused are often dismissed as pathological. But pathology suggests that the crime is the outcome of a deranged mind, a sick individual detached from society at large.

The three very feminine women who make up our case studies are far from the stereotypical monsters of film, psychiatry, or criminology, although the seriousness of their crimes rivals any of the monster stories. In addition to the headline murders in which they were implicated, they continue to attract media attention because they were attractive, white, middle-class young women at the time of their crimes. All are currently in prison. We focus on these sensational cases even while critiquing sensationalism. We do not see these women as presented by the media, but as women whose life experiences prior to their crimes were not unlike those of other women of their cultures and generations. They are not aliens but rather signifiers of the times and places in which they lived.

Leslie Van Houten

On August 9 and 10, 1969, in affluent neighbourhoods in Los Angeles County, two sets of murders were orchestrated by a cult guru who had spent most of his life in prison. Four men and three women were killed, and the name Charles Manson entered the lexicon of American popular culture, signifying an end to the idealism of the 1960s. Manson, in his mid-thirties, and three young women aged nineteen to twenty-one were arrested in late 1969. In July 1971 they were sentenced to death and transported to state prisons to await execution. The media were unrelenting in the attention given to the case until spring 1972, when the U.S. Supreme Court declared the death penalty unconstitutional and their sentences were amended to life in prison.

Manson had about twenty-five followers (aged thirteen to early twenties), any of whom would have been happy to have been selected for these murder missions. Most of these disciples had been extremely feminine young women when he met them — on streets, in parks, in hippie pads in San Francisco. Each of them, all white and most of them middle class, had been successfully socialized to be attractive, soft and feminine in appearance and demeanour. They were all skilled in the domestic arts, and they honoured men's hierarchical privilege in the social order. They excelled in submissiveness.

In the beginning Manson presented himself as a gentle man with spiritual wisdom and no fear. Through the use of drugs, especially lsd, and intensive, unrelenting mind-control games, his followers became convinced that he had supernatural powers. They revered him as the reincarnation of Jesus Christ. At a time when millions of young people throughout North America were rebelling against the hypocrisies and barbarities of the establishment, and seeking enlightenment from Eastern religions, these young people were convinced of Manson's higher authority. He looked up to Aboriginal peoples, he opposed the war in Vietnam, he preached peace and love. He had magical qualities. He played his guitar and sang self-penned songs with social commentary. Wild animals weren't afraid of him. Even rattlesnakes let him pet them. He washed the feet of his disciples, just as Christ had done. His followers were ready to follow him anywhere, which turned out to be "Helter Skelter." This was Manson's vision of the world in chaos, with himself, a white man, at the helm of a new revolution that would give the power back to the Black man and rain terror on "Whitie" for centuries of abuse against transported, enslaved Africans and their descendants. Manson, an undisguised sexist, recruited young trophy women to serve him and his male friends in every respect. His plan to start a race war was patronizingly racist; and his selection of victims was based on straightforward class antagonism against materialist consumer "piggies."

On August 9, 1969, Manson selected four of his followers, "Tex" and three of "the girls," and sent them out to start the revolution. (On this first night he didn't send Leslie, who stayed home at the communal ranch to take care of the family's babies.) He targeted a home formerly the residence of a music producer who had failed to satisfy Manson's ambition for a rock 'n' roll career. Unbeknownst to Manson, the house had been leased to a film director who was then away. At home were his pregnant wife, an actor, and several of her friends. Five people were mercilessly killed, and messages taken from lyrics in Beatles songs were left in blood on the walls. Manson himself didn't attend the killing; he just told his followers what to do and they obeyed. He was the general, and they were his soldiers.

When the crew reported back to Manson, he was displeased with their "messy" job. On the following night, August 10, he went along with a somewhat changed crew to make sure things were properly set up. Again, Tex was chosen to commit the murders along with two girls, Pat and Leslie. Like most of the other girls, Leslie had a wholesome upbringing. She sang in the church choir as a teen, and was a smart, popular, classic beauty, a homecoming princess, active in the community and just generally a well-admired middle-class Southern California girl. She had joined up with Manson in September 1968. In the spirit of the times, a period of great social upheaval and protest against universal injustices, Leslie was looking for answers to life's big questions, and she thought Manson had them. He promised to help her kill her ego. As his disciple, she gave up her name, her birthday, and every facet of her former self. She was just nineteen.

This second night, Manson chose a house at random, though significantly in another affluent neighbourhood and next door to a house where he had once partied as an aspiring rock 'n' roller. He and Tex went in first and tied up the occupants, Leno and Rosemary LaBianca, parents and owners of successful retail businesses. Manson then left the house, telling Pat and Leslie to go in and do whatever Tex told them to do. Manson himself drove to what he mistakenly thought was a Black neighbourhood, where, in a gas station restroom, he left the wallet he'd stolen from Mr. LaBianca. He expected Black men would be blamed for the crime, and that Black men would then rise up in a race war. The "family" would live in a hole in the desert, staying young and healthy somehow, until the war ended and they would surface as the ally of the victorious Blacks. Anything he said sounded like prophecy to those who believed in him, and they were prepared to do his bidding at any cost. Yet, in the LaBianca home, Leslie was unable to perform as a good soldier. She recoiled at the prospect of killing, and backed off into another room when the murders started. After Tex had already killed Leno Bianca, and had struck the fatal blow to Rosemary after Pat was unsuccessful, he then insisted that Leslie also come into the room and stab the by-now dead woman, which she did, fourteen to sixteen times in a brutal act of frenzy. She later described to a parole board that she both felt like a wild animal with its prey and was filled with fury at herself for having not lived up to Manson's faith in her.

As he was to later testify, and contrary to the women's boastful testimony at trial, later refuted, it was Tex Watson who dealt the death blow to all seven of the victims of Manson's forays into Helter Skelter. (Watson was tried separately, and continues to serve life in a California state prison.) All three of the women had proven inadequate to the task. Like any good girl would be, each was terrified at the murders. Each resisted, and each proved incompetent as murderers, even while trying to act the good soldier. As young women, they had no training for violence. It was not so much a matter of conscience that bothered Leslie afterward but rather frustration and disappointment at her inability to perform as instructed, and her failure to meet their leader's expectations.

The press routinely demonizes people who have been criminalized, and with Manson this practice did not require much journalistic imagination.

He presented himself as both a deity and Satan. (He was once booked in jail as Jesus Christ, Saviour and Lord.) As the mastermind conspirator, he was sentenced to death along with the three women who took credit for the killings on the two nights. During trial, on his instruction, they all shaved their heads, carved Xs into their foreheads, and taunted the judge. The press characterized the women as pathologically evil, and they did appear to be serving Satan. Compounding the theatrics were the numerous "Manson girls" who lived on the sidewalk outside the L.A. court building for almost two years in solidarity. They too shaved their heads and wore long cloaks that reinforced the witchy impressions.

In 1972, when the death penalty was rescinded throughout the United States (until 1976), Leslie and the others were still housed on death row in the California women's state prison. They continued to live in their six-by-nine-foot cells for four more years, when they were gradually transferred to the main prison. By 1974, five years after the trial, Leslie had completely shed her attachment to Manson. She was racked with remorse, and expressed her guilt with anorexia. In 1976 her case was separated from that of her co-defendants. Because she was not in her right mind at the time of the crime, had never killed anyone, had been the victim of cult conditioning, and, most relevantly, had never had a proper defence (her lawyer had drowned on a camping trip during the trial), her previous sentence (death, converted to life in prison) was overturned and she was granted a new trial. In this 1977 trial the jury was deadlocked as to her guilt, so a third trial was scheduled.

For six months prior to and during the third trial, Leslie was permitted to leave the county jail on bail, having now served over eight years, much of it in solitary. While on bail she worked as a legal secretary when not in court, and she was able to reunite with family and old friends. She lived a normal life and the media was respectful of her privacy. Reporters were startled to discover the change in her, from the 1971 clone of Satan to the calm young woman of 1977 who showed humility, remorse, compassion, integrity, and a grounded intelligence. This time she was convicted for robbery-murder (the wallet, some coins), rather than first-degree murder, and she was returned to state prison. She is still there, at the age of fifty-seven, in 2006.

The public first saw the rehabilitated Leslie in 1976 when she was interviewed on abc television by Barbara Walters. She did not disclaim responsibility for the crimes, and said she was as guilty as if she had taken the victims' lives. Her guilt was for following Manson, giving him her power. With that interview, the public began to see "the Manson girls" as individuals, not as robots who all used the same voice — saying the same words, using the same mannerisms — when they were under Manson's control. Subsequent interviews with Leslie by Larry King and Diane Sawyer further erased the monstrous images that had accompanied the first seven years of reportage on the case.

Over twenty-five years ago, while in her early twenties, Leslie returned to her "self" with help from therapists, family, friends, teachers, and sympathetic prison staff. She would have to live with the nightmare of the torment she helped cause and the enduring grief of the victims' family and her own. Permanently humbled, she lives as healthfully as anyone can while incarcerated, and she became a model prisoner who engages in service to her prison community and beyond. By day she works full-time at prison jobs, which rotate every several years, in the hospital, school, administrative and chaplain's offices. In her spare time she reads onto tape for the blind; makes quilts for the homeless; teaches English to women for whom it isn't a first language; and organizes talent for the annual AA dinner show. When she entered the prison, there were six hundred women there. Now there are two thousand. Younger women who come in learn from Leslie how to survive prison with grace. She's the oldtimer who doesn't complain. The parole board has turned her down in fifteen hearings, often reluctantly, it seems; they encourage her to remain hopeful that "one day soon" she'll be released.

The death penalty may have been a less painful punishment than living out a life sentence with a deeply injured conscience and no hope for making restitution. Life sentences commonly do not exceed twenty-five years, especially for someone like Leslie with an unblemished prison record and who poses no threat of violence or escape. If she is soon released her nightmares will accompany her, and getting out after almost forty years would not be getting off easy.

Karla Homolka

Normally, in making a release decision, the Canadian National Parole Board conducts a risk assessment, considering the applicant's criminal history, alcohol or drug use, violence on record, psychological state, information from experts, and, sometimes, victims of the crimes. Those convicted of first-degree murder must generally serve a minimum of twenty-five years. In the case of Karla Homolka, whom many consider dangerous, a deal was made in 1993 in which she was granted a maximum twelve-year sentence on manslaughter charges. In exchange she offered information about her husband, but without revealing the extent of her own role.

The story of Karla Homolka and Paul Bernardo erupted on the media landscape in February 1993 with Bernardo's arrest on charges of murder and sexual assault. The murder charges stemmed from the discovery of the cement-encased body-parts of fourteen-year-old Leslie Mahaffy and the abused body of fifteen-year-old Kristen French. Both young women had been kidnapped, raped, and tortured. Bernardo and Homolka were also implicated and subsequently charged with the murder of Homolka's younger sister, Tamylynn. It was subsequently discovered that Bernardo had routinely engaged in sexual assault between 1983 and 1993. He was charged with two counts of first-degree murder and forty-three counts of sexual assault. The extent to which Homolka was a willing accomplice in committing the murders was then a matter of conjecture. Bernardo's lawyers argued that she was actively involved, as "home movie" tapes later demonstrated. While the actions of both Bernardo and Homolka were equally brutal, the media spotlight and public attention were focused on and continue to dwell on Homolka.

The 1992–93 survey of print media on issues dealing with women and the criminal justice system yielded a preponderance of stories dealing with Homolka (Gordon, Faith, and Currie 1995). A total of 136 women and crime articles appeared in the Saturday editions of five urban Canadian newspapers. Twenty-one of these articles focused on Karla Homolka, all of them published between May and July. Eight articles, more than a third, were in the Toronto Star, given the provincial interest in the case, but for three months Homolka stories dominated the media nationwide.

Despite a court-ordered publication ban, there were more stories published on the Homolka and Bernardo case than on any other criminal case that year. The media tended to focus their initial coverage not on details of the crimes but rather on the freedom of the press and the public's right to know (Gordon, Faith, and Currie 1995; McCormick 1995). The publication ban itself incited speculation and rumours about the case, as well as a proliferation of Web sites and Internet news discussion groups (Regan Shade 1994). The cloud of secrecy intensified speculation when Bernardo's own lawyer argued against the ban (Walker 1994). In 1995 Homolka again dominated the airwaves and print media with her testimony at Bernardo's trial.

Initially Homolka's media representation alternated between heartless killer and victim slave. As with most media coverage, the tendency was to confine the figure or issue in easily understandable binary oppositions (bad versus good; savage versus civilized) (Hartley 1982). Yet this binary framing tended to collapse from the sheer velocity of the vacillations between competing representations. The oppositions relayed in news accounts were so extreme that the story became an exceptionally bizarre case of inconsistencies. For instance, a Globe and Mail article begins with a description of Homolka's "Barbie" image, describing her as "a stunning 23-year-old veterinarian's assistant ... long blonde hair and blue eyes ... peaches and cream complexion ... wouldn't hurt a fly." The same article refers to Bernardo as "26 ... accountant ... tall ... charming ... handsome enough to melt a young girl's heart. But behind the Ken and Barbie masks lurked the face of grotesque evil" (quoted in its entirety in McCormick 1995: 186).

Crime reporting is also based on the element of sensationalism, and much depends on how far a story departs from conventional standards and encapsulates an extreme (McCormick 1995). Homolka's crimes were unusual in the extreme. They were committed by a woman. They were taken as being crimes against humanity because they involved the torture and murder of adolescent women, one of whom was her sister. The pleasant, clean-cut news-photo images of Homolka and Bernardo were incompatible with the standard idea of sex murderers. The cognitive dissonance created by the juxtaposition of the stories with the photographs served to draw in readers who would not normally seek out stories about sex and violence. The sensationalism was supported by the unusualness of having a woman challenged and convicted of pornographic murders and by the offenders' disarmingly wholesome profiles.

Each time she appeared in the public arena, the media scrutinized and communicated Homolka's behaviour to fit into a conception of her as either cold psychopath or battered woman. At no time did the media engage in a critical analysis of the many women who are battered, murdered, raped, and mutilated throughout the world on any given day, or of the reality that most homicides are committed by men. Rather the media focus on the unusual event or situation, and especially one that becomes a "continuing story," with new developments day by day or from time to time (Connell 1980; Hartley 1982). In the case of Homolka, the continuity was ensured for a period of at least two years — until 1995, when she was called to testify at Bernardo's trial. Homolka's plea bargain, resulting in the twelve-year sentence on the lesser charge of manslaughter, generated intense and negative public reaction, which, in itself, became a media story. More than three hundred thousand signatures were collected on a petition opposing the Crown's settlement and the lenient sentence (Boritch 1997: 3).

This intense reaction can be explained in terms of the contradictory identification that Homolka evoked — as a daughter and sister, and as tormentor and killer. Not only did she symbolize the deepest betrayal of trust among women by killing those of her own kind, but she also offered a symbol of daughter, sister, or wife. She epitomized the potentiality of an evil that society seeks to constrain through the rationale of law and order, which gains its legitimacy at least partially through the media.

An additional but highly critical factor underpinning the moral outrage ignited by this case sprang from the identities and representations of the victims. The young women tortured, raped, and murdered were not "deserving" victims. They were not on the streets. They came from good homes. They were innocent, pretty, white schoolgirls whose parents were solid citizens. In contrast, Homolka and Bernardo represented the fractured identities of individuals who were not what they purported to be.

Crime reporting is incident-driven and decontextualized (Gordon, Faith, and Currie 1995; Schissel 1997). It is the lack of an overall social context that gives news stories their poignancy and dramatic flavour; the stories reveal the extremes of human behaviour without placing those extremes in context. Over a time the repeated stories and their common themes communicate a sense that the issue — whatever it is — is pervasive and increasing in intensity. The prevailing "new filter" — the means by which some details get into stories and others are left out — becomes entrenched, suggesting that the issue has always been problematic (Hall et al. 1978; Hall 1990). The most common example of this kind of entrenchment can be seen in news coverage of ethno-racial groups that are often presented as problematic immigrant groups who will not assimilate (Jiwani 1993).

From the start of the Homolka-Bernardo case, the media drew on entrenched filters to make sense of the story. For example, in one of the early articles published by the Globe and Mail the reporter notes, "The striking blonde is the daughter of Czechoslovakian refugees..." (Sept. 28, 1993: 24–25). That this bit of information was considered pertinent suggests the reporter's search for potential explanations that would resonate with the public imagination and make "common sense."

As the case unfolded in media reports, part of the "common sense" explanations included the rationale that Homolka was either devoid of a moral conscience or under Bernardo's power. During her trial, the coverage described her as "stone-faced" amidst the "gasps of horror" that greeted her testimony (Globe and Mail Sept. 28, 1993). She provided "chilling testimony" (Warwick 1995). Reporters who listened to the audio tracks of four Homolka–assisted rapes by Bernardo underlined the horror of the murder-rapes. As a means of conveying unprintable words, one reporter explained, "The words were the same as those uttered on most X-rated movies — expletives and crude instructions to perform sexual acts" (Galloway 1995). Reporters noted that "a stunned silence took over the courtroom" during the playing of an audio tape of a drug-induced rape. According to one reporter, "The scant dialogue was enough to send an eerie chill through the courtroom. For several moments after the tape stopped, nobody said anything" (Legall 1995).

The press alternately depicted Homolka as the devil's accomplice and a battered woman, helping to justify her short sentence and ensure Bernardo's conviction (Blackwell 1995a). By her own testimony, Homolka said she acquiesced and did everything she could to please Bernardo until she left him on January 5, 1993. She testified, "He treated me like a princess, like I was the only girl in the world" (Brown 1995), but said she feared for her life. Headlines communicated the press's skepticism of the use of the battered woman's syndrome to describe Homolka's actions by using such terms as "robo-victim defence" (Verburg 1995), despite photographic evidence of severe physical abuse (Blackwell 1995a).

These competing points of view accelerated as her testimony continued from late May to July 14, 1995, in what was described as "one of the longest and most dramatic appearances to take place in a Canadian courtroom" (Makin 1995b). Reports described Homolka as an extremely cold, manipulative, and possibly insane personality who has "a truly sick, twisted side" (Stepan 2000), and they used testimony from experts to legitimize this perspective. The media representation was bolstered by the very backlash it helped to foment. From most media perspectives, Karla Homolka personified evil — a kind of evil that the justice system cannot rehabilitate. The system is "soft" and thus allows for the likes of Karla Homolka to escape without retribution (Wente 1999).

On the victimization-criminalization continuum, where does Homolka stand on the level of guilt? The only agency permitted her is that of complicity in a series of heinous crimes with her apparently psychopathic husband/ abuser. Neither of them were aberrant in their observed everyday behaviours. As presented by the media, Bernardo and Homolka were oversocialized to the worst extremes of their respective gender possibilities. It would seem that Homolka's femininity was her nemesis. Her feminine passivity and fear led to her inability to resist Bernardo's sex, violence, and death games. Her external femininity also caused uneasiness, because her media-transmitted image of attractive, pleasant normality disrupts conventional notions of women who can be trusted not to hurt people. Paradoxically, her crimes were also consistent with her image: she was acting out the extreme end of the compliant femininity continuum — absolute obedience.

Once placed in the centre of the media spotlight, Homolka and Bernardo were mutually but separately challenged to recreate themselves through the lens of innocence; they had to be reconstructed, based on who they were — or who they appeared to be — before the violence — the previously undisclosed but now fully discussed identities based on the media-constructed reality of two incomplete human beings, sufficiently banal to be all the more terrifying. They appear to be inflicted with the "shallow personality syndrome," which is endemic to a materialistic, individualistic, image-obsessed society. They invite armchair psychologizing. In her demeanour, Homolka retains a superficial quality, that of a "material girl" gone berserk.

Given the limits on and biases in media coverage, the rest of us are backed up against the limits of the personal/political dialectic — the contradictions inherent in trying to understand crime at a societal level but believing that explanations for certain types of crime must come from within the individual — forced to retreat with the conservatives, from the search for internal logic to the paradigm of pathology. Given the conflicting details of the crimes, it would be difficult to formulate a reading of the case that goes beyond the boundaries of the mainstream print and television coverage, which vacillates so strongly between Karla the Monster and Karla the Victim. The relatively restrictive Canadian approach to criminal trials, even one as sensational as this, is a far cry from the circus of the simultaneous O.J. Simpson trial in Los Angeles. We can only speculate from our global knowledge of femicide, ritual rape, wife battering, and sex slavery that there is much more to the story than the newspapers and television stations are telling us, or than what Homolka and Bernardo themselves know, but aren't telling us — yet.

In 2005, after serving twelve years in federal prison, Karla Homolka was released in accordance with the deal she made prior to the court's knowledge of the extent of her involvement in the rapes and murders. Her release was not renegotiated despite protest from the public and the legal community.

In 2006 Karla is now living as anonymously as possible somewhere in the province of Quebec.

Kelly Marie Ellard

On November 14, 1997, seven girls (aged fourteen to sixteen years) and one sixteen-year-old boy brutally attacked Reena Virk, a young girl of South Asian origin, in a suburb of Victoria, B.C. As Reena left the scene of the beating to make her way home, she was followed by two members of the group — Kelly Ellard and Warren Glowatski. Kelly called out to her to ask if she was okay. Reena told them to leave her alone and staggered across the road. They followed her to the other side of a park, near a body of water. According to Glowatski's testimony, Kelly asked Reena to remove her jacket and shoes. Kelly then proceeded to beat her up again, smashing her head against a tree trunk to the point where Reena was rendered unconscious. Ellard and Glowatski dragged the unconscious body to the water, where Kelly hit Reena in the throat again and forcibly drowned her. According to Glowatski in his trial, Ellard stood in the water with her foot over Reena's head and smoked a cigarette. Neither Ellard, nor Glowatski, had met Virk until that night.

The discovery of Reena's body eight days later and the subsequent arrest of the teens involved in the initial attack resulted in intense media scrutiny and publicity. Both nationally and internationally, Reena Virk's murder came to symbolize the increasing violence of girls and young women, despite statistical evidence to the contrary.

The early media coverage advanced a "liberation thesis" to explain the murder, dwelling on the violence as an outcome of girls achieving gender equality. Reena, as a victim, was explained in terms of her inability to "fit" into her peer culture. She was described as being overweight, tall for her age, and plain in her looks. The news media failed to mention her South Asian origin or reflect on how her racial difference contributed to not fitting into the school culture (Jiwani 1999). She was not exotic enough in her difference to fit, nor was she acceptable according to the dominant, normative standards of her peer group or her family.

In March 2000, Kelly Marie Ellard was tried for the murder of Reena Virk. Media speculation about Ellard's role in the murder had continued throughout the two-year period prior to her trial. From January to April 21, more than a hundred local and national radio and television newscasts and press articles focused on the Virk murder. This sustained and, at times, heavy coverage appeared to be motivated by a desire to advance explanations of the crime that made "common sense." That desire to make sense emanated from the same cognitive dissonance that had occurred in the cases of Karla Homolka and Leslie Van Houten. Like them, Ellard came from a middle-class, white family. Although her parents were divorced, she appeared to have a close relationship with her family, which motivated one judge to rule that she could stay at home rather than be incarcerated in a youth detention centre. Her appearance did not fit her crime. As one columnist opined, "How do you match the sweet-looking teenage girl who doesn't stand five feet in her platform shoes, who's a little heavy in the hips, who speaks tremulously on the stand, with the image of an accused killer...?" (McMartin 2000).

From the beginning of the trial, the press presented Ellard as a normal-looking teenager "with straight black hair cut just above the shoulders," wearing "a gray sweater and black pants" (Stonebanks 2000). However, these descriptions were juxtaposed with photographs that portrayed Ellard with a smug expression, downcast eyes, and a hint of a smile. The pictures communicated an image of an individual cognizant of more than she was willing to reveal.

The coverage of the Ellard trial was influenced by a number of external factors. Reporters attending the trial had followed the story from its inception two years earlier. Hence they were privy to details revealed in the testimonies presented at the previous trial of Warren Glowatski, the co-accused, and the hearings of the other young women who were involved in the beating. It was not uncommon to see reporters gather outside the courtroom to verify what they had heard and identify common themes of relevancy for their particular articles and newscasts. Additionally, reporters were cautioned by the outcomes of a preceding event in which one newspaper was severely chastised by a particular judge for revealing details of a trial prior to the jury going out for deliberation. In the Ellard trial, the presiding judge, Madam Justice Morrison, had decreed that the jury would not be sequestered for the length of the trial. This meant that journalists could not report on anything other than what witnesses stated in their testimonies. The reportage was thus extremely factual and rarely included the same level of descriptive discourse that appeared in the Homolka case. Nonetheless, reporters used terms such as "chilling," "gang-murder," "savage," "cold-blooded killing" and "calculated" to describe both Ellard and the murder. They borrowed most of these words directly from testimony provided by witnesses.

From the testimonies, the media constructed an image of Ellard as a cold-blooded killer who had deliberately murdered Virk. They portrayed her as being the most aggressive and leading the assault. She was also described as having bragged about the murder to her friends. Throughout the trial, Ellard's composure, as reported, vacillated from being tearful to being calm, depending on who took the witness stand. Between the sessions in court, she was often seen, and captured on camera, laughing and joking with her family and defence counsel.

Some thirty witnesses were called to testify at the trial over a three-week period. The Crown maintained that Ellard had committed the crime to ensure that Reena would not "rat" on the members of the group who had beaten her up. The defence strategy was to portray Ellard as a helpless victim of a conspiracy organized by the co-accused, Warren Glowatski. Ellard and members of her family were the key witnesses for the defence. Together they wove a picture of middle-class normalcy and concern. Ellard was composed on the stand. She spoke softly and denied any involvement. She identified Glowatski and two other young women as having committed the murder. According to news reports, Ellard cried when asked to recount why she had delivered the first blow to Reena Virk. She replied, "I guess I was being like them, victimizing her" (Moore 2000a).

While the media coverage was contained and cautious throughout the trial, once the jury went into deliberation the press focused on the information presented in the voir dires — information not accepted as evidence by the judge or seen by the jury. The media pointed to the inconsistencies between Ellard's statements to the police and the testimonies presented by the various Crown witnesses. Despite this, the tenor of the articles was not as damning as the coverage that came after the verdict was announced. The jury's verdict was a conviction for second-degree murder. Justice Morrison set the eligibility for parole at five years.

The news media used stock theories to account for Ellard's criminal behaviour. In some instances they identified teen group loyalty as the main motive underpinning Ellard's actions, as well as those of Glowatski, who refused to testify as a Crown witness against Ellard (Teahen 2000). Other accounts drew on previous psychological assessments to demonstrate Ellard's pathological character, her inability to assume responsibility, and her lack of internalized social values (Hall 2000; see Appendix). Other news items focused on the need for increased law and order to control the increasingly violent actions of teens. This last point was underscored by Crown counsel, who stated to reporters, "I hope it will spur parents particularly to do whatever they can to make sure they know where their children are so that a little more control can be taken of the situation" (Canadian Press, March 31, 2000). Some of the coverage utilized the previous frame of girl violence, alleging that most of the girls involved in the attack on Virk had criminal records (Moore 2000b).

These same theories appear in letters to the editors. In an anonymous letter (April 4, 2000) printed in the Province (Vancouver), the author addresses "Killer Kelly Ellard" stating, "Perhaps we don't want to know how an attractive young woman like yourself, 15 at the time, could murder a younger school mate with a cruelty we've always preferred to believe was reserved for the vilest of villains — nearly always adult males." The author ends the letter by stating, "We'll just write you off as a whacky weirdo with a rotten childhood whose hatred of herself and the world is etched in her eyes. What else can we do? Except keep our fingers crossed that if the social network should fail, the jury system will prevail."

Significantly absent in the range of explanations put forward by the media was Reena Virk's marginalized positioning vis-à-vis those who had beaten and killed her. The issue of race and racism was either absent from the media discourse or presented in terms of her inability to fit. Rarely did the media question why she could not fit, and what she might have been attempting to fit into. Even though both Ellard and Glowatski are white, and both were convicted of killing a young South Asian girl, the issue of racism only surfaced when Justice Morrison stated in her sentencing, "Whatever the motive for this crime, it was not racism" (Ivens 2000). Justice Morrison went on to portray Ellard as someone who had shown remorse as well as the potential for rehabilitation. She spoke at length about Ellard's love for animals and the positive references she had seen in the twenty-nine letters she had received from Ellard's friends and family.

Although the media work in concert with other dominant/elite institutions in society to legitimize perspectives that are consonant with the views of those in power (Hall et al. 1978; Hall 1980; van Dijk 1993), the relationship between the media and dominant institutions is not a direct one. Rather, in putting forward competing explanations, the media favour the explanations that make "common sense," and "common sense" perspectives often work in support of the dominant ideology. In this particular case, Justice Morrison underlined Ellard's presumed innocence and thereby contributed to the media's more muted condemnation of the murder. The coverage is starkly different from that of the Homolka case. It colludes with dominant "common sense" definitions of racism as extremist behaviours confined to the actions of hate groups, or as overtly racial slurs and insults. Within the landscape of "multicultural" Canada, these dominant definitions do not include systemic and invisible forms of everyday racism.

If the crime were to be recast — if a South Asian girl murdered a white girl or, more dramatically, an Aboriginal boy murdered a white girl — the denial and erasure of racism in the Ellard case would become apparent. Public outrage would have been intense, and the crime would probably not have elicited the same light sentence of five years. Given the omission of the factor of racism and, with it, a profound denial of the unequal and hierarchical nature of society, we can only see the media as being complicit in presenting an image of a democratic society in which all members are equally vulnerable to victimization and equally accountable in the eyes of the law.

Media and Dangerous Girls and Women

When they occurred, these three cases incited considerable media coverage and public scrutiny. At the root of the public fascination and extensive coverage was that all three cases ruptured stereotypical notions of appropriate gender behaviour.

In numerous respects, these three women and their crimes have distinct commonalities. All three were involved in uniquely horrific murders. These were exceptional crimes in that the victims were also girls/women and primarily strangers. Van Houten and Homolka, and perhaps Ellard as well, explicitly committed their crimes in seeking a man's approval. None of them was a feminist. In the aftermath, all of them seemed unaffected by the consequences of their crimes, the immense pain caused by their actions. They were all from balanced, middle-class homes, which sets them apart from the majority of criminalized women. (This did not benefit Van Houten, who was declassed through her association with the outcast Manson.) According to contemporary, white femininity standards, all are good-looking with likeable personalities, which may well have been factors in the lenient deal/sentencing of Homolka and Ellard. (It didn't help Van Houten, who was originally sentenced to death.) None of them suffered from disabilities or was in any way stigmatized as "other" prior to their crimes. They all "fitted in." Thus their behaviours were regarded as radical aberrations of gender expectations. In short, they were marked as dangerous women.

Van Houten, along with twenty-five or so other young people, was a straightforward victim of brainwashing by a cult guru. Her decisive crime was in surrendering her power to him. Her reasons were of a spiritual nature; she was seeking truths and believed he had them. Although Homolka was similarly entranced by Bernardo, her motives weren't at all spiritual. Van Houten's crime occurred at the peak of a massive social movement that had disrupted traditional capitalist values. By contrast, Homolka's crimes, and Ellard's, occurred during a period of conformity, consumerism, and materialism. Whereas Van Houten rejected the consumer society, Homolka embraced it. According to the accounts, she was interested in the surface appearance of things.

The perception of dangerousness in each of these cases was heightened and exaggerated by intense media coverage. The coverage served to re-entrench the proverbial notion that women are as dangerous as men, and that an increasing proclivity to violence among women is a result of their liberation from patriarchal control. Certainly some women such as Homolka and/or Ellard can be readily perceived as dangerous, but men are ten times more likely to kill someone. The fear of "criminal women," as a generalized, stereotyped group, is irrational. However, the hardware invested in locking up women — the bars, fences, lasers, electronic locks, cameras, guards, and walls — are all signals to the public that these unseen women are dangerous. In a prison, every real or contrived crisis or emergency that gathers media interest is a means for correctional workers to express to the public the dangers of their occupations, and to be granted better wages, working conditions, and "danger pay."

Theories of female criminality and dangerousness have evolved from essentialist notions regarding women's innate nature. The dangerousness of women, after all, can be traced back to Biblical times and Eve. Notions of women's inherent dangerousness have also existed in other cultural milieus, in part as a result of colonization and the spread of the Judeo-Christian and Islamic traditions.3 Contradictory representations in this historical tradition clearly cohere around the notions of women as virgins or vamps, madonnas or whores.

The placing of some women on a pedestal of purity and innocence (representing woman as virginal) often comes at the expense of non-white, sexualized women in low-income households. To be effective, one representation is contrasted with another that is its opposite. We know that not all women are pure, innocent, or chaste. We do not understand quite as well how social class, race, age, sexuality, and ablebodyness influence a girl's or woman's vulnerability to violence as victim and/or perpetrator. The three cases demonstrate the need to complicate the analysis — to begin to consider interlocking forms of oppression (Razack 1998) and relations of power that have an impact upon and among women who are in different places in the social hierarchy. Media monopolies are gendered, race-based, and class-based. They are controlled by white, upper-class men. Media explanations for women's criminality borrow from an androcentric historical tradition and reflect the views of those who control them. From this perspective, women's "inherent proclivity" to criminality tends to be confined to the sexualized, racialized, and low-income classes. Women who break the mould are most newsworthy.

The three cases illustrate the media's strategic use of isolated examples of female criminals to establish a generalized female proclivity to crime. These cases were headlined simply because such cases are rare — that is what makes them sensational. The horrors of the crimes committed by Leslie Van Houten, Karla Homolka, and Kelly Marie Ellard are used to underscore how women in general are capable of committing violent crimes and becoming "like men." By this logic, women do not deserve any special consideration on the grounds of gender inequality; their criminality becomes a result of their achieving gender-parity. The media's decontextualized and case-specific reportage lends itself well to this kind of explanation.

Pathology occurs at extreme ends of a continuum of social values and behaviours. We are socialized for pathological behaviours as surely as we are socialized for acceptable behaviours. In focusing on these women's transgressions, the media reinforce the normative social and moral order. They imply the rewards that accrue if women stay "in their place." However few and far between are these cases of horrific violence by girls and women, their actions ignite the fears engendered by Adler's work in the 1970s and Pearson's book in the 1990s. Women who engage in "senseless violence" are demonized and, if they excite the media, permanently stigmatized. Their identities are lost to processing by the state: the literal replacement of a person's name with a number, and the social death and invisibility of living behind bars. Their identities are reduced to their crimes.

Gayle Horii, a woman who served a life sentence in Canada, writes of that experience:

I realized that probably less than five minutes of my life dictated my punishment, but it need not wipe out the woman I was for forty-two years previous to my particular madness, nor dictate how I live the remainder of my life. Because of the crime I committed, it may be difficult to accept my assertions that I should be granted human rights and that I could still maintain decent values. It is a most abstract conundrum, to wrap one's mind around the fact that a killer and/or prisoner could also be a good person. (Horii 2000: 104)

13 Looking Toward the Future

Since 2008, there has been a groundswell of political mobilization amongst young people. In June 2011, Senate page Brigette DePaper was ejected from the House of Commons and fired from her job when she silently held a sign stating "Stop Harper." In her words:

> This country needs a Canadian version of an Arab Spring, a flowering of popular movements that demonstrate that real power to change things lies not with Harper but in the hands of the people. When we act together in our streets, neighborhoods and workplaces …. I think everywhere is the right place to resist the Harper government. (*Globe and Mail* June 3, 2011)

The Arab Spring of 2010 saw hundreds of thousands of young people filling city streets in Yemen and Egypt, with smartphone-captured pictures and video footage of the uprisings that went viral, creating a global awareness of the political corruption and military oppression. The Twitterverse exploded with protest manifestos. Here in Canada, young people, shaken by the police brutality of the G20 protests in June 2010 and witnessing the Arab Spring online, continued to press for accountability of governments responsible for the largest (illegal) mass arrest and detention in Canadian history. By September 2011, Occupy Wall Street initiated North America's own pro-democracy movement. In April 2012, student protests in Quebec erupted over tuition fee increases, resulting in draconian "back to school" legislation that empowered police to arrest protestors. Ultimately, the student movement captured international attention of celebrities, including Arcade Fire and U.S. filmmaker Michael Moore (*Globe and Mail* May 20, 2012).

Young adults today are the most vulnerable to the effects of the economic recession and socially conservative government policies. Surveys indicate an ethos of pessimism exists in Canada, where 37 percent of Canadians believe youth today will have far fewer opportunities than their parents' generation (*Globe and Mail* May 31, 2012). As Canada ages and its infrastructure shifts towards meeting the needs of seniors but more so to recover from the devastation of the corporate greed of speculators and banks that forced government budgets into the red, thanks to multi-billion dollar bailouts, the economic, cultural political and environmental interests of youth appear to be under threat.

What can be done? Reform movements have gone global and viral. Legal battles are only one of the tactics used by activists seeking social transformation. Human rights, environmental protection and civil liberties are all important yet partial aspects of the struggle for social justice. In the following reading, young anti-poverty activists challenge the lack of affordable housing in Ottawa through the courts and on the streets.

"Squat the City, Rock the Courts: Challenging the Criminal Marginalization of Anti-Poverty Activism in Canada"

Lisa Freemen, in Diane Crocker and Val Marie Johnson (eds.), *Poverty, Regulation, and Social Justice* (Fernwood, 2010)

On September 27 2004, five anti-poverty activists entered a criminal court in Ottawa to defend their political action and to challenge the criminal charges that were brought against them. ... Two years earlier the five accused, along with seventeen other people squatted in an abandoned building on Gilmour Street in downtown Ottawa. During their trial the accused went beyond arguing the technicalities of the criminal charges brought against them. From their perspective as anti-poverty activists, they directly questioned whether the act of squatting should be defined and prosecuted as a criminal activity during a major housing crisis [such as a systemic lack of affordable rental housing]. ... Consequently, their trial reveals ways in which activists specifically squatters have resisted the criminalization of both poverty and anti-poverty activism in Canada.

The trial of the Gilmour Street squatters raises significant questions about the relationship between activism and the law. Does the criminalization of anti-poverty activism and the political techniques used to combat poverty (such as urban squatting) substantially demobilize political resistance? Can activists find a space for political resistance within the criminal courts of Canada?... I argue that activists as demonstrated in the Gilmour Street squatters' case, move beyond a simplistic understanding of a binary opposition between radical activism (squatting) and liberal legal procedure and reform (Sheldrick 2004). I demonstrate how the Gilmour Street squatters confronted the boundaries of legal conceptions of victory and the proper place of political activism in the courts. ...

Squatting: A People's History

Public and political squats in Europe gained attention through their affiliations with autonomous and anarchist social movements of the late 1960s, 1970s, and 1980s. Italy had approximately twenty thousand documented squatters between 1969 and 1975 while towards the of 1980 in Zurich, Switzerland "more than eleven hundred youth faced criminal charges" for squatting with more than sixty confrontations with police and over twenty-five hundred arrests. There were an estimated six or seven thousand squatted houses in Amsterdam in the spring of 1980 and squatters there had a strong influence on urban planning.[1] Denmark's squat in 1970 occupied a 54 acre site with over 175 buildings in Copenhagen, which represented one of the largest squatter settlements in Europe (Gimson 1980). Meanwhile several German squats were associated with the radical Autonomen movement and the fall of the Berlin wall. Berlin's squatter movement controlled approximately sixteen houses at its peak in the late 1970s, and by 1980 formed a squatters' council (Katsiaficas 1997). European social and legal struggles over squats continue today; police eviction of a squat in Copenhagen in March 2007 resulted in length police confrontations with anarchist squatters from around Europe joining the protest, resulting in over 500 arrests (Olsen 2007).

Police evictions, governmental responses, and legislation regulating squatters title vary significantly between European countries. For example, [in the U.K.] a squatter needs to possess the land for 10 years with few other restrictions before they are allowed to apply for Adverse Possession Rights. If the landowner does not reply to or challenge this request within three months, the squatter is then entitled to be registered as the new landowner. In the Netherlands a building can be squatted legally if it has been unoccupied for a minimum of one year. The criminal charges of the break and enter are applicable only if the police catch the squatters entering the building. If the squatters are simply found living in the building and the police did not intervene during the initial stages of the occupation, formal eviction notice and legal action are requested to evict the squatters (Wiegand 2004).

Unfortunately, Canadian laws around adverse possession are far stricter than European laws and are virtually impossible for Canadian squatters to put into practice. Provincial land holdings systems of Crown land (such as provincial parks) typically require a squatter to remain on the land for sixty years. For privately held land, the statutory period is ten years (Ziff 2000). The combination of restrictive property law and a lack of squatters' title makes squatting in Canada difficult and dangerous. Squats are viewed as illegal and occupants are vulnerable to arrest. Continual conflict with the criminal justice system is a reality for Canadian squatters.

Due to the legal landscape most squats in Canada occur covertly, making it difficult to document a comprehensive history of squatting and squatters' rights in Canada. Over the past ten years however the steady presence of public and politizied urban squatting in grassroots anti-poverty movements has drawn attention to plight of squatters and the related social problems of surrounding the lack of affordable housing (Katsiaficas 1997; Gimson 1980). From Montreal's Overdale squat (2001), the Infirmary Squat in Halifax (2002), Toronto's Pope Squat (2002) and Victoria's Pandora Street squat (2002) to Peterborough's Water Street squat (2003), Vancouver's Woodward's squat (2003), and Toronto Gatekeepers squat (2003), Jarvis Street squat (2004) and Women Against Poverty Collective squat (2007), occupations of abandoned properties have created temporary shelter and ignited heated debate on the lack of affordable housing. Most of these squat actions have occurred as part of a mass rally or protest and have involved squatter demands on municipal governments. The actions have also tended to cumulate in police-led evictions, multiple arrests, criminal charges, and occasional trials (Arsenault 2003; Patriquin 2001; Levine 2002).[2]

Public squats in Canada are perceived by the media, mainstream anti-poverty groups, and housing agencies as a marginal tactic used by a few radical activists; however these squats have received a significant amount of media attention and community support. While most Canadian squats have been short lived, with some lasting only for a few hours and the longest enduring three months, these actions have resulted in identifiable if limited achievements.[3] In Montreal, Toronto, and Vancouver these achievements have included the establishment of temporary deals with the government consisting of the reconnection of electricity, the promise of city council discussions focused on alternative housing projects, and monetary support. In the case of Montreal's Overdale squat, the squatters moved to a city-owned abandoned building with advice and approval from the municipal government, intending to create long-term affordable housing, only to be evicted in a police led operation shortly thereafter (MacAfee 2001). Attempts to negotiate long-term housing settlements with municipal governments have generally been unsuccessful. With a history of limited and inconsistent municipal support, the majority of Canadian squatters are cautious of any negotiations and collaboration with politicians. Still, these squats are not marginal and socially unsupported as the reported municipal responses suggest.

Recent public squats have relied heavily on moral and financial support from an extended community of social work agencies, shelters, unions, neighbors, and individual city councilors. In many instances, union support has been invaluable. For example, during the Ontario Coalition Against Poverty's Pope squat, the Canadian Autoworkers Union pledged $50,000 to help renovate the building. Several national unions donated money and supplies to Ottawa's Gilmour Street squatters, and lent support even after the squatters were evicted (*Canadian Press Newswire* 2001). John Baglow, then president of the Public Service Alliance of Canada, was a supportive witness for the squatters in court.[4] While limited in scope, these examples suggest that squatting has the potential to be a unifying strategy among social justice groups in the fight against poverty and its criminalization.

Even as a potentially unifying force, political squats are unfortunately only a temporary tactic in the present struggle against poverty in Canada. A relatively uniform state response consisting of regular police surveillance, lack of municipal government support, and brutal police-led evictions and arrests has criminalized and marginalized squatters, making it difficult to create permanent housing from public squats (Lamble and Freeman 2004). However, from Halifax to Vancouver, lessons learned from evictions are informally shared amongst anti-poverty organizers and squatters. Knowledge of policing tactics during evictions, failed and successful negotiations with landlords and municipal governments, and legal defence strategies (including the effectiveness of Charter arguments), build an on-the-ground archive of accessible information for anti-poverty activists working together in the fight against the criminalization of poverty.

246 Gilmour Street, Ottawa

The criminalization of urban squatting may appear to push the efforts of anti-poverty activism out of the public eye, but the case of the Gilmour Street squat reveals that when people challenge the criminal marginalization of such direct actions, the space for political resistance may also be redefined. When the Gilmour Street building was occupied on June 28, 2002, during a mass demonstration against the economic summit of the Group of Eight nations[5] it was the first public squat that Ottawa had witnessed in approximately forty years. The action received substantial community and media attention, and the activists pursued an innovative defence strategy in their criminal trial. These factors make the Gilmour Street squat significant in its implications for future squats, legal challenges, and anti-poverty organizing in Canada.

The abandoned, privately owned house at 246 Gilmour Street was located in a trendy section of the Centretown neighbourhood, a few city blocks away from Parliament Hill. Shortly after the occupation began, the squatters presented a list of demands to city officials, and through media interviews they posed the central question: why would a house remain unused and neglected for seven years despite the city's shortage of affordable housing? According to defendant Dan Sawyer, the Gilmour Street squat "reignited a debate about poverty… during one of the worst housing crises the city had seen."[6] The squat garnered substantial support from neighbours, community activist groups, national unions, affordable housing and tenant support organizations, and a local city councillor. Daily newspaper articles and letters to the editors indicate that both skeptical and supportive Ottawa residents and municipal politicians perceived the Gilmour Street squat as a novel political action. The actual occupation lasted only seven days and the squatters' interactions with municipal government officials — who acted as negotiators for the mayor — and police enforcement were predictably ineffective and full of empty promises.

The police response was excessive. The deployment of various gas substances and the use of force during the eviction of the Gilmour Street squat were reminiscent of earlier police responses to politicized squats in Montreal and Toronto (*Ottawa Citizen* 2002). According to defendant Mandy Hiscocks:

> The way the police arrested people was pretty typical of a squat action. Coming in strong when they decide to arrest, forcing people out. Other squats in Toronto that has been what has happened. This arrest was [at a] different level, because it was really brutal. The police were a little more armed. A guy with a machine gun, I don't think that is very common in a political operation to evict people from an

empty building. A battery arm may be common, smashing the house. It seemed over the top.[7]

The six-hour eviction process involved multiple city vehicles, including fire engines, city buses, and paramedic vans (Freeman and Lamble 2004). In addition to a police force armed with the "regular weapons [as well as] a MP-5 machine gun, rubber bullets and… a gas gun," a battering ram was used to breach several window frames on the third floor of the house in order to deploy the gas substances.[8] The entire city block surrounding 246 Gilmour Street, including several other privately owned properties, was cordoned off by crime scene tape, and supporters were forced to keep away.

Upon their arrest the squatters were held in police custody for thirty-six hours. They were released despite their refusal to sign the original bail conditions, which included a curfew, a clause forbidding the defendants from associating with each other, a ban on all participation in political activity, and a restriction barring them from being within 500 metres of 246 Gilmour Street.[9] The ban on political activity and the non-association clause are fairly standard bail conditions for activists charged by the police in Ontario, but the curfew and geographical restrictions placed on these squatters went beyond this scope.[10]

Each of the twenty-two squatters was initially charged with break and enter with intention to commit mischief, three counts of mischief over $5,000, and obstruction of a peace officer.[11] Over the two years of administrative court proceedings, fifteen of the squatters opted to make a deal with the crown prosecutor and obtained court diversions instructing them each to complete forty hours of community service in lieu of standing trial. The criminal trial of five remaining squat defendants (*R. v. Ackerley et al.*) ensued from September 27 to October 22, 2004. Ultimately, the jury did not find the squatters guilty of a single criminal offence. A couple of months after this verdict was announced, the crown declared a mistrial instead of opting for a retrial. The squatters declared victory.

On Trial

While it is not unusual for activists to appear before a criminal court, the level of cooperation between activists and legal actors varies. Some activists refuse to acknowledge hierarchical authority in the courtroom, by refusing to stand when the judge enters the room, for example, and primarily use the courtroom as a stage to vocalize their political dissent. Others actively engage with the court system, using the law as a tool for achieving their political goals. The approach taken by the Gilmour Street squatters strategically deviated from these two approaches; the squat defendants did not openly dismiss the hierarchical organization of the courts, nor did they wholeheartedly embrace the law as a tool for progressive social change. The squatters were skeptical of modifying their politics to fit within the technical arguments of criminal law, yet at the same time recognized the importance of fighting the criminalization of squatting. For them, going to court was not a choice. However, deciding to work *with* the courts was.

In choosing to actively fight the criminalization of squatting in court, the Gilmour Street squat defendants did more than avoid a conviction or act according to a particular type of politics. They challenged the liberal separation of politics and law in the courtroom and redefined what constitutes a legal victory. Participating in a criminal trial hardly necessitates radical politics or a comprehensive strategy for social change, but the Gilmour Street squatters utilized their position as accused to fight the further criminalization of anti-poverty activism. They expanded the scope for political resistance by inserting political claims and social context into the proceedings of a criminal trial, by refusing to abandon their grassroots politics, and by defending themselves along these lines without the aid of legal counsel.

On the surface, [the case] proceeded like any other criminal trial. Crown prosecutor David Elhadad began with an opening statement describing the details of the occupation of 246 Gilmour Street, the interactions between the squatters and the property owners, and the criminal charges. The self-represented accused prepared for trial, followed court procedures assiduously, deployed their knowledge of applicable case law, and predominantly conducted their case in a manner respectful of court decorum; they submitted factums, wrote opening and closing arguments, examined and cross-examined witnesses, participated in jury selection, and utilized the traditional defences of necessity and colour of right.[12] During the six weeks of trial, interactions between the squatters, the judge, and the crown appeared to be professional, cordial, and mutually respectful.[14]

In his arguments and closing statement, Elhadad stuck to the technicalities of the criminal charges and relied heavily on video evidence supplied by the Ottawa police. He went through painstakingly detailed accounts of minute damages to the inside of the building, the particulars of the real estate transactions before and after the squat, and highlighted the whereabouts and arrests of each accused. The crown emphasized that the squatters committed mischief by damaging the building, "rendering the property so that the owner could not use it, preventing him from lawfully using and enjoying his property," and refusing to leave the premises.[13] Elhadad also made it clear that it was not his job to "bring to the forefront social issues and decide that those are more important than dealing with the law."[14] The crown representative also voiced his perspective on squatting an abandoned house by stating, "you do not take property which belongs to other people simply to promote your social cause."[15] In contrast to the squatter's defence, the crown's case did not budge from a strictly legal perspective and adhered to the norms of private property ownership.

The squatters' defence strategy made the social context of the housing crisis in Ottawa the basis for their legal arguments. They did not deny that they had entered the house or even that they modified parts of the property.

They made it clear that the occupation of the house was a direct response to the housing crisis in Ottawa and should therefore not be viewed as criminal activity. The defendants used the courtroom strategically. Even though the accused never took the stand themselves, the witnesses they called, the content of their opening and closing statements, and their overall approach all demonstrated how politics were relevant to this trial.

Witnesses called to the stand included John Baglow, neighbour to the Gilmour Street residence and then-president of the Public Service Alliance of Canada, and housing advocate Robert MacDonald. Both men commented on the social consequences of the local housing crisis on the stand:

> When this squat took place, it managed to put the whole issue of homelessness on the front burner, to attract attention to it, to attract debate, to attract interest broadly across the region in the problem [of homelessness]. I would have to say [the squatters] were more effective than any means that I have employed personally or that my union has employed up to that time.

> I think what the squatters did was manage to put that agenda and turn it into a very high profile issue in a way that a lot of the agencies who actually work [on] homelessness on a daily basis were not able to do. I mean, they made an impact; there's no doubt about that.[16]

The witnesses for the defence helped shape the political relevance of this trial. They linked the Gilmour squat to broader campaigns for the rights of the poor and re-affirmed the role of local anti-poverty organizing in Ottawa.

The closing arguments of the defence, presented in turn by each of the accused, similarly emphasized the political significance of the squat by highlighting its community support and the non-criminal intentions behind it. The defendants framed the political necessity of this squat with reference to the traditional legal defences of necessity and colour of right. Defendant Rachelle Sauvé, in her section of the closing arguments, applied the defence of necessity to the squat by asking the jury the following:

> Was there really a choice? Were [we] really wrong to act? Could we have protected the right to housing without taking shelter and occupying it? In the reality and extremity of a housing crisis, where people in the city needed housing immediately, while buildings sat abandoned, a decision needed to be made.[17]

Occasionally Justice MacKinnon reprimanded the accused for bringing political claims not directly related to the evidence into their legal arguments. For the most part, however, the squatters were able to integrate the political grounds of the squat within their case. Justice McKinnon's instructions for the jury regarding the defences of colour of right and of necessity highlighted the extent to which the squatters had successfully made the social context of homelessness and the criminalization of poverty the grounding for this trial. In his closing remarks to the jury Justice McKinnon emphasized how the jury could substantiate both the defence of colour of right and necessity when he stated: "In this instance, the accused's honest belief must be that each of them had a right to the property which is the subject matter of the charge," and "here you will evaluate whether homelessness in Ottawa had become a situation so desperate and the peril of the homeless so pressing that it cried out for the actions taken by the accused."[18]

The jury's inability to make a decision on the charge of break and enter with intent to commit mischief illustrates the extent to which the defendants' emphasis on the squat's political context affected the outcome of [the case]. By submitting pamphlets, witness testimonies, and videotape evidence, the defendants emphasized that the intention of the squat was to create permanent housing, not to commit the crime of mischief.[19] The squatters challenged the legal notion that there is no place for politics in a court of law by incorporating the political motivation and social context of the squat within their legal arguments. Their physical presence in and approach to the trial challenged individualistic liberal conceptions of the role of activism in court. Most of the squatters remained apprehensive about working within the confines of the legal system. Consequently they organized their case in a collective manner resembling the politics that they used to organize the squat. According to defendant Mandy Hiscocks:

> We brought politics into the courtroom in how we were organized. When we had ten people with no lawyers, we [still] worked by consensus. The court had to adjust their own process to accommodate us. The judges didn't really mind it as an effective way for a lot of people to represent themselves... stop, huddle, take discussion outside. Then one person would speak for everyone. Highly abnormal for the courts [but it] ran smoothly. Judges were really tolerant of that, all the way through to the end. A big shift they had to make, [it] worked really well.[20]

This consensus-based, collective approach to the act of self-representation enabled the squatters to conduct their case in a manner consistent with their politics as they navigated their way through the regimented aspects of trial.

In fact, skeptics of self-representation on both sides of the legal system viewed the actions of the defendants in a positive light. On the last day of trial, Justice MacKinnon thanked the accused for the "responsible way they acted in their defence" and for the respect they showed the court.[21] After the trial, several of the defendants commented on how proud they were of their achievements in court and referred to the experience as empowering, remarking that it was "one of the more worthwhile activist projects" they had been involved in. They approached the task of self-representation as part of a broader political struggle, and thus were successful in more than their immediate, personal objectives of not being convicted.

The squatters' grassroots politics may not have been as visible in court as they were during the occupation at 246 Gilmour Street, but they were present nonetheless. The decision to represent themselves in court enabled them to structure their defence in the current political context of the state of affordable housing and poverty in Canada. This led to the establishment of what I term non-legal (but legally produced) social precedents. In this way, [the Gilmour Street legal case] ... is ... noteworthy [as] it reveals how the legal apparatus does not always extinguish grassroots politics through arrests and criminal trials.

Moving On

From a strict case law perspective, nothing new was gained from [this case]. A new formal legal precedent concerning the criminality of squatting was not established, alternative uses for traditional defences were not created and (due to the nature of Canadian jury trials), a written legal reasoning for the decision was not produced. If we measure political resistance only in a strict legal framework, and within a definition of effectiveness along those lines, the full meanings attached to political acts such as fighting the criminal marginalization of squatting and anti-poverty activism in Canada are obscured. From this limited perspective, perhaps law does demobilize anti-poverty activism. But fighting the criminalization of political actions, like urban squatting, does more than challenge legal discourse and criminal court procedure.

The case of the Gilmour Street squat is significant beyond narrowly defined legal goals. An informal social precedent was established through the trial that altered how those acting against poverty can form and sustain resistance. Broader positive social change could occur as a result of this precedent because other activists and the public at large have observed how it is possible for activists to fight their charges in court and win. Ottawa-based civil liberties lawyer Yavar Hameed has noted that, by going to trial, self-representing, and not being convicted, the squatters set a social precedent that extended beyond the immediate needs of the squatters.[22] Recognizing the social precedent set by [the case] contributes to future anti-poverty organizing efforts, reveals how the courts may react to self-represented accused, and redefines the interaction between the legal system and political activism.

Specific gains in social precedent established through [the case] can lead to the possible development of new resources for self-represented accused. With recently revised eligibility restrictions for Ontario legal aid support, many poor people have difficulty accessing the criminal courts.[23] Any new resources for self-represented accused gained from [the case] may present a useful tool and framework for future unrepresented accused in Ontario courts. During pre-trial motions the squatters presented an argument outlining why they (as self-represented accused) deserved financial support from Legal Aid Ontario.[24] Even though the legal aid documentation and testimony clearly indicated that a trial judge did not have the authority to grant the squatters' request, the presiding judge suggested that the crown appeal to the Attorney General for a set sum of money in order to ensure a fair trial. In the end, the Attorney General's office supplied financial support for the basic costs of trial, including daily court transcripts, photocopies, and other court-related costs, amounting to over $1,000.[25]

While the allocation of this money was a victory for these defendants, it did not establish any formal legal precedent. The crown clearly indicated that the circumstances of [the case] were exceptional and that future self-represented accused may not receive the same funding.[26] Despite the lack of a formal legal precedent, though, this victory may have established two social precedents. First, Justice McKinnon and followers of the trial gained awareness about the ineligibility of self-represented accused for legal aid. Second, the case law used by the squatters to ask for financial support may provide an unofficial guideline and motivation for other defendants.[27] The knowledge produced through this specific situation has the potential to be disseminated by personal connections, internet list-serves, and news articles throughout the extended network of anti-poverty activists in Ontario.[28]

The defendants also illustrated how grassroots activists can interact with the criminal courts without demobilizing their politics. Nonetheless, despite the positive verdict, compliments from the judge, and the generally positive experience of the trial, most of the defendants remained critical and wary of political activism in the context of the legal system. Days after the trial ended, two defendants in particular continued to vocalize their apprehension about using the courts as a venue for political activism. In a comparison with the political challenges posed by the Gilmour squat action itself, Dan Sawyer commented: "Court is different. In court we were not calling [political powers] into legitimacy."[29] He concluded that court should be "one of the packages of last resort [and] not part of a comprehensive strategy" for activism.[30] Similarly, defendant Mandy Hiscocks remarked:

> Once I thought that the best way to make social change was to get arrested, change the law. Law is not a good place to make social change but people are going to end up there if they are trying to make social change. Might as well get something out of it. I think you can affect change in the court, not through the laws. Trial shouldn't be the goal of activism.[31]

This critical attitude toward achieving justice through the legal system strengthened the defendants' political convictions and actions in court. As a result, they were meticulous and thorough in making decisions that would coincide with their political values. The defendants did not view the criminal courts as a harbinger for change and thus they defined their victories beyond the confines of traditional legal discourse. A criminal trial was expected to challenge the defendants' anarchist politics and the gains that they made in court were conscious and deliberate. This willingness to engage with the courts while remaining skeptical of them reveals an astute recognition of and resistance to the ways in which the law effectively demobilizes political activism.

Even though the accused in [this case] successfully navigated their way through trial procedures and established several social precedents, the courts are still inaccessible to most people, and are thus not necessarily the best venue for promoting social change. Nonetheless, while numerous legally defined gains may not have resulted, the occupation of 246 Gilmour Street and the accompanying trial highlight how one political action can influence social understandings of urban poverty and of activist engagement against it, both outside and within the criminal courts.

Conclusion

Challenging the criminalization of anti-poverty political actions like squatting is important, but going to court should not always be the goal of activism. In the case of urban squatting, fighting the criminal marginalization of direct actions for housing is necessary. The criminality of squatting an abandoned house during a housing crisis should be challenged. Even though this social precedent is not binding in a strictly defined legal way, it has the potential to foster social change.

Activist engagement with the criminal courts does not fit in dichotomous categories. Criminal prosecution does not necessarily demobilize political activism, nor do activists consistently ascribe to liberal notions of individualized rights that inhere in the criminal justice system. The Gilmour Street squatters balanced on a tenuous political line. They did not dismiss the law altogether or make a mockery of the hierarchy of the criminal courts, but neither did they idealize the courts as the holy grail of justice. The Gilmour Street squat defendants worked within the court when necessary and transferred to their trial the grassroots politics that they had cultivated during their squat.

The Gilmour Street defendants pushed the boundaries of liberal definitions of legal process and victory and made a space for political activism in the criminal courts. By weaving the social context of poverty, homelessness, and affordable housing into legal arguments and procedure, the defendants consistently kept their politics at the forefront of this trial. The criminality of squatting and anti-poverty activism was questioned and a legally defined acquittal was not the only victory achieved.

Five anti-poverty activists represented themselves in court and were not convicted of an indictable criminal offence. Through media interviews, magazine articles, and other public forums these activists engaged significant segments of community from Ottawa and beyond — including but not limited to national union presidents and workers, representatives of the mayor's office, and prominent city councillors — in a public debate on housing and homelessness that was not present before the squat and trial. The squatters also set a social precedent for future anti-poverty political actions in Canada.

The trial of the Gilmour Street squatters gives hope and leads us to seriously reconsider how we view the victories resulting from political activism, both in the streets and the courts. Progressive social change may not be bundled in a neat package. As seen in the case of the Gilmour Street squatters, social gains can easily be lost within traditional legal discourse and procedures. When we push beyond established categories, however, a space for political resistance can be made. Challenging the criminality of squatting and of anti-poverty activism in court is a necessary part of, but not the only tool in, the fight against the criminalization of poverty.

Notes

Chapter 5

1. For more discussion and information on the idea of exploitation and economic crisis see Bowles, Gordon and Weisskopf, "Power and Profits"; Brenner, *The Boom and the Bubble;* Chernomas and Hudson, *Social Murder;* Dumenil and Levy, *Capital Resurgent;* Greider, "Father Greenspan"; Moseley, *The Falling Rate of Profit;* Phillips, *Inside Capitalism;* Pollin, *Contours of Descent;* Shaikh, "An Introduction to the History"; Smith, *Invisible Leviathan;* and Stanford, *Economics for Everyone.*
2. Cited in Cohen, "Gambling with Our Future."
3. Greenspan, "Testimony before the Committee on the Budget."
4. Mishel, Bernstein and Schmitt, pp. 225–26

Chapter 9

1. Keynesian policies or Keynesianism: the terms are named after John Maynard Keynes (1884–1946), a British economist whose theories greatly influenced the economic policies of many governments after the Second World War. His book *General Theory of Employment, Interest, and Money* is considered one of the most important theoretical works of the century. It was published in 1936 during the Great Depression, the worst crisis to affect Western countries since the Industrial Revolution. In it he argued that there was no self-correcting measure to lift an economy out of a depression. Because of boom-or-bust cycles inherent in capitalist economies, governments should not rely on private investment to maintain high employment levels or a flow of money in the economy. They should instead use their powers to spend money, vary taxes and control the money supply to cushion the effects. In a depression, a government should increase its spending to counteract the effect of the decrease in private spending; during a boom, it should decrease its spending to control speculation and inflation. His ideas radically affected the way in which capitalism worked in Western countries, leading to the adoption of the welfare state.
2. See Roberts and Bullen (1984: 112–18); Palmer (1992: 268 ff.).
3. In their essay, "The Rise and Fall of the Golden Age," Glyn et al. provide data on productivity growth and capital investment during the postwar period in the advanced capitalist world (Glyn, Hughes, Lipietz and Singh, 1990). Readers interested in the profit rates between 1947 to 1991 in Canada should consult Smith and Taylor (1996).
4. The author has first-hand experience in the mandatory Employment Insurance jobs training program. See also Sears' (2003) very insightful analysis of the kind of skills employers are actually seeking from workers today.
5. Under state capitalism (the former U.S.S.R. and Peoples Republic of China), the state maintained control of civil society by monopolizing its representation under the guise of an identity of interests — the state and party purportedly representing the interests of the workers. All the organizations and associations of civil society, then, were state or party controlled, denying the existence of civil society as distinct from the state. Terrorism in the U.S.S.R. and the PRC was employed to prevent a reality for civil society separate from the state, to maintain a monopoly of power for the state and ruling party, thereby maintaining the illusion of socialism, which was really socialized capital centrally control-

led. They comprised forms of state capitalism premised on state ownership of the main means of production; the state and party controlled capital, and the workers continued as workers. The principal contradiction remained between labour and capital, although here the state as capitalist. Legitimacy was based on the provision of social reforms and the pretence of democracy — both camouflaging a *de facto* class divide. This illusion of socialism, with the state as capitalist parading as representative of labour and workers without control of their own destiny could only be held together in the end as a police state, marked by pervasive terror.

6. None of this is to say that the U.S.S.R. and China should not be criticized for their repressive regimes that passed for socialism and the terror employed to maintain them. If socialism implies the subordination of the state to society, then these regimes are more appropriately seen as state capitalist. They did, however, represent significant social advancement for tens of millions of people. They never had the resources to spend on the military that the West did, and they never had the hundreds of military bases with tens of thousands of active military personnel around the world. For the West, the real danger they represented was two-fold. Their economic model as socialized and not private corporate capital was a threat but not nearly as much if it had been a genuinely worker-run economy; that is, state capitalism still left all the fundamental capitalist relations intact. The other main issue was the exclusion of their populations and resources from the global markets.

7. The anti-communism of the West met with an unwitting "confirmation" from the socialist states themselves. Among other issues, revelations about the crimes of Stalin in the mid-1950s, Russian troops in Hungary in 1956 and Czechoslovakia in 1968, the excesses of the "cultural revolution" in China roughly between 1966 and 1976, and the tyranny in North Korea were significant blows to the credibility of the idea of socialism, compounded by China's turn to capitalism in the 1970s and the collapse of the Soviet Bloc in the late 1980s. That "actually existing socialism" proved not to be genuine socialism does not negate the hope that the working classes saw in it as freedom from the insecurity and unfreedom of the market, from a system that did not embody their interests.

Chapter 13

1. This chapter is based on ethnographic research including interviews with the Gilmour Street squatters, Ottawa-based lawyers, participant observation, and an analysis of court transcripts. The research was completed for my M.A. thesis, L. Freeman, 2005, "The Legal Geography of Urban Squatting: The Case of Ottawa's Gilmour Street Squatters," Carleton University. My personal experience with the Gilmour Street squat case informs this chapter — being arrested at the squat, defending myself and representing others at administrative trials, conducting community service instead of being prosecuted through a trial, supporting the squatters during their trial, and writing magazine articles about the squat, as well as casual correspondence with other Canadian squatters and anti-poverty activists.

2. See P. Conradi, 2004, "Tenants from Hell with the Law on their Side," (London) Sunday Times, April 18; Katsiaficas 1997.

3. R. v. Clarke (O.J. No. 5259 1998). Montreal's Overdale squat began with a march

of 500 people, Toronto's Pope squat was led by a march of 1,000 anti-poverty demonstrators, and Ottawa's Gilmour Street squat was part of an anti-Group of Eight rally of approximately 3,500 demonstrators. On the G-8 see note 9 below.

4. Vancouver's Woodward's squat and Toronto's Pope squat both lasted approximately three months, whereas Ottawa's Gilmour Street squat and Peterborough's Water Street squat lasted a week. Many other squats have lasted mere hours. Toronto's most recent squat (June 2007), conducted by members of the Women Against Poverty Collective, was evicted approximately six hours after it was publicly acknowledged.

5. R. v. Ackerley et al. (Ottawa Sup. CT.J. Crim-div October 21, 2004)

6. The Group of Eight (G-8) is a political forum where government leaders gather to discuss global economic issues. G-8 member countries are Canada, France, Germany, Italy, Japan, Russia, the United Kingdom, and the United States. For more information on the G-8, refer to the Halifax Initiatives report: "The G8, Globalization and Human Security: A Resource Package and Facilitator's Guide," Halifax Initiative, available at <halifaxinitiative.org>. For articles critical of the G-8 refer to S. Hodkinson, 2005, "Inside the Murky World of the UK's Make Poverty History Campaign," Znet, available at <zmag.org/content/showarticle.cfm?ItemID=8181>; M. Jarman, 2005, "G8 Climate," Znet, available at <zmag.org/content/showarticle.cfm?ItemID=8188>; G. Monbiot, 2005, "The Man Who Betrayed the Poor," Znet, available at <zmag.org/content/showarticle.cfm?ItemID=8685>.

7. Dan Sawyer, interviewed by author, December 14, 2004.

8. Mandy Hiscocks, interviewed by author, tape recording, December 2, 2004.

9. R. v. Ackerley et al. (October 21, 2004).

10. R. v. Ackerley et al. (October 21, 2004), Official Disclosure of Evidence (2002).

11. Law student and Peterborough Coalition Against Poverty activist Nitti Simmonds informed me that in her experience working with anti-poverty groups across Ontario, non-association clauses and bans on political activity are common bail conditions when activists affiliated with anti-poverty groups are arrested. Bail conditions are seldom recorded in the media, thus records of activist bail conditions are informally acknowledged within activist networks. Nitti Simmonds, telephone interview by author, February 2007.

12. R. v. Ackerley et al. (October 21, 2004), Official Disclosure of Evidence (2002).

13. R. v. Ackerley et al. (October 21, 2004).

14. Field notes, observed by author, September 28–October 12, 2004.

15. R. v. Ackerley et al. (October 21, 2004).

16. R. v. Ackerley et al. (October 21, 2004).

17. R. v. Ackerley et al. (October 21, 2004).

18. R. v. Ackerley et al. (October 21, 2004).

19. Rachelle Sauvé, interviewed by author, tape recording, December 2, 2004. In his charge to the Jury, J. McKinnon described colour of right as "a honest belief in a state of facts which, if it existed, would be a lawful justification or excuse for a person's conduct." According to J. McKinnon, the defence of necessity "recognizes that a liberal and humane criminal law cannot require strict obedience to laws in genuine emergencies where normal human instincts, whether of self-preservation or helping others, overwhelmingly inspired disobedience" and

"is only available to those whose wrongful acts are committed under pressure which no reasonable person could withstand." R. v. Ackerley et al. (October 21, 2004). For more information on colour of right see: R. v. Howson (1966). On the defence of necessity see R. v. Latimer (1 S.C.R. 3, 193 D.L.R. (4th) 577, 2001 SCC1 [2001].

20. R. v. Ackerley et al. (October 21, 2004).

21. Field notes, September 28–October 12, 2004.

22. Hiscocks interview, December 2, 2004.

23. Field notes, September 28–October 12, 2004.

24. Yavar Hameed, interviewed by author, tape recording, January 7, 2005.

25. Information on the increase of self-represented accused in Ottawa's criminal court is based on casual observations with legal actors and defendants conducted during research from September 28–October 12, 2004.

26. Hiscocks interview, December 2, 2004.

27. R. v. Ackerley et al. (October 21, 2004).

28. R. v. Ackerley et al. (October 21, 2004).

29. According to self-represented accused Dan Sawyer, there was not any case law used for this decision. The squat defendants were asking for money for disbursements (photocopies, etc.) and were not asking to be paid for their labour. A legal aid lawyer attended court and (with the squatters present) the presiding judge asked if Legal Aid Ontario would be comfortable with allocating money to the accused. The legal aid lawyer answered in the affirmative and the crown representative disbursed the funds to the squatters many months after the trial. This decision, according to Sawyer, may be the only case law where self-represented accused were allocated money to mount a defence. Sawyer interview, December 14, 2004.

30. Discussions and announcements were posted on activist list-serves and web-based news sources: A-Infos: Anarchist News Service <www.ainfos.ca>; Thunder Bay Indy Media <http://thunderbay.indymedia.org/>; "Montreal Activist Arrest and Trial Calendar (2000–2005)" <http://www.ainfos.ca/05/jan/ainfos00363. html>, <www.cmaq.net>, and <www.infoshop.org>. Information about the trial was also disseminated through informal publications such as Mandy Hiscocks, "Stunning Legal Victory for Ottawa Squatters," Critical Times 2, 3 (CUPE 3903, York University Faculty Association, CUPE 1281 Grad Students Association, 2004); Mandy Hiscocks and Amy Miller, "In the Streets and in the Courts: How the Seven-Year Squat Fought and Won," The Rabble-Rouser's Guide to Surviving Law School: A Disorientation Handbook McGill Radical Law Committee (McGill Radical Law Community, 2006).

31. Dan Sawyer interview, December 14, 2004.

32. Dan Sawyer interview, December 14, 2004.

33. Hiscocks interview, December 2, 2004.

References

Adler, F. 1975. *Sisters in Crime: The Rise of the New Female Criminal*. New York: McGraw Hill.

Agamben, G. 2000. *Means without End: Notes on Politics*. Minneapolis: University of Minnesota Press.

Ahmed, N.M. 2002. *The War on Freedom*. Joshua Tree: Tree of Life Publications.

___. 2005 *The War on Truth: 9/11, Disinformation, and the Anatomy of Terrorism*. Northampton, MA: Olive Branch Press.

___. 2007. *The London Bombings, An Independent Inquiry*. London: Duckworth.

Allen, T.W. 1994. *The Invention of the White Race, Volume One: Racial Oppression and Social Control* and *Volume Two: The Origins of Racial Oppression in Anglo-America*. London: Verso.

Alleyne, J., I. Papadopoulos and M. Tilki. 1994. "Anti-Racism within Transcultural Nurse Education." *British Journal of Nursing* 3(15).

Alvi, S. 2000. *Youth and Canadian Criminal Justice System*. Cincinnati: Anderson.

Amnesty International. 2004. *Stolen Sisters: A Human Rights Response to Discrimination and Violence Against Indigenous Women in Canada*. Toronto: Amnesty International.

Anderson, A.B. 2005. "Socio-Demographic Study of Aboriginal Population." In J. Anderson, 2000. "Gender, Race, Poverty, Health and Discourses of Health Reform in the Context of Globalization: A Post-Colonial Feminist Perspective in Policy Research." *Nursing Inquiry* 7(4).

Andrews, C. 1995. *Profit Fever*. Monroe: Common Courage Press.

Armstrong, J. 2002a. "The Short Tragic Life of Sereena." *Globe and Mail* February 27.

___. 2002b. "Inquiry into Handling of Disappearances Urged." *Globe and Mail* February 11.

Arsenault, C. 2003. "From Street to Squat in Halifax." *Canadian Dimension* 37,1

Artz, S. 1998. *Sex, Power and the Violent School Girl*. Toronto: Trifolium.

Assembly of First Nations. 2007. *First Nations Regional Longitudinal Health Survey*. Ottawa.

Associated Press/CBS News. 2007. "Tattoos Lose Their Cool: Want a Blasting Berry Tattoo with That Fruit Roll-Up?" December 4. <cbsnews.com/stories/2007/12/04/entertainment/main3573970.shtml>.

Atkinson, M. 2002. "Pretty in Ink: Conformity, Resistance, and Negotiation in Women's Tattooing." *Sex Roles* 47.

Avert. 2008. "Wolrdwide HIV and AIDS Statistics." <avert.org/worldstats.htm>.

Babad, M. 2011. "Steve Jobs' Salary Is just $1, but his Apple Stock Is Soaring." *Globe and Mail* January 7 <theglobeandmail.com/report-on-business/top-business-stories/steve-jobs-salary-is-just-1-but-his-apple-stock-is-soaring/article1861380/>.

Bauman, Z. 1989. *Modernity and the Holocaust*. Ithaca, NY: Cornell University Press

BBC News. 1999. "Health: Six Diseases Threaten the World." June 18. <news.bbc.co.uk/2/hi/health/371522.stm>.

___. 2004 "Iraq Death Toll 'Soared Post-war." October 29. < news.bbc.co.uk/go/pr/fr/-/2/hi/middle_east/3962969.stm>.

___. 2006. "Iraqi Civilian Deaths Shrouded in Secrecy." March 22. <news.bbc.co.uk/2/hi/middle_east/4830782.stm>.

Begley, S. 1996. "Three Is Not Enough: Surprising New Lessons from the Controversial Science of Race." *Newsweek* 13.

Beirne, P., and J. Messerchmidt. 2006. *Criminology*. Los Angeles: Roxbury.

Bell, S.J. 1999. *Young Offenders and Juvenile Justice*. Toronto: Nelson.

Bernard, W. 2002. "Including Black Women in Health and Social Policy Development: Winning over Addictions." In C. Amaratunga (ed.), *Race, Ethnicity and Women's Health*. Halifax, NS: Halcraft Printers.

Bertrand, M.A. 1969. "Self-Image and Delinquency: A Contribution to the Study of Female Criminality and Woman's Image." *Acta Criminologica* 2.

Birch, H. (ed.). 1993. *Moving Targets: Women, Murder and Representation*. London: Virago.

Blackstock, N. 1975. *COINTELPRO: The FBI's Secret War on Political Freedom*. New York: Vintage.

Blackwell, T. 1995a. "Jury Faces Question of Homolka's Role: Was She a Battered, Blackmailed Handmaiden to a Driven Murder or a Willing Participant in Killing?" *Vancouver Sun*, June 17.

Blum, Wm. 1998. *Killing Hope, U.S. Military and CIA Interventions Since World War II*. Montreal: Black Rose Books.

___. 2000. *Rogue State*. Munroe: Common Courage Press.

Bonefield, W. 1993. *The Recomposition of the British State During the 1980s*. Dartmouth, UK: Aldershot

Boritch, H. 1997. *Fallen Women: Female Crime and Criminal Justice in Canada*. Scarborough, ON: ITP Nelson.

Brady, R.A. 1937. *The Spirit and Structure of German Fascism*. London: Victor Gollancz.

Brancati, F.L., L. Kao, A.R. Folsom, R.L. Watson and M. Szklo. 2000. "Incident Type 2 Diabetes Mellitus in African American and White Adults: The Atherosclerosis Risk in Community Study." *Journal of the American Medical Association* 283(17).

Braunberger, C. 2000. "Revolting Bodies: The Monster Beauty of Tattooed Women." *NWSA Journal* 12, 2.

Breen, N., M. Wesley, R. Merril and K. Johnson. 2004. "The Relationship of Socioeconomic Status and Access to Minimum Expected Therapy among Female Breast Cancer Patients in the Black-White Cancer Survival Study." *Ethnicity and Disease* 9.

Brohm, J.M. 1978. *Sport: A Prison of Measured Time*. London: Pluto Press.

Brondolo, E., and E. Love, M. Pencille, A. Schoenthaler and G. Ogedegbe. 2011. "Racism and Hypertension: A Review of the Empirical Evidence and Implications for Clinical Practice." *American Journal of Hypertension* 24 (May): 518–29.

Brown, B. 1995. "Homolka Says She Watched Killing of 2 Girls in Bedroom: 'Paul Strangled Them with a Black Electrical Cord,' Ex-Wife Tells Court." *Vancouver Sun*, June 20.

Brown, C. (ed.). 2003. *Lost Liberties, Ashcroft and the Assault on Personal Freedom*. New York: The New Press.

Burke, M., and J. Shields. 2000. "Tracking Inequality in the New Canadian Labour Market." In M. Burke and C. Moores and J. Shields (eds), *Restructing and Resistance: Canadian Public Policy in an Age of Global Capitalism*. Halifax: Fernwood.

Cameron, S. 2007. *The Pickton File*. Toronto: A.A. Knopf Canada.

Campaign Against Sanctions on Iraq. 1999. "Starving Iraq: One Humanitarian Disaster We Can Stop." March.

Canada. 1996. "Office of the Correctional Investigator Backgrounder: Aboriginal Inmates: The Numbers Reveal a Critical Situation." Ottawa: The Correctional

Investigator Canada.

Canadian Press. 2000. "Teen Girl Begins Life [sic] Sentence for Killing Reena Virk." March 31.

Canadian Press Newswire. 2001. "Community Alliances Ready to Renovate Pope Squat." November 11.

Caplan, J. 2000. "Introduction." In J. Caplan (ed.), *Written on the Body: The Tattoo in European and American History*. London, UK: Reaktion Books.

CCJS (Canadian Centre for Justice Statistics). 1999. *Canadian Crime Statistics: Annual Catalogue*. Ottawa: Statistics Canada.

Chang, N. 2002. *Silencing Political Dissent*. New York: Seven Stories.

Chavez, L., and D. Gray. 2004. *Betrayal: How Union Bosses Shake Down Their Members and Corrupt American Politics*. New York: Crown Forum.

Chesney-Lind M. 1997. *The Female Offender: Girls, Women and Crime*. Thousand Oaks, CA: Sage.

___. 1999. "Review: P. Pearson, When She Was Bad." *Women and Criminal Justice* 10 (4): 113–18.

Chester, E.T. 1985. *Cover Network*. Armonk: M.E. Sharpe.

Chomsky, N. 1992. *Deterring Democracy*. New York: Hill and Wang.

Chomsky, N., and E.S. Herman. 1988. *Manufacturing Consent: The Political Economy of the Mass Media*. New York: Pantheon.

Church Council on Justice and Corrections. 2011. "Prison Facts: The Costs — A Letter to the Prime Minister." January 21. <ccjc.ca/2011/01/12/prison-facts-the-costs/>.

Clark, W. 1989. "Residential Segregation in American Cities: Common Ground to Differences of Interpretation." *Population Research and Policy Review* 8.

Clinard, M., and P. Yeager. 1980. *Corporate Crime*. New York: Free Press.

Cole, D., and J. Dempsey. 2002. *Terrorism and the Constitution: Sacrificing Civil Liberties in the Name of National Security*. New York: The New Press.

Connell, I. 1980. "Television News and the Social Contract." In Stuart Hall, Dorothy Hobson, Andrew Lowe and Paul Willis (eds.), *Culture, Media, Language*. London, UK: Hutchinson Press and the Centre for Contemporary Cultural Studies, University of Birmingham.

Corn, D. 2003. *The Lies of George Bush*. New York: Crown Publishing.

Cox, J. 1981. *Overkill*. Harmondsworth: Penguin.

Curtis, K.M. 2008. "The Fatality Inquiries Act." Report by Provincial Judge on Inquest Respecting the Death of Matthew Adam Joseph Dumas. Winnipeg: The Provincial Court of Manitoba. <manitobacourts.mb.ca/pdf/dumas_inquest_report.pdf> December 9.

Davis, J.K. 1997. *Assault on the Left*. Westport: Praeger.

Davis, M. 2001. *Late Victorian Holocausts: El Nino Farmers and the Making of the Third World*. London: Verso.

DeKeseredy, W.S. 2000. *Women, Crime and the Canadian Criminal Justice System*. Cincinnati: Anderson.

DeKeseredy, W.S., D.G. Saunders, M.D. Schwartz, and S. Alvi. 1997. "The Meanings and Motives for Women's Use of Violence in Canadian College Dating Relationships: Results from a National Survey." *Sociological Spectrum* 17.

DeMello, M. 1995. "Not Just For Bikers Anymore: Popular Representations of American Tattooing." *Journal of Popular Culture* 29, 3.

Doyal, L. 1979 *The Political Economy of Health*. Boston: South End Press.

Drevdahl, D.J., M.K. Canales, and K.S. Dorcy. 2008. "Of Goldfish Tanks and Moonlight Tricks: Can Cultural Competence Ameliorate Health Disparities?" *Advances in Nursing Science* 51(1).

Earle, C., L. Venditti, P. Neuman, R. Gelber, M. Weinstein, A. Potosky et al. 2000. "Who Gets Chemotherapy for Metastatic Lung Cancer?" *Chest* 117.

Ehrenreich, B., and D. English. 1973. *Witches, Midwives, and Nurses: A History of Women Healers*. Old Westbury: Feminist Press.

Elkins, C. 2005. *Imperial Reckoning: The Untold Story of Britain's Gulag in Kenya*. New York: Holt.

Enang [Etowa], J.E. 1999. "Childbirth Experiences of African Nova Scotian Women." Master of Nursing thesis, Dalhousie University, Halifax, NS.

___. 2002. "Black Women's Health: Health Research Relevant to Black Nova Scotians." In C. Amaratunga (ed.), *Race, Ethnicity and Women's Health*. Halifax, NS: Halcraft Printers.

Enders, W., and T. Sandler. 2002. "Patterns of Transnational Terrorism, 1970–1999: Alternative Time-Series. Estimates." *International Studies Quarterly* 46.

Ericson, R.V., P.M. Baranek, and J.B.L. Chan. 1991. *Representing Order: Crime, Law, and Justice in the News Media*. Toronto: University of Toronto Press.

Essed, P. 1991. *Understanding Everyday Racism: An Interdisciplinary Theory*. Newbury Park, CA: Sage Publications.

Etowa, J. 2005. "Fostering Diversity in the Nursing Workforce: The Worklife Experiences of African Canadian Nurses." International Council of Nurses (ICN) 23rd Quadrennial Congress. Taipei, Taiwan.

Etowa, J., B. Keddy, J. Egbeyemi and F. Eghan. 2007. "Depression: The 'Invisible Grey Fog': Influencing the Mental Health of African Canadian Women." *International Journal of Mental Health Nursing* 16.

Etowa, J., J. Weins, W.T. Bernard and B. Clow. 2007. "Determinants of Black Women's Health in Rural and Remote Communities." *Canadian Journal of Nursing Research* 39(3).

Faith, K. 1993a. *Unruly Women: The Politics of Confinement and Resistance*. Vancouver: Press Gang Publishers.

___. 1993b. "Media, Myths and Masculinization: Images of Women in Prison." In E. Adelberg and C. Currie (eds.), *In Conflict with the Law: Women in the Canadian Justice System*. Vancouver: Press Gang.

Fann, K.T., and D.C. Hodges (eds.). 1971. *Readings in U.S. Imperialism*. Boston: Porter Sargent.

Fitch, R. 2006. *Solidarity for Sale: How Corruption Destroyed the Labor Movement*. New York: Public Affairs.

Forbes. 2009. "NBA Team Valuations." December 9 <http://www.forbes.com/lists/2009/32/basketball-values-09_nba-Team-Valuations_Rank.html>.

___. 2011. "The NBA's Most Valuable Teams." January 26 <http://www.forbes.com/lists/2011/32/basketball-valuations-11_land.html>.

Fraser, N. "Jersey Jetsam." 2010. <http://www.newyorker.com/arts/critics/television/2010/01/18/100118crte_television_franklin?current page=all>.

Gabriel, C. 2001. "Restructuring at the Margins: Women of Colour and the Changing Economy." In E. Dua and A. Robertson (eds.), *Scratching the Surface: Canadian Anti-Racist Feminist Thought*. Toronto: Women's Press.

Galabuzi, G. 2006. *Canada's Economic Apartheid: The Social Exclusion of Racialized Groups in the New Century*. Toronto: Canadian Scholars Press.

Galloway, G. 1995. "Bernardo Jury Stoic as 'Disturbing' Videotape of Rape Played." *Vancouver Sun*, June 1

Galnoor, I. (ed.). 1977. *Government Secrecy in Democracies*. New York: Harper and Row.

Gannon, M. 2005. *General Social Survey on Victimization, Cycle 18: An Overview of Findings*. Ottawa: Statistics Canada.

Garrett, S.A. 2004. "Terror Bombing of German Cities in World War II." In I. Primoratz (ed.), *Terrorism: The Philosophical Issues*. London: Palgrave/Macmillan.

Gelbspan, R. 1991. *Break-ins, Death Threats and the FBI*. Boston: South End Press.

George, A. (ed.). 1991. *Western State Terrorism*. Oxford: Polity Press.

Gimson, M. 1980. "Everybody's Doing It." In N. Wates and C. Wolmar (eds.), *Squatting: The Real Story*. London: Bay Leaf Books.

Girard, D. 2002a. "All We Can Do Is Keep Waiting." *Toronto Star*, February 9.

___. 2002b. "Despair Stalks Hookers on Mean Streets." *Toronto Star*, February 10.

___. 2002c. "The Little Sister Behind the Statistic." *Toronto Star*, February 15.

___. 2002d. "Police Slow to Accept Crime Link." *Toronto Star*, February 8.

___. 2002e. "Relatives of Missing Demand Inquiry." *Toronto Star*, February 12.

Giroux, H.A. 2004. *The Terror of Neoliberalism*. Aurora: Garamond.

Glasbeek, Harry. 2002. *Wealth by Stealth: Corporate Crime, Corporate Law and the Perversion of Democracy*. Toronto: Between the Lines.

Glaze, W.D., K.N. Anderson and L.E. Anderson (eds.). 1994. *Mosby's Medical, Nursing and Allied Health Dictionary*. St. Louis, MO: Mosby, Inc.

Globe and Mail. 2002. "Asking How 50 Could Just Disappear." February 27.

___. 2011. "'Stop Harper' Placard Gets Senate Page Turfed from Throne Speech." June 3. <http://www.theglobeandmail.com/news/politics/ottawa-notebook/stop-harper-placard-gets-senate-page-turfed-from-throne-speech/article620231/>.

___. 2011. "Emergency Law Celebrity Support Giving Oxygen to Quebec Protestors." May 20. <http://www.theglobeandmail.com/news/national/emergency-law-celebrity-support-giving-oxygen-to-quebec-protesters/article4198126/>.

___. 2011. "Polls Reveal Age of Pessimism." May 31. <http://www.theglobeandmail.com/news/politics/ottawa-notebook/poll-reveals-an-age-of-pessimism/article4219798/>.

Glueck, Sheldon, and Eleanor Glueck. 1965 [1934]. *Five Hundred Delinquent Women*. New York: Kraus Reprint.

Goff, C. 2011. *Criminal Justice in Canada*. Fifth edition. Toronto: Nelson.

___. 1999. *Corrections in Canada*. Cincinnati: Anderson.

Goldstein, R.J. 1978. *Political Repression in Modern America*. New York: Schenkman.

Gomme, Ian. 2007. *The Shadow Line: Deviance and Crime in Canada*. Toronto: Thomson-Nelson.

Gordon, J. 2002. "Cool War: Economic Sanctions as a Weapon of Mass Destruction." *Harper's Magazine* November.

Gordon, J., K. Faith, and D. Currie. 1995. "The Case of Karla Homolka: Crime, Media and Gender Politics." Unpublished data, President's Research Grant, School of Criminology, Simon Fraser University.

Gordon, R., and I. Coneybeer. 1995. "Corporate Crime." In M. Jackson and C. Griffiths (eds.), *Canadian Criminology*. Toronto: Harcourt Brace.

Govenar, A. 2000. "The Changing Image of Tattooing in American Culture, 1846–1966." In J. Caplan (ed.), *Written on the Body: The Tattoo in European and American History*. London, UK: Reaktion Books.

Green, C.R., K.O. Anderson, T.A. Baker, L.C. Campbell, S. Decker, R. Fillingim et al. 2003. "The Unequal Burden of Pain: Confronting Racial and Ethnic Disparities in Pain." *Pain Medicine* 4(3).

Griffin, D.R. 2004. *The New Pearl Harbor: Disturbing Questions about the Bush Administration and 9/11*. Norhampton, MA: Olive Branch Press.

Griffith, B., S. Iliffe, and G. Rayner. 1987. *Banking on Sickness*. London: Lawrence and Wishart.

Guardian. 2005. "One Huge US Jail." March 19.

Guerin, D. 1973. *Fascism and Big Business*. New York: Pathfinder.

Hackett, R.A., and W.K. Carroll. 2006. *Remaking Media: The Struggle to Democratize Public Communication*. New York: Routledge.

Hagan, J. 1992. "White Collar and Corporate Crime." In R. Linden (ed.), *Criminology: A Canadian Perspective*. Second edition. Toronto: Harcourt Brace.

Hagan, J., and R. Linden. 2009. "Corporate and White Collar Crime." In R. Linden (ed.), *Criminology: A Canadian Perspective*. Sixth edition. Toronto: Nelson

Hall, S., C. Critcher, T. Jefferson, J. Clarke, and B. Roberts. 1978. *Policing the Crisis: Mugging, the State, and Law and Order*. London: Macmillan.

___. 1990. "The Whites of Their Eyes." In M. Alvarado and J.O. Thompson (eds.), *The Media Reader*. London: British Film Institute.

Hartley, John. 1982. *Understanding News*. London & New York: Methuen.

Hawkes, D., C.Y. Senn, and C. Thorn. 2004. "Factors That Influence Attitudes Toward Women with Tattoos." *Sex Roles* 50.

Hayman, S. 2000. "Prison Reform and Incorporation." In K. Hannah-Moffat and M. Shaw (eds.), *An Ideal Prison? Critical Essays on Women's Imprisonment in Canada*. Halifax: Fernwood Publishing.

Hayter, T. 1971. *Aid as Imperialism*. Harmondsworth: Penguin Books.

Heidensohn, F. 1968. "The Deviance of Women: A Critique and an Enquiry." *British Journal of Sociology* 19 (2).

Henry, Frances, and Carol Tater. 2002. *Discourses of Domination: Racial Bias in the Canadian English Language Press*. Toronto: University of Toronto Press.

Henry, F., C. Tater, W. Mattis and T. Rees. 2000. *The Color of Democracy: Racism in Canadian Society*. Toronto: Harcourt Canada.

Herman, E.S. 2004. "The War of Terrorism." *Znet Commentary* 11, September.

Hochschild, A. 1999. *King Leopold's Ghost*. London: Pan Macmillan.

Hoffer, E. 1951. *The True Believer: Thoughts on the Nature of Mass Movements*. New York: Harper Collins.

Hoffman, H., and Klabunde. 2003. "Racial Differences in Initial Treatment for Clinically Localized Prostate Cancer." *Medscape News* 11(11). At <http://www.medscape.com/viewarticle/462914>.

hooks, b. 1992. *Black Looks: Race and Representation*. Cambridge, MA: South End Press.

hooks, b. 2004. *Where We Stand: Class Matters*. New York: Routledge.

Horii, G. 2000. "Processing Humans." In K. Hannah-Moffat and M. Shaw (eds.), *An Ideal Prison? Critical Essays on Women's Imprisonment in Canada*. Halifax: Fernwood Publishing.

Houston, M., and J.T. Wood. 1996. "Difficult Dialogues, Expanded Horizons:

Communicating across Race and Class." In J.T. Wood (ed.), *Gendered Relationships*. Mountainview, CA: Mayfield Publishing.

Hume, M., and I. Bailey. 2002. "Police Told About Farm Many Times." *National Post* February 9.

Ignatieff, M. 2004. *The Lesser Evil: Political Ethics in an Age of Terror.* Toronto: Penguin.

Ivens, A. 2000. "No Apology by Killer, She got the Lightest Sentence Possible: Five Years without Parole." *Vancouver Province*, April 21.

Jacobs, J.B. 2006. *Mobsters, Unions, and Feds: The Mafia and the American Labor Movement.* New York: New York University Press.

Jersey Shore Quotes. June 2012. <http://www.jerseyshorequotes.com/best-quotes-from-jersey-shore.htm>

Jiwani, Y. 1993. "By Omission and Commission: 'Race' and Representation in Canadian Television News." Unpublished doctoral dissertation, School of Communications, Simon Fraser University.

___. 1999. "Erasing Race: The Story of Reena Virk." *Canadian Woman Studies* 19 (3).

Jiwani, Y., and M.L.Young. 2006. "Missing and Murdered Women: Reproducing Marginality in News Discourse." *Canadian Journal of Communication* 31: 895–917.

Joe, K., and M. Chesney-Lind. 1993. "Just Every Mother's Angel." Paper presented at meetings of the American Society of Criminology. Phoenix, Arizona, October.

Johnson, L.K. 1989. *America's Secret Power: The CIA in a Democratic Society.* New York: Oxford University Press.

Johnstone, M.J., and O. Kanitsaki. 2010. "The Neglect of Racism as an Ethical Issue in Health Care." *Journal of Immigrant and Minority Health* 12(4).

Katsiaficas, G. 1997. *The Subversion of Politics: European Autonomous Social Movements and the Decolonization of Everyday Life.* New Jersey: Humanities Press.

Kauffman, J.S., and R.S. Cooper. 1996. "Descriptive Studies of Racial Differences in Disease: In Search of the Hypothesis." *Public Health Reports* 110.

Keck, J. 2002 "Remembering Kimberly Roger." *Perception* 25, 314.

Kendall, K. 1999. "Beyond Grace: Criminal Lunatic Women in Victorian Canada." *Canadian Woman Studies* 19 (1&2).

Kershaw, A., and M. Lasovitch. 1991. *Rock-a-Bye-Baby: A Death Behind Bars.* Toronto: McClelland and Stewart.

Kim, J., K.T. Ashing-Giwa, M. Kagawa-Singer and J.S. Tejero. 2006. "Breast Cancer Among Asian Americans: Is Acculturation Related to Health-Related Quality of Life?" *Oncology Nursing Forum* 33(6).

Kines, L. 1998a. "Police Target Big Increase in Missing Women." *Vancouver Sun*, July 3.

___. 1998b. "Cases Probed: Vancouver Police Will Review 40 Unsolved Cases Dating from 1971, but They Doubt a Serial Killer Was Involved." *Vancouver Sun*, September 18.

Kines, L., and L. Culbert. 1999. "3 Officers Join Hunt for Missing Women." *Vancouver Sun*, July 14.

King, W.R., and T.M. Dunn. 2004. "Dumping: Police-initiated Transjurisdictional Transport of Troublesome Persons." *Police Quarterly* 7 (3).

Klaits, J. 1985. *Servants of Satan: The Age of the Witch Hunts.* Bloomington: Indiana University Press.

Klein, D. 1973. "The Etiology of Female Crime: A Review of the Literature." *Issues in Criminology* 8 (2).

Koshul, B.B. 2005. *The Postmodern Significance of Max Weber's Legacy: Disenchanting*

Disenchantment. London: Palgrave Macmillan

Kreiger, N. 2003. "Does Racism Harm Health? Did Child Abuse Exist before 1962? On Explicit Questions, Critical Science, and Current Controversies: An Ecosocial Perspective." *American Journal of Public Health* 93(2).

Krieger, N., D.L. Rowley, A.A. Herman, B. Avery and M.T. Phillips. 1993. "Racism, Sexism, and Social Class: Implications for Studies of Health, Disease, and Well-being." *American Journal of Preventive Medicine* 9(6).

Krueger, A.B., and D.D. Laitin. 2004. "'Misunderestimating' Terrorism, The State Department's Big Mistake." *Foreign Affairs* September/October.

LA Times. 2007. "Poll: Civilian Toll in Iraq May Top 1m." September 14.

Lackey, D. 2004. "The Evolution of the Modern Terrorist State: Area Bombing and Nuclear Deterrence." In I. Primoratz (ed.), *Terrorism: The Philosophical Issues*. London: Palgrave Macmillan.

Lamble, S. L. Freeman. 2004. "No Room for Squatters Except in the Big House." *Briarpatch Magazine* October: 19–21.

Laqueur, W. 1986. "Reflections on Terrorism." *Foreign Affairs* Fall.

Legall, P. 1995a. "Graphic Dialogue Sends Eerie Chill through Court: 200 Spectators Hear 6 Minutes of Drug-Induced Rape of Homolka Sister." *Vancouver Sun*, June 1.

Levitz, S. 2007. "Lessons from Tragedy: How Vancouver's Missing Women Changed Police." Canadian Press, January 7. <http://www.missingpeople.net/lessons_from_tragedy.htm>.

Lifton, R,J., and R. Falk. 1982. *Indefensible Weapons*. Toronto: CBC

Logan, S.M.L., E.M. Freeman and R.G. McRoy (eds.). 1990. *Social Work Practice with Black Families: A Culturally Specific Perspective*. NY: Longman.

Lombroso, C., and W. Ferrero. 1895. *The Female Offender*. New York: Philosophical Library.

MacAfee, M. 2001. "Seven People Arrested as Montreal Police Evict About 30 Squatters." Canadian Press Newswire, October 3.

MacFarlane, A. 1970. *Witchcraft in Tudor and Stuart England: A Regional and Comparative Study*. New York: Harper and Row.

Mackenzie, A. 1997. *Secrets: The CIA's War at Home*. Berkeley: University of California Press.

Magdoff, H. 1969. *The Age of Imperialism*. New York: Monthly Review.

Makin, K. 1995a. "Homolka Chose Kristen for Abduction, Lawyer Says: Bernardo's Ex-Wife Keeps up Verbal Battle with Defence over Her Role in Girl's Death, Tells Court Her Level of Intelligence Is 'Very Debatable.'" *Globe and Mail*, July 13.

Maliski, S.L., S. Connor, A. Fink and M.S. Litwin. 2006. "Information Desired and Acquired by Men with Prostate Cancer: Data from Ethnic Focus Groups." *Health Education & Behavior* 33(3).

Marrs, J. 2004. *Inside Job, Unmasking the 9/11 Conspiracies*. San Rafael: Origin Press.

Marwick, M. (ed.). 1975. *Witchcraft and Sorcery*. Harmondsworth, Middlesex: Penguin.

Marx, K., and F. Engels. *The Communist Manifesto*. Halifax: Fernwood Publishing.

Matas, R. 2002. "B.C. Police Lashed over Probe; Response by Police under Fire." *Globe and Mail*, February 9.

McCamant, J.F. 1984. "Governance Without Blood: Social Science's Antiseptic View of Rule; or, The Neglect of Political Repression." In M. Stohl and G.A. Lopez (eds.), *The State as Terrorist*. Westport: Greenwood Press.

McCormick, C. 1995. *Constructing Danger: The Mis/Representation of Crime in the News*.

Halifax: Fernwood Publishing.

McGibbon, E., P. Didham, D. Smith, M. Malaudzi, A. Sochan and S. Barton. 2009. *Decolonization of Nursing Education: A Paradigm Shift for the New Millennium*. Book of abstracts published from the Proceedings of the Canadian Association of Schools of Nursing National Conference, Moncton, NB, May.

McGibbon, E., and J. Etowa. 2009. *Anti-Racist Health Care Practice*. Toronto: Canadian Scholar's Press.

McMartin, P. 2000. "Shock of Virk Trial is Ordinary Appearance of Accused Teen — A Scared Little 17-year-old in Person Comes as a Surprise after Grisly Testimony and a Smug-Looking Photo." *Vancouver Sun*, March 23.

McMullan, J., and S. Smith. 1997. "Toxic Steel: State-Corporate Crime and the Contamination of the Environment." In John McMullan et al, *Crimes, Laws and Communities*. Halifax: Fernwood.

Mead, George Herbert. 1948. *Mind, Self and Society: From the Standpoint of a Social Behaviorist*. Seventh edition. John W. Petras (editor). Chicago: University of Chicago Press.

Media Lens. 2007. October 3. Available at <www.medialens.org>.

Merkin, S.S., S. Stevenson and N. Powe. 2002. "Geographic Socioeconomic Status, Race, and Advanced-stage Breast Cancer in New York City." *American Journal of Public Health* 92(1).

Mifflin, M. 2001. *Bodies of Subversion: A Secret History of Women and Tattoo*. New York: Juno Books.

Mikkonen, J., and D. Raphael. 2010. *Social Determinants of Health: The Canadian Facts*. Toronto: York University. <thecanadianfacts.org/>.

Milloy, J. 1999. *A National Crime: The Canadian Government and the Residential School System, 1879 to 1986*. Winnipeg: University of Manitoba Press.

Missing Women Task Force. 2007. "Missing Women: Vancouver, British Columbia, Canada." Missing persons poster. Vancouver: Missing Women Task Force, updated January 25.

Moody, K. 1999. *Workers in a Lean World: Unions in the International Economy*. London: Verso.

Moore, D. 2000a. "Accused Teen Killer Says She Wasn't There when Virk Killed." Canadian Press, March 23.

___. 2000b. "Girls Who Beat Virk Had Long Histories of Violence." Canadian Press, April 1.

Morgan, D. 1996. "Threats to Use Nuclear Weapons: The Sixteen Known Nuclear Crises of the Cold War, 1946–1985." <www.vana.ca/articles/threatsofwar.html>.

Mosher, J. 2002. "The Shrinking of the Public and Private Spaces of the Poor." In J.Mosher and J. Hermer (eds.), *Disorderly People: Law and the Politics of Exclusion in Ontario*. Halifax: Fernwood.

Moynihan, R., and A. Cassels. 2005. *Selling Sickness*. Vancouver: Douglas and McIntyre.

MSNBC. 2007. "Tattoo Ads Turn People into 'Walking Billboards'." November 26. <msnbc.msn.com/id/21979076/ns/business-us_business/t/tattoo-ads-turn-people-walking-billboards/#.Tr7WmPFZQZc>.

National Post. 2002. "Corporate Abuse Crackdown." October 11: 1.

___. 2005. "$1.5 M in AD Fraud, No Jail: Sponsorship Scandals' Coffin Sentenced to Speak on Ethics." September 20: 1.

Nguyenlo, M., M. Ugarte, I. Fuller, G. Haas and R.K. Portenoy. 2005. "Access to Care for Chronic Pain: Racial and Ethnic Differences." *The Journal of Pain* 6(5).

Nutter, J.J. 2000. *The CIA's Black Ops*. Amherst: Prometheus.

Oakley-Girvan, I., L. Kolonel, R. Gallagher, A. Wu, A. Felberg and A. Whittemore. 2003. "Stage at Diagnosis and Survival in a Multiethnic Cohort of Prostate Cancer Patients." *American Journal of Public Health* 93(10).

Oetterman, S. 2000. "On Display: Tattooed Entertainers in America and Germany." In J. Caplan (ed.), *Written on the Body: The Tattoo in European and American History*. London, UK: Reaktion Books.

Olsen, J. 2007. "European Anarchists Join Rioters in Danish Capital." *Globe and Mail*, March 3.

Ontario. 1995. "Report of the Commission on Systemic Racism in the Ontario Criminal Justice System." (Margaret Gittens and David Cole, Co-Chairs). Toronto: Queen's Printer.

Ottawa Citizen. 2002. Police Tactics Bring Quiet End to House Occupation: More Takeovers Likely, Politicians Warn." July 4: B1.

Overholser, G., and K. Hall Jamieson. 2005. *Institutions of American Democracy: The Press*. New York: Oxford University Press.

Panitch, L., and D. Swartz. 1993. *The Assault on Trade Union Freedoms*. Toronto: Garamond Press.

Parenti, M. 1993. *Inventing Reality: The Politics of Mass Media*. New York: St. Martin's Press.

Parrinder, G. 1963. *Witchcraft: European and African*. London: Faber & Faber.

Parry, R. 2006. "George W. Bush Is a Liar." April 14. <consortiumnews. com/2006/041306.html>.

Pate, K. 1999. "Young Women and Violent Offences: Myths and Realities." *Canadian Woman Studies* 19 (1&2).

Payer, C. 1974. *The Debt Trap, The IMF and the Third World*. Harmondsworth: Penguin Books.

Pearson, P. 1998. *When She Was Bad*. Toronto: Vintage.

Peck, J. 2001. *Workfare States*. New York: Guilford.

Periago, M. 2004. "Women Bear Burden of Home Care." Press release, March 8. Pan American Health Organization, World Health Organization. Washington, DC.

Perkins, J. 2004. *Confessions of an Economic Hit Man*. San Francisco: Berrett-Koehler.

Phillips, R. A. 1999. "Mayor: No Reward in Missing Hookers Case." apbnews.com, April 9. <http://www.missingpeople.net/mayor_no_reward-april_9,1999. htm>.

Pitman, B. 2002. "Re-Mediating the Spaces of Reality Television: America's Most Wanted and the Case of Vancouver's Missing Women." *Environment and Planning* 34 (1): 167–84.

Polanyi, K. 1944. *The Great Transformation*. Boston: Beacon Press.

Porteous, T. 2006. "The Al Qaeda Myth." April 12. <tompaine.com/arti-cles/2006/04/12/the_al_qaeda_myth.php>.

Poulantzas, N. 1974 [1970]. *Fascism and Dictatorship: The Third International and the Problem of Fascism*. London: NLB.

Pratt, M. 1991. "Art of the Contact Zone." *Profession* 91: 33–40.

Price, D.H. 2004. *Threatening Anthropology: McCarthyism and the FBI's Surveillance of Activist*

Anthropologists. Durham: Duke University Press.

Prins, G. (ed.). 1983. *Defended to Death*. Harmondsworth: Penguin.

Quan, H., A. Fong, C. De Coster, J. Wang, R. Musto, T.W. Noseworthy and W.A. Ghali. 2006. "Variation in Health Services Utilization Among Ethnic Populations." *Canadian Medical Association Journal* 174(6).

Rampton, S., and J. Stauber. 2003. *Weapons of Mass Deception*. New York: Penguin.

Raphael, D. 2009a. "Social Determinants of Health: An Overview of Key Issues and Themes." In D. Raphael (ed.), *Social Determinants of Health*. Toronto: Canadian Scholars Press.

___. 2004. "Strengthening the Social Determinants of Health: The Toronto Charter for a Healthy Canada." In Dennis Raphael (ed.). *The Social Determinants of Health: Canadian Perspectives*. Toronto: Canadian Scholars Press.

Razack, S. H. 1998. *Looking White People in the Eye: Gender, Race, and Culture in Courtrooms and Classrooms*. Toronto: University of Toronto Press.

Reasons, C., L. Ross, and C. Patterson. 1986. "Your Money or Your Life: Workers' Health in Canada." In S. Brickey and E. Comack (eds.), *The Social Basis of Law*. Toronto: Garamond.

Reber, S., and R. Renaud. 2005. *Starlight Tour: The Last, Lonely Night of Neil Stonechild*. Toronto: Random House Canada.

Reich, W. 1993 [1946]. *The Mass Psychology of Fascism*. Third edition, translated by Theodore P. Wolfe. New York: Orgone Institute. <http://www.whale.to/b/reich.pdf>.

Reiman, J. 2007. *The Rich Get Richer and the Poor Get Prison*. Eighth edition. Boston: Pearson.

Reiman, J., and P. Leighton. 2010. *The Rich Get Richer and the Poor Get Poorer*. Boston: Allyn and Bacon.

Reitsma-Street, M. 1999. "Justice for Canadian Girls: A 1990s Update." *Canadian Journal of Criminology* 41 (3).

Ritzer, G. 1999. *Enchanting a Disenchanted World: Revolutionizing the Means of Consumption*. Pine Forge Press, Thousand Oaks,

___. 2008a *The McDonaldization of Society*. Fifth edition. Thousand Oaks, CA: Pine Forge Press.

Robidoux, M. 2001. "Power, Play and Powerlessness." In *Men at Play*. Montreal: McGill-Queen's University Press.

Rodney, W. 1981. *How Europe Underdeveloped Africa*. Washington, DC: Howard University Press.

Rossiter, C. 1963 *Constitutional Dictatorship, Crisis Government in the Modern Democracies*. New York: Harcourt, Brace and World.

Rubin, M. 2001 "Sanctions on Iraq: A Valid Anti-American Grievance?" *Meria Journal* 5, 4 (December).

Russell, B. 2000. "From the Workhouse to Workfare: The Welfare State and Shifting Policy Terrains." In M. Burke, C. Moores and J. Shields (eds.), *Restructuring and Resistance: Canadian Public Policy in an Age of Global Capitalism*. Halifax: Fernwood.

Salvemini, G. 1973. *The Origins of Fascism in Italy*. New York: Harper and Row.

Schissel, B. 1997. *Blaming Children: Youth Crime, Moral Panics and the Politics of Hate*. Halifax: Fernwood Publishing.

Schmalleger, F. 2007. *Criminal Justice Today*. Upper Saddle River, NJ: Pearson-Prentice Hall.

Schramm, H. 1998. *Young Women Who Use Violence: Myths and Facts*. Calgary: Elizabeth Fry Society of Calgary.

Schrecher, E. 1986. *No Ivory Tower: McCarthyism and the Universities*. New York: Oxford University Press.

____. 1998. *Many Are the Crimes: McCarthyism in America*. New York: Little, Brown.

Sears, A. 1999. "The Lean State and Capitalist Restructuring: Towards a Theoretical Account. *Studies in Political Economy* 59.

____. 2003. *Retooling the Mind Factory: Education and Lean State*. Aurora: Garamond Press.

Sharpe. J.A. 1984. *Crime in Early Modern England, 1550–1750*. New York: Longman.

Simmons, Tony. Forthcoming. *Revitalizing the Classics*. Halifax & Winnipeg: Fernwood.

Smart, C. 1976. *Women, Crime and Criminology: A Feminist Critique*. London: Routledge & Kegan Paul.

Snider, L. 1994. "The Regulatory Dance: Understanding Reform Processes in Corporate Crime." In R. Hinch (ed.), *Readings in Critical Criminology*. Scarborough, ON: Prentice.

____. 2002. "'But They're Not Real Criminals': Downsizing Corporate Crime." In Bernard Schissel and Carolyn Brooks (eds.), *Marginality and Condemnation: An Introduction to Critical Criminology*. Black Point, NS: Fernwood Publishing.

Stall, B. 1999a. "Mayor to Propose Skid Row Reward." *The Province*, April 25.

____. 1999b. "Mayor to Propose Skid Row Reward: Mayor Backs Reward in Hooker Mystery." *The Province* July 14. <http://www.missingpeople.net/mayor.htm>.

Star Phoenix. 2006. "Three-Strikes Bill Will Hit Natives." October 18: A10.

Statistics Canada. 1999. "Psychological Health—Depression." *Health Reports* 11, 3. Ottawa: Statistics Canada. Catalogue no. 82-003.

____. 2001. "Aboriginal Peoples' Survey, Canadian Community Health Survey." Ottawa: Statistics Canada. Catalogue no. 89-589-XIE2000/2001.

____. 2006. "Violence Against Aboriginal Women." Ottawa: Statistics Canada. <http://www.statcan.gc.ca/pub/85-570-x/2006001/findings-resultats/4054081-eng.htm>.

____. 2005. "General Social Survey, Cycle 18 Overview: Personal Safety and Perceptions of the Criminal Justice System." Ottawa: Statistics Canada.

____. 2006b. "Measuring Violence Against Women: Statistical Trends." Ottawa: Statistics Canada. Catalogue no. 85-570-XIE.

____. 2006c. "Low-Income Cutoffs for 2005 and Low-Income for 2004." *The Daily* Thursday, April 6.

____. 2003. "Canadian Statistics: Visible Minority Population, Census Metropolitan Areas." <statscan.ca/enlish/Pgdb/demo40e.htm>.

Stohl, M., and G.A. Lopez (eds.). 1986. *Government Violence and Repression*. New York: Greenwood Press.

____. 1988. *Terrible Beyond Endurance? The Foreign Policy of State Terrorism*. New York: Greenwood Press.

Stonebanks, R. 2000. "The Last Accused in Reena's Death: Families Gather to Witness Final Trial in Teen Tragedy." *Victoria Times Colonist*, March 7.

Strange, C. 1985–86. "'The Criminal and Fallen' of Their Sex: The Establishment of Canada's First Women's Prison, 1874–1901." *Canadian Journal of Women and the Law/Revue juridique "La femme et le droit"* 1 (1).

Sutherland, E.H. 1977. "Crimes of Corporations." In G. Geis and R. Meier (eds.), *White-Collar Crime: Offences in Business, Politics, and the Professions*. New York: Free

Press.

Swanson, J. 20001. *Poor Bashing: The Politics of Exclusion.* Toronto: Between the Lines.

Taras, D. 1990. *The Newsmakers: The Media's Influence on Canadian Politics.* Scarborough: Nelson Canada.

Tarpley, W.G. 2005. *9/11: Synthetic Terror — Made in the USA.* Joshua Tree: Progressive Press.

Taylor, C.S. 1993. *Girls, Gangs, Women and Drugs.* East Lansing: Michigan State University Press.

Taylor, T., C. Williams, K. Makambi, C. Mouton, J. Harrell, Y. Cozier et al. 2007. "Racial Discrimination and Breast Cancer Incidence in US Black Women: The Black Women's Health Study." *American Journal of Epidemiology* 166(1).

Teahen, K. 2000. "When Loyalty turns Threatening." *London Free Press,* Opinion, April 4.

Teotonio, I. 2009. "School Backpack of Missing Teen Mariam Found." *Toronto Star,* October 9.

Tilly, C. 2005. "Terror as Strategy and Relational Process." *International Journal of Comparative Sociology* 46 (1–2).

Thompson, E.P. 1963. *The Making of the English Working Class.* London: Penguin.

Toronto Sun. 2010. "Canada's Richest Own a Third of Country's Wealth." December 1. <torontosun.com/money/2010/12/01/16388411.html>.

Trevor-Roper, H.R. 1975. "The European Witch-Craze." In M. Marwick (ed.), *Witchcraft and Sorcery.* Harmondsworth, Middlesex: Penguin.

Trotsky, L. 1961. *Terrorism and Communism: A Reply to Karl Kautsky.* Ann Arbor: University of Michigan Press.

UNAIDS. 2008. "2008 Report in the Global AIDS Epidemic." <unaids.org/en/KnowledgeCentre/HIVData/GlobalReport/2008>.

Underdown, D.E. 1985. "The Taming of the Scold: The Enforcement of Patriarchal Authority in Early Modern England." In A. Fletcher and J. Stevenson (eds.), *Order and Disorder in Early Modern England.* Cambridge: Cambridge University Press.

UNICEF. 2005. *Child Poverty in Rich Countries.* Florence: UNICEF Innocenti Research Center.

Utsey, S.O., J.G. Ponterotto, A.L. Reynolds and A.A. Cancelli. 2000. "Racial Discrimination, Coping, Life Satisfaction, and Self-Esteem Among African Americans." *Journal of Counseling and Development* 78(1).

Van Bergen, J. 2005. "The New CIA Gulag of Secret Foreign Prisons: Why It Violates both Domestic and International Law." <http://writ.news.findlaw.com/commentary/20051107_bergen.html>.

Van Dijk, T. 1993. *Elite Discourse and Racism.* California: Sage Publications.

Van Riper, T. 2010. "The NBA's Best for the Buck." *Forbes,* December 7 <forbes.com/2010/12/07/lebron-james-rondo-durant-business-sports-nba-best-players-buck.html>.

Vancouver Sun. 2002. "How Lindsay Kines and *Sun* Reporters Broke Missing Women Story." November 6.

Vann Woodward, C. 1974. *The Strange Career of Jim Crow.* New York: Oxford University Press.

Verburg, P. 1995. "'Battered Wife Syndrome' on Trial: Homolka's Complicity in the Bernardo Atrocities Dealt a Heavy Blow to the 'Robo-Victim' Defence." *Western Report* 10 (22). June 26.

Verdun-Jones, S. 2007. *Criminal Law in Canada*. Toronto: Thomson-Nelson.

Walker, R. 1994. "Publication Ban Doing More Harm than Good, Lawyer Argues." *Montreal Gazette*, February 7.

Walton, J., and D. Seddon. 1994. *Free Markets and Food Riots: The Politics of Global Adjustment*. Cambridge: Blackwell.

Warwick, L. 1995. "Violent Women." *Ottawa Citizen*, August 1.

Washington Post. 2005. "CIA Holds Terror Suspects in Secret Prisons." November 2.

___. 2007. "U.S. Holds 18,000 Suspects in Secret Prisons." April 15.

Weber, M. 1994. *Political Writings*. (Cambridge Texts in the History of Political Thought.) Ed. Peter Lassman. Trans. Ronald Speirs. Cambridge: UP.

Wente, M. 1999. "The New and Self-Improved Karla Homolka." *Globe and Mail*, November 6.

White House. 2002. "The National Security Strategy." <http://whitehouse.gov/nsc/nss>.

Widdicombe, S., and R. Wooffitt. 1995. *The Language of Youth Subcultures: Social Identity in Action*. New York: Prentice Hall.

Wiegand, E. 2004. "Tresspass at Will: Squatting as Direct Action, Human Rights, and Justified Theft." *LIP Magazine*.

Wilkinson, R., and M. Marmot. 2005. "Income Inequality and Population Health: A Review and Explanation of the Wvidence." *Social Science and Medicine* 16: 1768–84.

Williams, D.R. 1999. "Race, Socioeconomic Status, and Health: The Added Effects of Racism and Discrimination." *Annals of the New York Academy of Sciences* 896.

Wilson, N.K. 1993. "Taming Women and Nature: The Criminal Justice System and the Creation of Crime in Salem Village." In R. Muraskin and T. Alleman (eds.), *It's a Crime: Women and Justice*. Englewood Cliffs, NJ: Regents/Prentice Hall.

Winderman, I. 2010. "LeBron James to join Chris Bosh, Heat's Dwayne Wade." *South Florida Sun-Sentinel*, July 8. <http://articles.sun-sentinel.com/2010-07-08/sports/sfl-lebron-james-decision-070810_1_james-and-bosh-dwyane-wade-lebron-james>.

Wise, D. 1976. *The American Police State*. New York: Random House.

Wise, D., and T.P. Ross. 1964. *The Invisible Government*. New York: Random House.

Witzig, R. 1996. "The Medicalization of Race: Scientific Legitimization of a Flawed Social Construct." *Annals of Internal Medicine* 125(8).

Wood, D. 2004. "House Rules." *Vancouver Magazine* April.

Woods, M. 2010. "Cultural Safety and the Socioethical Nurse." *Nursing Ethics* 17(6).

World Health Organization. 1996. "The World Health Report 1996 — Fighting Disease, Fostering Development." <who.int/whr/1996/en>.

Wright, Justice D.H. (Commissioner). 2004. "Report of the Commission of Inquiry into Matters Relating to the Death of Neil Stonechild." <justice.gov.sk.ca/stonechild/finalreport/Stonechild.pdf>.

Zakreski, D. 2000. "Witness Recalls Native Man Struggling with Police: Man Who Sparked Internal Probe Tells Horror Story." *Saskatoon StarPhoenix*, February 18.

Ziff, B. 2000. *Principles of Property Law*. Third edition. Toronto: Thompson Canada.

Zwolinski, M. 2011. "Bautista Set to Sign 5-Year, $65 Million Contract." *Toronto Star*, February 16. <http://www.thestar.com/sports/baseball/mlb/bluejays/article/939888-bautista-set-to-sign-5-year-65-million-contract>.